What others
Detou

MW00896888

An inspiring story of a remarkable man and his entire family pursuing their vision with clarity, integrity, and hard work. They overcame extraordinary challenges and hardships along the way but persevered with dedication to their faith and their values. Elling is a true Living Legend of Aviation—always optimistic about the outcome, never quitting, and achieving great success. I have known him and his family for nearly 50 years, and they have my highest respect and admiration.

—Bruce R. McCaw, Seattle Businessman and Philanthropist

This engaging memoir teaches all of us to search for solutions to our challenges, our detours in life. A compelling, urgent read for anyone who commits to succeed—or even more, to achieve significance in their business or personal life.

—Gary Carlberg, President, Simutech International, Inc., and
Gregoriann "Greg" Hanna, Managing Broker, John L. Scott Real Estate

In sharing his remarkable story, Elling Halvorson teaches us about the possibilities that await when we embrace the unexpected. Through his core values of hard work, fortitude, faith, and humility, he has achieved an extraordinary level of success that enables him to embody the meaning of generosity. Elling is generous with his big ideas, contagious can-do spirit, and in giving back to the community. One shining example is the Elling & Barbara Halvorson Cancer Center at EvergreenHealth. This world-class facility for treating people facing cancer encourages healing and inspires patients daily to have faith and hope. After reading Elling Halvorson's memoir, I think you will be inspired to view life's detours as pathways to your own remarkable destiny.

—Robert Malte, CEO Emeritus, EvergreenHealth, Kirkland, WA

I just finished reading every word of Elling Halvorson's fascinating memoir, *Detours to Destiny*. Full of high-risk adventures, significant setbacks, and amazing recoveries, one might say that Elling has really made a name for himself. But Elling would disagree. Woven throughout every chapter of his life (and recorded in these pages) are core values that give much deeper meaning to life than self-promotion. Easy to read, and rich with knowledge, humor, honesty, and wisdom, Elling's memoir brings hope and confidence to those detours we all experience, and it teaches us how to make the most of this precious life we've been given. A read like this is truly a faith-builder!

— *Rev. Steven J. Brue, Past President of Hillcrest Lutheran Academy, Fergus Falls, MN*

LWTech is so fortunate to have had Elling Halvorson serve as a Trustee of the College for over eight years. His visionary, generous, and kind leadership . . . led to his reputation on campus as the father of the institute of technology . . . Moreover, Elling and Barbara have both kept a close eye on the college after Elling's term as trustee concluded . . . They even created the Elling and Barbara Halvorson Endowed Scholarship for Outstanding Nurses . . . He embodies the motto of Service above Self. It has been an honor and a privilege to come to know Elling, Barbara, and their family. I am so pleased his story is being told.

— *Dr. Amy Morrison Goings, President, Lake Washington Institute of Technology*

DETOURS TO DESTINY: A MEMOIR

Elling Halvorson

with Diana Savage
and Gerald D. Gawne

Canyon Flight Trading Company, LLC
Grand Canyon, AZ 86023

Canyon Flight Trading Company, LLC
Grand Canyon, AZ 86023
Printed in the United States of America

ISBN-13: 978-1-7241-9773-3

Interior design by Diana Savage of Savage Creative Services, LLC
Cover design by Lynnette Bonner of Indie Cover Design

DEDICATION

The longer I live, the more grateful I am for my outstanding family. In an age when so many families are falling apart, I am tremendously blessed that my loved ones not only like each other, but they also work together cooperatively, argue companionably, and love fiercely. This family togetherness is what has given me the strength to navigate life's detours.

Therefore, I dedicate this book to my wife, Barbara, who has been my greatest cheerleader during our 65 years of marriage;

To my children: Brenda, Kent, Lon, Randy, and Rod;

And to my grandchildren and great-grandchildren.

My life is better in every way because of all of you.

Definitions

Detour

Noun: deviation from the usual procedure or a direct course
Verb: to avoid by going around; to send by a circuitous route

Destiny

Noun: something to which a person is destined;
a calling, purpose

CONTENTS

Part V: Giving Back

Preface 1: How This Book Came About

Elling Halvorson had lost count of how many people told him he should write a book. He knew they were probably right, but he had better things to do than sit all day and copy down his stories. Then around the year 2010, his friend Gerry Gawne joined the chorus. "You've had such a fascinating life, you should write a book!"

Elling started to brush the idea aside until he remembered Gerry wrote narration for all the videos he produced. "Well," Elling said, "if you're so convinced I should write a book, I'll let you help me write it."

Gerry compiled stories, gathered photos, and added his creative touch to the narrative. When a change in his health required him to step down, I was contacted about moving the project forward, as I'd done for dozens of other authors.

My first step was to Google "Elling Halvorson." I quickly learned what a legend he is in the fields of aviation, construction, and philanthropy. His name and picture were everywhere. But then, if you own or are the principal of some 20 companies, that's bound to happen. When I finally met him and started to read the first few chapters, I knew his story needed to be published.

Although Gerry and I typed the words, Elling directed the project. Often, when attempting to explain an engineering concept or an invention he'd created, he would grab a pen and sketch the item on whatever piece of paper was handy so I could describe it accurately.

Barbara Halvorson gets a gold star for urging her husband to finish the book whenever life events delayed it. She unearthed photos, correspondence, and other documents to help with the storytelling.

You may be reading this because you're related to Elling, work for him, are his friend, have benefitted from his philanthropy, or simply because you enjoy reading great memoirs. Whatever the reason, you'll be inspired. And maybe you'll pick up a pointer or two on turning your own detours into highways to destiny.

– Diana Savage

Preface 2: The Power of Story

In many ways, family stories are treasure chests holding a wealth of shared experiences. They teach members of the younger generation about their parents, grandparents, and the legions of people and traditions from which they've come. The stories of hard times, good times, afflictions, losses, and recoveries are the collected wisdom of us all, to be passed along to the newest and most vulnerable among us.

"If history were taught in the form of stories," said famed British author Rudyard Kipling, "it would never be forgotten." Stories of our families help teach younger ones how to live, how to handle challenges, and how to find their own place in a complicated world.

Science has found that humans remember stories better than information communicated in any other way. No doubt that's why Jesus told so many parables when teaching important spiritual truths.

The following stories reveal how the maze of detours I encountered had the potential to veer me—and those I cared about—permanently off course. Instead, they created a zigzag path to greater successes than I ever could have imagined.

Please keep in mind that this book reflects my present recollection of experiences over time. While some names and characteristics have been changed and some dialogue has been recreated, I have done my best to present the most truthful account that memory will allow.

My hope is that this memoir might inspire you to navigate each detour you encounter with the knowledge that creativity, hard work, and a spirit of generosity truly are the keys to success.

– Elling Halvorson
October 2018

PART I: DEVELOPING A RISK-TAKING REPUTATION

✦ ✦ ✦ ✦

1

FALL FROM THE SKY

At midday, black clouds tumbled across the Arizona sky, blocking out the sun and turning daylight to darkness. Light rain grew in intensity, until over the next 36 hours, an unprecedented downpour dumped some 18 inches of water right where my company was completing its major construction project on the floor of the Grand Canyon.

Two days after the rain had begun, I awoke Monday morning, December 5, 1965, to clear skies. Worried about what the weekend of rain might have done to the underground pipeline we'd constructed from the North Rim to the South Rim, I rushed out early in a helicopter to be the first to survey the situation.

I saw destruction everywhere. Cliffs, some 200 to 300 feet high, had collapsed. Side trails had been wiped out, along with six of the seven bridges we'd built over the creek to carry conduit. Dozens of segments of the once-buried pipe had been reduced to twisted aluminum. Even from the air I could see we'd lost from eight to 10 miles of pipeline.

As we flew toward the starting point of our project where Bright Angel Creek normally emerges from the canyon wall as a tidy little waterfall, I was astounded to see millions of gallons of water gushing from cracks in the cliff wall across an expanse of nearly one and a half miles. The incredible cascade was so enormous, it was almost like looking at Victoria Falls in southern Africa.

After the short flight back, I exited the helicopter to face the assembled crew of around 50 men who were ready to go to work on the

1

canyon floor. On our loudspeaker system, I told them about the destruction I'd seen in the canyon. The trails they were to dress had been wiped out. The pipeline they were about to test had been ripped up. With a heavy heart I explained that because there was no work for them to do, they were all terminated as of that morning. They would receive their final paychecks as soon as we could process them.

After flying back to Washington State, I consulted with my Bremerton project partners, Lent's Mechanical Contractors, to decide on the best course of action. We agreed we had to assess the damage more accurately. To do so, I would take a couple of managers with me and spend a week in the canyon measuring and photographing as much as possible to put a value on our losses. At least it was a place to start.

I returned to the canyon on Friday. The following Monday, December 12, one week after first viewing the flood's destruction, my pilot, job superintendent, and I took off in a helicopter from Yaqui Point. I told the rest of my team to stand by.

As we flew slowly over the confluence of the Colorado River and Bright Angel Creek, I saw the exhaust stack of a Caterpillar crawler tractor sticking up from the water like a periscope. We'd purchased the D-6 crawler six months earlier and still owed payments on it. From all appearances, it had tumbled downstream about one and a half miles.

We landed. I stepped carefully across rock to examine the tractor. It was then I noticed that all of the cottonwood trees in that formerly lush part of the canyon—some trees as tall as 10-story buildings—had been swept away. The entire area was barren.

I felt sick as I returned to the helicopter. "Fly low and slow," I told the pilot. "We need to photograph this damage."

We lifted off again, flying 40 miles an hour at 75 to 100 feet above the canyon floor. Suddenly, we slammed into an antenna wire, formerly hidden by cottonwood branches. It had been strung from the side of the cliff down to an old Civil Conservation Corps bunkhouse on the canyon floor. The wire snapped and whipped around the helicopter, winding into the mast that held control rods for the main rotor blades.

Keeping his composure, the pilot remembered a nearby landing spot we'd used many times during pipeline construction. He tipped the helicopter for an approach. But at that second, the other end of the wire struck the tail and ripped it completely off. Now the tail rotor, gearbox, and blades were gone.

With the helicopter's center of gravity knocked forward, we spun out of control and crashed on the rocky shore below. The collision didn't stop the high-energy main rotor system, however. It continued to thrash what was left of the aircraft.

I'd been sitting in the center seat with the strap of a Polaroid camera around my neck. As the chopper broke up with a wild roar, I was thrust violently forward into the metal control console. The impact shoved the camera into my body, causing my chest to throb with massive pain. Hot blood sluiced around in my mouth. I spit it out again and again as more blood dripped over my eyes and down my face. Pain stabbed throughout my legs.

Then I smelled aviation fuel. *I've got to get out of here! We're going to burn!* I fumbled with the seatbelt. Although I can't remember it, I'm told I staggered away from the wreck and collapsed like a rag doll at the side of the Rim-to-Rim trail.

Slipping in and out of consciousness, I saw members of my crew hurry to my side. Another burst of hot blood flooded my mouth and choked me. I knew I had to clear my airway. "Help me turn so the blood can drain!" I begged.

Afraid that moving me at all might be fatal, no one touched me.

I knew I didn't have much time before I drowned in my own blood. So, ignoring the tremendous pain, I managed to turn. Finally, blood ran from my mouth, and I could gulp small gasps of air. Then I saw another man hurry toward me. Sensing a soft touch on my head, I saw dimly that it was Bob, a rowdy but faithful employee on my crew.

"Sir, I am so sorry," Bob said. "It should have been me, not you. You are a good man." He explained that the pilot and job superintendent had been thrown free from the wreckage.

As I lay on the rocks, bleeding, struggling to breathe, and fighting to stay conscious, I could feel my body getting cold. I knew without a doubt I was dying. With what breath I could draw in, I asked Bob to give my love to my wife, children, and two brothers and to tell them I would see them in heaven.

Bob assured me, "A helicopter has been called to come get you."

Would it arrive in time? Slipping into hypothermia, I realized something was terribly wrong with my chest. I gasped out, "Tell them to bring oxygen!"

Was this a huge detour for me? Or had I reached a dead end?

Journey to the Bottom of the Canyon

Perhaps I shouldn't have been surprised at ending up in such a dire situation. My construction company had developed the reputation of undertaking risky jobs few others would even consider.

Eleven years earlier, in 1955, I'd gotten my start by going to work for H. Halvorson Inc., one of the major construction firms in the Pacific Northwest. My brother Hal in Spokane, Washington, had founded the company and had built a trusted reputation in the construction industry.

Arriving at the job site, I saw a familiar face. Ole Orsted, a man my dad loved and had brought into construction, served as general superintendent for Hal for 30 years or more. People in the trade viewed Ole as one of the top construction-site managers in the region.

As a successful builder of many school buildings and other substantial projects throughout the Pacific Northwest, Hal's firm won a contract to construct Shoreline High School near Richmond Beach, Washington. The morning I arrived at the job site, the roof was starting to go on. Ole put me on the roof to "face-nail" it using seven-inch-long spikes to fasten down the wood decking. The decking itself was four-inch-thick double tongue-in-groove Douglas fir fastened to a four-inch by four-inch nailer bolted to the top of a steel-bar joist.

The method they used was to hit the spike eight times or so with a two-pound hammer until it sank all the way into the wood rafter. I came up with a possibly "cheaper, faster, better" way of getting the job done in only two strokes. My plan was to use the hammer just once to set the seven-inch spike into the wood about an inch or so and later drive the spike the rest of the way with one blow of an eight-pound sledge hammer. I explained my idea to Ole, and he gave me the okay to try it. From below, Ole watched me often and seemed to approve what I was doing.

I would "set" a full row of those seven-inch spikes with the two-pound hammer. Then I would come in reverse with the eight-pound sledge hammer, hitting each spike just once and driving it in completely with a single, powerful stroke. Since this was an exceptionally large school building, many of those rows were 50 feet or longer. My idea worked and reduced hammer strokes from roughly eight strokes per spike to two.

But this novice inventor overlooked two key elements in the system: *my two hands*. As a recently graduated college student with soft hands and muscles, I didn't anticipate the strain on my hands and arms. Going along a 50-foot-long row of those seven-inch spikes, I'd swing that heavy sledge hammer over and over, as if trying to set a new record. All too soon, my hands were red-hot and felt as if they were melting. I tried to hide my discomfort, but the pain in my swollen hands was excruciating.

So that Ole wouldn't notice, I just waved a quick goodbye at the end of the day and jumped into my car. But once I was driving, I was shocked to realize I couldn't even open my hands. They were so swollen and puffed out, they looked more like boxing gloves than human hands. When I walked in the door of our new home to be welcomed by my wife, Barbara, she was holding our baby, Brenda. Seeing my injury, Barbara's eyes widened, and she was so horrified, she wanted to cry. The next day at work—Friday—my hands became even more damaged.

Happily, we learned that the weekend was a four-day holiday—George Washington's birthday was on Tuesday, the 22nd of February. So my swollen hands had Saturday, Sunday, Monday, and Tuesday to heal. And they did, to a fair degree. When I showed up at the jobsite Wednesday morning, Ole told me he'd calculated that the roof decking was being placed at the lowest cost per board foot that Hal's company had ever done. That made me proud. I knew coming up with that idea wouldn't hurt my reputation. And I was quietly grateful Ole didn't try to shake my hand, because it was still sore.

Over the next week or two, I developed a less frantic pace that didn't result in my hands falling off my body. Soon, I face-nailed all the roofs on that new school. And since it was a big school, with acres of roof, I got very good at my task. Ole continued to tell me how pleased he was. It felt good to be making a positive impression early on with Ole, and through him, on my brother Hal. The job went smoothly, right through the summer of 1955.

Promotion from Roof to Office

Then one day, without notice, Hal showed up at the jobsite where I was near the top of a high ladder. He'd come from the company's headquarters in Spokane. He hollered up at me as he grinned and waved. "Hey, Elling. C'mon down."

When I descended, he said, "I want you to come work in my Seattle office." I'd briefly seen it before and remembered that it was a small place where Hal had a superintendent. He'd also had an estimator and secretary, but he'd recently laid them both off. Hal continued, "I want you to be secretary for a while. It'll help me, and it'll help you learn the business."

Without a second of delay, I said, "Sure!"

My brother turned out to be right about the knowledge I would receive. For a number of months as I learned the ropes, I was transformed into a one-man construction company. I kept the payroll—including typing out the payroll checks—wrote letters to clients, talked to

I worked hard to learn how to do accurate cost estimating.

and corresponded with city and state government agencies, and maintained the office totally. My efforts seemed to impress Hal enough for him to fly to Seattle and sit down with me on a new bid opportunity he wanted me to work on. He was about to make me solely responsible for a *take off*, a term in the construction business that means the major part of the cost-estimating process that all builders must do.[1]

Another dimension of construction bidding is that some contracts, particularly public works and military contracts, require the construction firm to post a bid bond which often is 5 percent of the amount of the bid. That means the contractor bears risk and responsibility should it be necessary to walk away from a low bid.

When a contract is awarded, especially in the case of public works, the contractor is required to provide a 100 percent performance and payment bond. Therefore, if the contractor is unable to complete the project for any reason, the bonding company would complete it—either using the contractor's work force or using another contractor at no cost to the owner.

Smaller contractors must assign to the bonding company everything they own, often including their personal property, such as a home. This arrangement is typical until a contracting company has built a solid

---

[1] The first step was to thoroughly analyze the construction specifications and then "take off" specific quantities of needed items from those specifications and the working drawings in order to prepare the overall estimate and bid. For example, we would start with the dirt work, the cut and fill required, and then categorize the types of excavation needed. Next we'd determine what type of equipment would be used to do the site work. After computing the cubic yardage and distance of movement for site-work materials, we would calculate the building excavation for footings, foundations, basement, crawl space, etc. Then we'd calculate the square footage of form work that would be in contact with concrete, plus the amount of concrete required for footings, basement walls, foundations, and any other concrete work. Next we would calculate all the lumber, steel, and other materials necessary to build the floor and wall systems. By making a quantity survey of everything that would eventually go into constructing the building, we could price the cost of materials and labor. If you do your estimating right, you may make a profit. If you do it incorrectly, you could face a substantial loss.

reputation and has significant cash resources and relationships. So there's a lot on the line for a contractor.

My own rule of thumb is that the contractor has to build the project three times.

1. The first "build" is the quantity survey and pricing of the work. That estimate is often so detailed, it's as if the project is being built right there in one's office. Every component used in the project takes place on paper as seriously as it happens in the real-life build-out.

2. The second building of the project involves frugal purchase of all the materials needed to complete the job, wisely selecting subcontractors for plumbing, heating, ventilation, electrical, and other specialized trades, and finally choosing the right management team.

3. With build number three, everything shifts from paper projections and estimates to the physical build. Earth is moved, workers are hired, contractors are scheduled, and the job must be managed within critical labor budgets, including scheduling of trades. The three "builds" described must be in concert with each other to have a successful outcome.

Soon enough, Hal arrived with a seriously large roll of plans under his arm. "Elling," he said, "I want you to hire a secretary, and then I want you to work full time on a quantity survey. Here's a set of drawings. Please get the specifications out of my car."

I could hardly carry all the notebooks.

Well, I was an untrained take-off man. But I was a makeshift engineer, and I'd been around the business all my life, so I said, "Man, I'd like to do that, Hal. But I don't trust myself." The project was the approach control facility for the Minot, North Dakota, Air Force Base. The set of specifications was six inches thick, with maybe 120 sheets or more of plans. When I opened those sheets and blueprints, I almost stopped breathing. I had absolutely no idea how to read those specifications.

Developed by the US Corps of Engineers, the plans were professional and complex.

Meanwhile, Hal smiled and said, "I'll be back in three weeks, and I figure you'll get all this taken off properly."

I replied, "I will be scraping the bottom of my intelligence. I'll have to start from ground zero."

Hal nodded and began a short and valuable briefing. After about 20 minutes, he gave me a grin and said he had to be going. The office door closed, and I put my head down on my desk. I felt like I'd been ordered to assemble a jet plane from spare parts in maybe three weeks. I tried to keep cool and not freak out.

High-Pressure Calculations

That evening, the pillow talk between Barbara and me was about how worried I was at this challenge. Barbara was hurting for me, knowing I would never let my brother down.

In the office the next morning, my coffee was steaming, but my brain was already confused. I leafed through the enormous specifications book, and my heartbeat kicked up a few notches. Flipping through page after page, I felt overwhelmed, drowning in statistics. But when I finally stopped feeling sorry for myself, I recognized I had just one choice: *get the job done.*

"Get to work on it," I chided myself. "Open the first page of the specifications book, and start reading and understanding. Then turn to the second page. Then the third!" Soon, nervous as a pickpocket at a police convention, I started the work. But my confidence didn't go up. It sank. By the end of the day, I was incredibly underwater.

I was always a guy to take on challenges, but this was so different, with such a short deadline, and it mattered so much to Hal. There was nothing to do but go forward, despite my fears of making mistakes. I promised myself I would read and learn to understand each item, come hell or high water.

Initially, almost everything was foreign to me. I couldn't even understand the organization of the specifications. I struggled with it and had to look up information constantly. Day after day, night after long night, I worked well past midnight. Finally, my comfort level went up a notch. I thought I had it mostly figured out.

But after mastering the specifications book, I had another dragon to slay, and that was studying hundreds of drawings. It was then I first realized this project wasn't just one building, it was many buildings, all linked together by utility ducts. I did my best with my limited knowledge and ultimately put that bid together. I worked especially hard to make *sure* I had not missed anything.

But as if my fear levels weren't high enough already, Hal phoned out of the blue to say, "Elling, get an airplane ticket to Minot, North Dakota, and I'll meet you there next Tuesday. I've decided we're going to bid this job."

So I purchased my ticket, bundled up all my paperwork, and flew off to Minot to meet him in his hotel room. Hal had brought some of his most capable staff along to take telephone prices for materials and subcontracts. Other staff members computed and summarized a final composite price for the bid.

I watched with more than a little nervousness as my brother slowly went through my estimate and priced the labor cost page by page by page. My throat was so dry, I couldn't say much. After coming to the end of my estimate, Hal pushed back from the desk and told me he liked the work and trusted it.

Relieved, I felt great, but deep down I still obsessed about possible errors and oversights. Did we miss something? Were there any miscalculations? Did we resolve the tax questions? Did we allow enough money for travel and housing? Did we include the builder's all-risk insurance? It is so easy to make a mistake in these complex bids. But Hal's growing confidence that our price was okay—based on my take-offs plus Hal's learned ability to see the job as a whole—gave me some badly needed comfort at a tense moment.

We ended up being the low bidder. As I learned from that and subsequent experiences, if the bid is accurate, you're probably in good shape.

Being awarded the contract for the Air Force base in Minot was a great win for my brother, bringing his firm more than a year of good work and revenue flow. It was also hugely significant to me. As I worked that contract and several other challenging projects over the next couple of years—1955 through 1957—I gained genuine confidence in my construction skills. I had become so proficient at estimating that I began to think I was ready to leave my brother's nest.

It wasn't a new thought. During the first month of working for my brother, I'd told him I had ambitions to go into the construction business on my own. I'd watched Dad build his company, then Hal develop his own, and our brother Carl follow suit. I told Hal, "I figure I've been preparing my whole life to be in the business for myself."

Hal grinned and agreed. As always, his only interest was to help me anytime, anywhere, anyhow. Hal is gone now, but he remains in my heart and memories. I'll never stop missing his skills, his good nature, and his love of life and fun.

Deciding My Future Path

Making construction my career had not been an easy decision. I'd struggled whether to follow in my family's footsteps or start a new life by ministering to others through the church. Influencing my decision was something Dad had included in his will.

> It has always been my desire that someone in my family be in full-time Christian service. Since my older children are established in business, I bequeath to Elling 50 percent of my estate, if within five years of the date of my passing, he is involved in either full-time Christian work of some sort of studying to that end.

Of course, Dad's hopes for me added to my dilemma. I was truly conflicted and unable to make up my mind. But all that changed one memorable day when a friend told me how much he enjoyed a book by one of America's great inventors, Robert "R. G." LeTourneau. Dad knew the gifted engineer well, and I'd met the man as well. LeTourneau's biography, *God Runs My Business*, gave me an immediate insight to my dilemma by prompting me to realize I had given myself a false choice: ministry life or business life?

Bob LeTourneau lived a combination of ministry *and* business throughout his life. Why hadn't I seen that possibility? As far back as I could remember, conversation around our dinner table had centered on the construction business, and my family had always demonstrated the core values of honesty, integrity, and generosity. I felt confident I could establish my own company based on those core values, which I had already realized were the real keys to success. After all, one must be successful in business in order to be successful in charitable areas. And true charity goes beyond finances. It has to do with respecting others.

I felt as if a light had been switched on in a dark corner of my mind. For the first time in a couple of years, I saw a pathway I'd be spiritually comfortable with for the rest of my life.

With that internal conflict settled, I began focusing on what it would take to set up a construction business of my own. I was confident I could do it. After all, when I was young, our family's dinner-table talk was often about construction—its ups and downs, its hazards and rewards. My father was one of the top executives in the field. Even my quiet but awesomely smart sister, Evelyn, learned how to keep a construction-business office humming in Montana—and keep her brothers from fighting.

With both hot ambition and the happy ignorance of youth, I began visualizing a new construction firm—a trailblazing one. After all, there was no shortage of construction firms. Often there were too many. In asking how I could make my new firm stand out in the crowd, I developed some ideas.

2
I Launch a Construction Company

Near the end of 1957, my entire focus was on starting my own construction firm. I figured that if Dad, Carl, and Hal could do it, why couldn't I? I'd learned the estimating process. I'd been part of the management on a number of Hal's construction projects. That not only provided me with several years of invaluable training, but I'd also earned a significant income that made funding the new venture possible.

Raised in a family of builders who watched economic changes like farmers watch the weather, I liked the predictions concerning America's healthy economy in 1958. The newspaper hitting my front steps the morning of January 1 reported that families were earning a record amount of $3,800 annually, with new home purchases averaging $12,000. People grumbled about gas prices at 20 cents a gallon, yet they were still buying lots of fuel for their cars.

Many were following the progress of the USA's first-ever satellite, Explorer 1, which was about to be sent up to compete with Russia's Sputnik launched the previous year. The Explorer 1 satellite didn't amount to much—cylindrical, only six feet long and not quite 31 pounds. It was outgunned by Russia's 180-pound Sputnik 2. People were nervous about Sputnik passing over the US seven times a day. Soon a flurry of new US rockets would shoot into space. In fact, in a single year, our nation created a brand-new industry called *aerospace*.

New Twist to New Plans

As I was about to open for business, Hal called me. "Elling," he said, "I'm going to close my office in Seattle. But you can take it over if you wish." I did. For my new team, I brought in an estimator—who was also an architect—and a secretary. It was a tiny but talented team.

Our first task was estimating a substation construction project for the Bonneville Power Administration (BPA) in the Covington area near Auburn,

Washington. My brother Carl had done a lot of work for the BPA. In fact, for many years, his firm was one of several top builders constructing most of the dams along the Columbia River. That produced a long-lasting relationship of trust with the Administration. So, upon receiving my bid for the substation, the BPA called Carl and asked, "Do you know this Elling Halvorson? We've never heard of Elling Halvorson Inc."

"Sure," Carl answered. "He's my brother."

"Well, we can't find out anything about him," the official said. "He's the low bidder on the Covington substation in Washington State."

Carl replied, "If you take a chance on him, you'll be okay."

Since I was a start-up, the BPA was skittish about me. Experienced clients avoid startups for good reason. Too many get into trouble, fail to complete the project, and end up filing for bankruptcy. The fact is, choosing a new startup construction company to build a project is like hiring a heart surgeon fresh out of medical school. The new doctor knows what to do but doesn't have enough experience to cope with unexpected events during surgery.

However, due to my father's good name in construction and the solid reputations of Carl and Hal, I had the benefit of a head start I wouldn't have had any other way. Our good family name also enabled me to get surety bonding for each project I bid on.

Normally, startup companies rarely qualify for bonding. But 20 years or so earlier, my dad had encouraged the Travelers Insurance Company of Saint Paul, Minnesota, to set up shop on the West Coast. The Halvorsons were the original family of contractors that Travelers did surety bonding for as they came west. That's why Travelers had kept an eye on me while I did bidding and building for my brothers. My brothers told Travelers, "You'll never lose any money betting on Elling, so you ought to bond him."

First Contracts

As a result, despite my youthful age of 25 and some competitors tagging me as the "Boy Contractor," my new company, Elling Halvorson Inc., was awarded the first contract we bid on, the BPA substation. I suspect some competitors thought my youth meant I'd do amateur work on cost estimating. Of course, the opposite was true.

One example of careful work versus careless work happened on our next successful bid for the US Army Corps of Engineers on a project named, "Railroad Relocation Facilities," a somewhat misleading title. When I received the actual plans, I was startled to see that except for some rail contractors, I was the only general contractor who'd ordered the bidding documents.

If, like me, they had requested the plans, they'd have learned this wasn't about relocating a railroad—a tough assignment. Actually, that step had already been completed. The plans showed this assignment to be the construction of a new railroad station and its facilities near the Howard A. Hanson Dam construction project. As I read the plans, I thought to myself, "Man, this is really our type of work!" Sure enough, we were the only bidder on what proved to be a moneymaker.

My brother Hal was always a competitive advantage for me in growing my new construction business. In one important instance, Hal brought me in to bid on building new supermarkets in Western states. Hal had a personal relationship of trust with Joe Albertson, a great guy and a true innovator. He was the first person to create an in-store bakery in all his grocery stores, and it brought him great success. Now most other chains have copied his idea. My brother and I built a total of 43 new Albertsons stores for Joe. My firm built six or seven of them, and Hal built the rest. A lot of those Albertson's projects were confirmed with nothing more than a handshake.

As a newcomer to the construction field, I was often in a David-versus-Goliath fight. My small company competed against much larger and more experienced firms. Since all the construction firms were fishing in one pond, I realized it would be wise for me to look for a different pond that wasn't so crowded.

Dangerous Routes

Like all contractors, I paid close attention to every published bid request. I began to notice that the big construction firms rarely bid on specialized jobs, so I focused a lot of my energies on searching for those particular projects. Without fully realizing it, I often left the normal world of construction and took my small staff with me into an unknown environment full of unique problems and dangers to life and limb.

I'm not sure what led me down the dangerous routes no one else chose. It might have been the arrogance of youth. I was, after all, just in my twenties, full of energy, ready to tackle anything. Still, I didn't make decisions because of youthful energy alone. I learned that meticulous advance planning (known as project logistics) could help me overcome obstacles few other construction firms would touch. However, I have to admit I don't recall ever asking myself, "Are all those other experienced construction companies wrong, and I'm the only guy who has it right?" Perhaps necessity and competitive pressures forced me to think outside the box.

One profitable early bid I won was part of a guidance system for the Federal Aviation Administration (FAA). We were to build an aviation facility high atop a mountain peak in the Cascade Range east of Seattle, just past the Snoqualmie Pass summit. We called it a "billy-goat project." Everything about it was difficult and dangerous. No wonder no other firm submitted a bid.

One key part of the job was to construct a road leading to the proposed facility. The second part was to build the facility that would allow a radar approach for all flights coming into the Seattle area.

I knew if I focused on each logistic challenge, we could get the dangerous job done. Our first task was to punch in a mountain road several miles to the top. Then my people used that super steep road to haul all the materials and equipment they needed to build the facility itself. Much of the job was high-risk and high-logistics, but we succeeded.

I'd found a competitive pathway for the years ahead. Whenever possible, my company would focus on the toughest, most demanding, and often, the most profitable jobs. While we continued to build many conventional projects such as schools, hospitals, and stores, we also had another pond not many competitors fished in. Those out-of-the-ordinary jobs were rare, but they *were* out there. I was finding them throughout the West. And looking back, I realize I was still too young to be frightened about the dangers.

Investing in a Private Airplane

It wasn't long before I realized I could see more potential projects and sign up more business if I had my own airplane. Flying by commercial airline has just the appearance of speed. For a one-hour flight, you waste two additional hours parking your car, standing in line, waiting for your bags, and more.

I'd always dreamed about being a pilot. In *Popular Mechanics* I'd read about airplanes, and then I got interested in free-flight model airplanes. With the models, I used a small Olson 23 liquid-fuel spark-ignition engine.

Now, in 1957, I had a compelling reason to take flight lessons, so I looked into the best light plane to buy or lease for that training. I homed in on a new type of private plane that had come on the market a couple of years earlier—the new twin-engine Piper Apache. The four-place (four-seat) aircraft cruised at just under 200 statute miles per hour, which would get me around pretty quickly. After choosing the type of plane I wanted, I had to locate one for sale at the right price.

Knowing my wife wouldn't be comfortable with me in a single-engine plane, I told her I had a friend with a Piper Apache who wanted to take her on a flight at Christmas time to see holiday light displays. She accepted. As we were enjoying Seattle's twinkling lights below, I said, "Barbara, would you feel comfortable with me in an airplane like this?"

"Yes," she replied.

"Oh, that's good," I said, "because this is your airplane." I'd already purchased it. I suppose that had been a little devious of me, but Barbara didn't seem to mind.

The grass-and-dirt landing field I learned to fly on, located near Seattle, was just 318 feet longer than an aircraft carrier. Scary! Remembering that tiny field makes me shudder even today. Not only was it short, but it also had high-tension power-line towers on one end and tall fir trees at the other. Setting the Piper Apache down between the towering trees and the power lines meant no mistakes were allowed. None. I had to hit the start of the runway on landing, and I had to get my takeoff absolutely right also, or I'd be toast. With hindsight I realize that to save a few bucks, I had trusted my life to the lowest bidders.

When I finished training, I was ready to apply for my license, which meant taking a required physical to prove I was in good health and also that I could read without glasses. Although I was a bit nearsighted, I didn't need glasses to see distances, so I had high hopes. Those hopes were dashed when, on the afternoon I took my eye exam, I didn't pass.

The same thing had happened to me in college when, during the time of the Korean conflict, I couldn't pass an Air Force ROTC flight test without my glasses. At the time, the Air Force was taking pilots only, so I was forced to drop out of the ROTC program. That disappointment had been bad enough, but I couldn't bear the thought of failing to get my pilot's license now.

The doctor, however, was encouraging. He said, "Elling, you're very close to seeing well enough without glasses. Why don't you come in again tomorrow morning before going to work, and take the test again with rested eyes?"

I wanted that license so much, I was willing to do just about anything to pass the exam. So, the next morning, I asked Barbara to drive me back to the doctor, and I sat in the passenger seat with my eyes closed and covered so I wouldn't be tempted to look at anything until I viewed the eye charts. My plan worked. I passed the exam and got my license.

Risks Increase

My ability to speed up and down the West Coast energized our construction company. One new project the airplane helped me bid on and build was the University of Oregon's Institute of Marine Biology on Newport Bay. Every contractor had to come from Portland, Salem, and other distant spots to the remote location. The use of the Piper Apache meant I could fly there from Seattle within an hour or so. If I'd gone by traditional means, it easily would have taken me a full day. Now I could go to the job site and return home to my family quite easily the same day.

The Piper Apache saved time, but it also made life a bit more exciting than I anticipated.

I used that airplane a lot. I actually flew around 1,500 hours in it and another 1,500 hours or so in larger, higher-performance aircraft. Overall, the move to using private aircraft proved to be a smart competitive advantage for my young company.

What I didn't see clearly was the growing number of risks to my family, my company, and my life. Maybe I was becoming immune to risk since I dealt with it every day. For example, I flew to look at a possible construction project in Madras, Oregon, a small town surrounded by mountain ranges in the north-central part of the state. An Army Air Corps base had been built there during World War II. The job that caught my attention was a microwave relay station for the military to be built on a mountain above Madras. Building on mountaintops? No problem! Look how well we did it near Seattle. However, it was wintertime when we flew into Madras. I had to park on the ramp because there was no room in the hangar.

A storm was forecast, and that first night was already bitterly cold. After spending a couple of days at Madras bidding the job, we got ready to leave the next morning.

The weather had turned so cold, the twin Apache's propellers wouldn't even turn over. We had to use portable heaters to melt the snow off the plane and get the engines decently warmed up so the starters could crank them. That cost us at least a couple of hours in the freezing weather. But our labor paid off, and I was able to start the engines. Then, piloting along the runway, I stayed on the lee side of snowdrifts on the strip and took off with no problem.

About 15 minutes out of Madras, heading toward Seattle, we were going fine when we heard a big bang—*kapow!* Oil splattered all over the windshield and front of our plane. I immediately turned off the engine and feathered the propeller so it wouldn't turn.

In that moment of crisis, I thought of stories I'd heard about pilots mistakenly turning off the only engine that was still working. But I had turned off the correct engine, and we were able to fly back to the Madras airport.

It turned out that during a previous tune-up, the oil-breather tube had been bent down slightly. Condensation collected at that low point and then froze about 10 minutes into our flight. Ice plugging the breather line caused oil pressure to increase and blow out the prop seal. Thankfully, we were able to land safely on the lee side of those snowdrifts.

I refused to fly the airplane home, so I called the Piper dealer in Portland and told him my plight. He sent a pilot to Madras, who said he would fly my airplane to the Portland airport, and I could fly his airplane, an Aztec slightly larger than mine, home to Seattle.

"Don't worry," he said. "It flies the same." He went over the dashboard a bit with me and then left. We never had any discussion about insurance; I didn't sign any papers. I simply took his more expensive airplane and, with some trepidation due to never having flown that airplane before, returned with it to Seattle. Everything went well. In about five days, the mechanic flew my airplane to me and took his back to Portland. Of course, a casual exchange like that would never happen today.

Detour in the Sky

I continued to use our airplane a tremendous amount. From Seattle, I flew to California's Bay Area at least every other week. That was when air navigation wasn't at all like it is now. For one thing, there was no such thing as GPS. And the navigation aids we did have were primitive, such as radio navigation by means of a trailing antenna that I could let out through the tail of the aircraft to give us longer-range radio reception. I could then home in on a commercial AM radio station and have a directional needle to that station. For example, when I was flying across the mountains, I knew the heights of the highest peaks and could follow the AM needle directly to a city. My primary navigation aid was an omnidirectional flight instrument called an Omnigator. In those days, every such instrument was constructed with vacuum tubes, which meant it wasn't nearly as powerful or accurate as today's digital equipment.

I even recall flying several times through the Rocky Mountains at night and steering just by light navigation. The government had light towers set up on certain mountain peaks so pilots could fly from one light to the next. I got over mountain passes a number of times that way. Thinking back, it gives me kind of an eerie feeling.

But that eerie feeling is nothing compared to what happened on a flight from Seattle to Eureka, California, where we were completing a new high school. I talked with the FAA Flight Service Center and got a complete report on weather along my route. The forecast reported clear skies in Seattle, but from about Olympia south, it was pretty much solid overcast with fog to the ground, with no wind anywhere in the region. It covered the southern half of Washington, all of Oregon, and the northern part of California. Eureka was clear, and the airport at Crescent City—which is a little north of Eureka—was open. However, the overcast hovered along the edge of Crescent City's coastline, which the airport paralleled.

Then I learned that the navigation systems were out of service at North Bend, about two-thirds of the way down the Oregon coast.

I knew from the weather report that I would have to fly over the top of the overcast all the way from Olympia to Eureka. No problem. I was used to doing that in such conditions, and dead-reckoning the 400 miles from Astoria, Oregon, to Crescent City, California, where the next working navigation aid was located, would be no problem either. I filed my flight plan without any major concern.

Taking off from Seattle, I climbed over the clouds and overcast. My little twin engine Apache was flying very well, and I was at ease as I headed directly to Astoria, Oregon. Situation normal.

Then just past Astoria, I noticed that when I compared the reading on the magnetic compass to the gyrocompass—my primary instrument for dead-reckoning to California—the gyro-compass had precessed an unusual amount. In fact, it was a greater change than I'd ever seen. Strange! I was sure I had reset the instrument for accuracy in Seattle before and after takeoff. But now I was beginning to doubt myself. Had I forgotten to reset it? Or had it simply not engaged? Since it had been working perfectly in the past, I didn't get overly worried and just corrected the gyrocompass to the magnetic compass reading. Still, my eyes kept darting over to the gyrocompass more often than normal.

I took a heading, picked it up on the gyrocompass, and flew for about 45 minutes toward Eureka. The gyro was holding firm to the magnetic compass, so I quit worrying about any precessing. From previous flights I'd made in this region, I knew I'd soon be picking up the Crescent City aviation radio. But strangely, I couldn't get a signal. My brain and body clicked into alert.

Something was out of whack, something I couldn't see or hadn't noticed. A pilot's heartbeat kicks up a few notches in uncertainty like this. I decided to maintain my current course for only another 15 minutes, then make a decision.

Fifteen minutes later, I was still flying without receiving any radio calls. I made some outgoing calls to the airport frequency but got only silence in return. Working to suppress a natural panic and suspecting I was in serious trouble, I then turned to the emergency frequency, VHF 121.5, and put out emergency calls to see if anyone would respond. The radio was dead silent. My heartbeat ratcheted up so quickly, it startled me. It was almost as if the radio silence told me I didn't exist.

Searching for the problem, I wondered if I'd made an error entering the airport radio-frequency settings. To check that out, I reached for Jeppesen's *Private Pilot Manual*, nicknamed "The Pilot's Bible." It's packed with information on every airport, including highly detailed airport diagrams and all radio frequencies. In the split-second it took me to reach over slightly and lift my Jeppesen guide off the dash, my eye caught a glimpse of my magnetic compass making a big spin. Whoa!

My heart nearly stopped beating. I did stop breathing.

In that flash of a second, I realized the truth. The metal spine of the Jeppesen manual had corrupted the magnetic compass into giving me false information. It had told me I was flying south, when I was actually flying west over the Pacific Ocean, heading into a certain doom!

In a millisecond, I instinctively wheeled my plane around to a heading I thought might be the general direction of the California coastline. My mouth went dry as I frantically reset my plane's course and sent a flurry of prayers heavenward.

I was in huge trouble—unable to see anything because of the thick overcast below, unable to hear any airport radio transmission since I had flown out of range, and unable to be heard by any airport or ship on the emergency frequency.

For the next 20 to 30 minutes of nonstop terror, I realized I was lost somewhere over the Pacific Ocean. If I went down over this vast space, no one would ever know it. They'd never discover where or when I disappeared.

By now fuel was running low. I continued to ask God for help in finding my way back to land and to sustain me in flight. Instinctively, I started to conserve fuel every way I knew. I throttled back the engines and adjusted the propellers to their most economical slow-flight performance mode, trying to squeeze every mile possible out of each ounce of gas left. But despite my fuel-saving efforts, the fuel-gauge needle dipped lower and lower. That gauge took on another dimension. Now it was also a life gauge, predicting my life span.

Suddenly, I saw the needle on my Omni gauge move, and in a few minutes, I heard the static of an airport radio coming into range. It was the best thing I'd ever heard since Barbara had said "I do."

The radio receiver was now bringing in the Crescent City airport signal. As soon as it grew strong enough for me to use it to get a direction, I learned that I was flying exactly on the right coordinate. I thanked God for this turn of fortune, feeling maybe he still had things for me to do on this earth.

When I arrived at Crescent City, I got another good break. The bank of fog lay just off the edge of the airport, making the runways easily visible. Still I got on my radio to declare an emergency landing because my fuel gauges were now showing empty. In fact, I purposely glided my aircraft from flight level down onto the runway. Later, I learned that because I had not arrived in Eureka, the FAA staff at the Eureka airport was about to initiate an inquiry to other airports, sites, and stations in the system along my submitted flight plan.

As I climbed out of the Piper Apache, my legs still a bit shaky, I was nearly overwhelmed with the realization of what had just happened. If I had not caught that brief glimpse of the magnetic compass's spin when I removed the Jeppesen guide, I would have continued in the wrong direction until it was too late. That brief glimpse had definitely been a God-moment, preventing me from plunging to my death in the Pacific Ocean.

Still, in spite of God's protection over my life, it was several years before I told Barbara about my nearly disastrous sky detour. We were growing a family of five kids, and her life was busier than mine. I figured she already had plenty to worry about.

My business continued to depend more and more on my use of a small private plane. I set up an office in San Mateo, near Palo Alto, just south of San Francisco. Working there was a general superintendent of construction, along with Kendall Peterson, an estimator. We did a lot of work in the region building state office buildings, some college dormitories, and a couple of hospitals. But our biggest challenge lay ahead—on another mountain peak.

3
MISSION IMPOSSIBLE

Having successfully completed the microwave-station job atop the remote mountain peak near Madras, we didn't hesitate in 1959 to bid on another huge microwave-communications facility, a radio relay station for AT&T's telephone service from New York to Los Angeles.

The facility was to be built above Echo Summit pass on US Route 50 in California's Sierra Nevada Range. At normal elevation, constructing such a facility would be routine. But the summit was about 3,000 feet above the highway pass itself, with no roads of any kind going to the top.

Nothing about the job was easy. As my small team and I started cost-estimating, we were intimidated by logistics problems. How on earth do you get tons upon tons of cement, steel, and other building materials—plus machines and workers—up to a mountain peak that has no road but does have such stringent environmental restrictions that road possibilities are pretty much eliminated? Yes, on our first billy-goat project, we were required to punch in a mountain road that ascended what seemed like straight up for some two miles. But the Echo Summit project presented additional challenges.

Getting to the peak was so immensely difficult, we considered *everything*, no matter how outlandish an idea it was, from unique vehicles to pack horses to mules. But studying ski hills that had similar access problems, I decided to build our own cableway, the type seen at ski resorts everywhere from Switzerland to Colorado.

The cableway would be one and a half miles long, with the first span a mile in length and climbing 2,500 feet to the supporting break-over tower. Then the second span was about a half mile to the building site. It worked great, allowing us to run the cableway 24 hours a day, seven days a week, 365 days a year. We used it to haul up many materials: sacks of cement, rebar, sand, gravel, structural steel, and even food and water, since many of our crew tent-camped on the peak. That cableway still operates reliably, day in and day out, at Echo Summit, overlooking Lake Tahoe.

This daredevil project captured regional attention, becoming the featured picture on the cover of the San Francisco telephone directory one year. A film of it also was made to be shown at the 1961 annual meeting of AT&T's board of directors.

Facing Lofty Challenges

Getting materials and people to the peak each day prompted me to purchase my first helicopter in 1960. It was only a three-place (three-seat) machine, but in the early sixties, helicopters were just then getting turbo-charged engines and the mechanical ability to fly as high as 9,500 feet. In fact, our machine, designated as a 47G3B1, was the first turbo-charged, three-place helicopter Bell ever built. I bought it slightly used, since it was the machine Bell Helicopters had used to get their type certificate from the FAA. It was also the only one available for sale. I paid $46,000 for it, which I thought was excessively high at the time. However, we now pay over $3 million for a seven-place helicopter.

Eventually, we recognized we simply could not avoid building a primitive road to the peak, since many objects, such as the huge antennas that were to go atop the completed facility, were too heavy for the helicopter and either too heavy or too clumsy for the cableway. The facility also had to have large diesel generators for producing power. Each of those weighed a ton or more. And we knew we would have to have a 15-ton mobile crane to pour concrete, lift structural steel, and other building materials, as well as lift major pieces of equipment into the building as it was being constructed. Clearly, there was no choice but to punch in a "pioneer road."

But we needed permission to build such a road. After much discussion and many promises to AT&T and the US Forest Service not to cut any trees—along with our firm written commitment to restore everything back to the natural environment when we were done constructing the facility—we received permission. However, the cableway and helicopter were to remain as our primary transportation.

Those of us who built the road were proud of our accomplishment, but the terrain was so steep, rugged, and dangerous, only a handful of vehicles could negotiate the road. The incline was even too much for a Jeep to handle. Still, we did find a couple of rigs that could make it up and down. A commercial, four-wheel-drive Dodge truck was able to handle it, even with a load. We took film footage of the truck, loaded with radomes (weatherproof enclosures for microwave antenna), as it climbed up our billy-goat road.

Since the facility had emergency diesel generators to produce electricity, another part of our task was to build a 30,000-gallon-capacity diesel-fuel storage tank.

We encountered yet another challenge in building the facility itself. At the height of the Cold War in the late fifties and early sixties, the world's two super powers, Russia and the

A four-wheel-drive truck hauls part of a radome up the steep, snowy mountainside.

United States, experienced several nuclear showdowns, including the Cuban Missile Crisis of 1962. That caused both governments to construct critical buildings that might survive nuclear war. The Echo Summit communications facility would hopefully be one of those, since AT&T and the US government required us to use huge, extremely thick concrete walls. As a result, we needed endless tons of concrete.

Ironically, while the Echo Peak summit was buried in tons of snow each winter, it didn't have enough water in summer. During June, July, and August, we had to haul water up to the peak for the concrete we were mixing daily. So we tested an idea I had for a reservoir. I placed a portable swimming pool at the peak. Sometimes water in it would freeze. At other times we would shovel snow into it when we were short of water. We laid a steam-cleaner wand in the pool to melt the snow or ice and circulate the water. Our temporary reservoir for construction cost us less than $1,000.

The biggest accomplishment in terms of weight-challenges was our success in hauling the 15-ton crane up to the peak using two D-8 caterpillar tractors—one pulling from the front with a cable and the other pushing from behind.

We couldn't let any problem get in the way of mixing and pouring concrete on that high mountain peak. Since no Ready-Mix concrete truck could get near us, all we could do was haul up bagged cement on the cableway and mix it with aggregate and sand at the top. After much work, we did succeed in transporting a 16S skip loader/concrete mixer and a Bin-a-Batch aggregate dispenser up there by taking the entire mixer apart. Then we helicoptered components of it in packages that were light enough for the aircraft to lift safely, and we transported heavy components using the tram. We reassembled the entire mixer at the peak.

The Bin-A-Batch aggregate-batching system was essentially a bottom-gated bucket that moved on a trolley beam to a point under each bin of various rock and sand components that would go into the mix. Each bin was equipped with a scale to measure the precise amount of material deposited in the bucket. A worker would operate the levers to dispense the material, and the trolley would move the bucket to where it would dump the mix into the mixer's skip loader. This system maintained the integrity of our designed mix to produce quality concrete.

Other workers then added powdered cement from bags into the skip loader and pulled a lever depositing premeasured amounts of water. The little mixer would whip up a batch of concrete to be dumped into power buggies (motorized wheelbarrows) or the crane bucket, and the concrete was placed where it was needed.

Given the restrictions of our equipment, we made a small batch every three minutes or so for what seemed like forever. This system allowed us to produce 40 yards of concrete per day, which is the equivalent of five concrete-truck loads a day. Not bad for a job on top of a mountain peak.

Our familiarity with primitive equipment and this style of batching gave us an edge. The equipment had been state of the art in the 1930s and was still being manufactured for projects in Africa and other places around the world, so we were able to buy new machines. However, nearly all US contractors were familiar only with updated designs.

This project was so extremely challenging to engineer and build that our work on that mountaintop was almost a Mission Impossible. A lot of fresh ideas and

The completed Echo Summit microwave station perched atop a mountain peak.

many unusual pieces of equipment were needed. Our company ended up owning some very interesting gear, including helicopters, special concrete batching equipment, eight-person snow tractors—such as are used at ski resorts for grooming large slopes—and other self-sustaining equipment.

Sometimes the weather would close in, and we couldn't fly, so we built an emergency camp atop the mountain for our workers. Some union organizations tried to unionize us and attempted to picket us at the locations from where we normally flew employees in the morning. Helicopters allowed us to be flexible, so we daily changed the pickup points—an airport here or a field there. As a result, we ended up never having much of a problem in that regard.

We bid Echo Summit as a lump-sum project, and we did well, calculating all of the logistics involved. Our success gave our young company bragging rights. The extreme job required all of us to use our imaginations, but we got the project done in record time. There were far too many unknowns, even with the best preplanning, so many changes had to be made in the contract. I am proud of the ingenuity we showed in getting this job accomplished, and I'm proud of the great relationship we built with AT&T.

A Regrettable Death

Given the high altitude, the steep inclines, the cold, the wind, and countless other dangers at every hand, we had remarkably few injuries. But we did suffer a death.

Near the end of our job, a workman climbed into our three-place helicopter to catch a ride down from the top of the mountain. The chopper had side baskets like those you might have seen on the TV series M*A*S*H. While the pilot and the ground attendant were looking in another direction, the workman put his lunchbox in the basket as he entered the helicopter.

We never allowed loose items in the side baskets. We posted warnings on the baskets, at each helispot we operated from, at the job site, and in our regular safety meetings regarding helicopter safety. Anything that went in the side baskets had to be safely roped down.

When the chopper lifted off, the lunchbox flew into the air during the fast descent of almost 3,000 feet, and hit the tail rotor, causing the helicopter to lose directional control. The machine plunged into a meadow. Although the workmen survived, the pilot was killed—the result of a simple, thoughtless act.

4

THE MOST UNUSUAL PIPELINE IN THE WORLD

Shortly after wrapping up our work at the Echo Summit project in 1963, I considered a federal government Request for Proposal for a job in Arizona. The project was to design and construct a freshwater pipeline, 13 and a half miles long, to be laid in a trench mostly underneath the trans-canyon trail from Rim to Rim in the Grand Canyon. My immediate thought was, "That's my kind of challenge!" I ordered the specifications and information and soon realized this would be the most unusual pipeline in the world.

Buried below the canyon's hard rock, the pipeline would carry water from the North Rim, which has an abundance of water, over to Indian Gardens, 2,000 feet below the summit of the South Rim, which has a shortage of water. The reason for the shortage is connected with the Canyon's nearly 40 sedimentary rock layers. On the North Rim, the water table is located just a few layers down. But where that rock layer is cut off in the chasm that forms the canyon, the water runs out of the rock and down to the canyon floor. The corresponding rock layer on South Rim, therefore, has no way of accessing that drained water table. The government's plan was for a pipeline to solve that problem.

Several "Plan Holders," or construction companies, including mine, requested all the government's plans and documents related to the job. The plans package contained enough detailed information and specifications to allow contractors to make reasonably intelligent bids on the proposed project, which required us to do the engineering and final designs for the pipeline. Among other specifications, this unique pipeline had to be capable of delivering 600 gallons of water per minute from its North Rim source at Roaring Springs to its South Rim destination at Indian Gardens. Only three of us bid the job—Elling Halvorson Inc., and two international pipeline companies.

The National Park Service encouraged all potential bidders to take advantage of the time before bidding closed in a couple more weeks and visit the canyon so they could assess the pipeline route. My guys and I were eager to do that. "After all," we told ourselves, "if we can be masters of a mountaintop, why can't we be masters of a canyon?"

I was told to call Fred Harvey for hotel reservations and to reserve mules for the ride down to the canyon floor. Being pretty young at the time, I'd never heard of the Fred Harvey Company that owned Harvey House restaurants, hotels, and other hospitality businesses in several states, as well as being concessionaires at various state and national parks and providing all the food service for the Santa Fe Railway.

I called the number and said, "I'd like to speak with Fred."

"Fred who?"

"Well, Fred Harvey, of course," I replied. "It says right here in this invitation to call Fred Harvey. So that's what I'm doing."

The person on the phone explained that there wasn't any Fred Harvey anymore and that the name referred to a large organization. So I made room reservations and then spoke to someone in the mule barn.

Within a few days, I piloted our company airplane, with my San Mateo general superintendent and our estimator on board, and landed at Flagstaff, Arizona, where there was a bit of snow on the runway. From there, we drove a rental car to Grand Canyon Village, which in 1963, was a small settlement along the edge of the South Rim—then and now the most visited section of the canyon. We checked into a hotel and prepared to meet the park service people the following morning.

The sun rose over the Grand Canyon at 5:00 AM. I left the hotel early, walked to the canyon's edge, and looked down in open-mouth amazement at the scope, the sweep, the size, and the sheer visual impact of it all. It made me feel so small, I felt as if I could sit on a sheet of paper and dangle my legs. It was a spiritual experience, and, thrilled to my bones, I realized I couldn't possibly walk away from the project in that most astonishing place. I felt an energy and enthusiasm for a job I was convinced my team and I could excel at.

The insights I would gain about how unusual and how *tough* this unique job could be began with the mules that would take us down into the canyon. At the mule barn, a staff member took one look at me and asked what I weighed. When I told him, he replied, "Mr. Halvorson, you have a choice. You can either rent two mules—riding one for half an hour and then changing to the other for half an hour—or you can

After experiencing the magnificence of the Grand Canyon, I was eager to share the view with Barbara.

rent just one mule, ride him for half an hour, then carry *him* for a half hour." This brought snickers from my crew.

I settled for two mules named Scotch and Bourbon, making me wonder about the sobriety of their owner. These mules were not the smaller burro breed. They were larger than many horses and more suited to this exacting trail work, but after riding them all day, my legs looked like parentheses. I did gain more confidence in these animals that were bred for their strength, endurance, temperament, and gentleness. The steepness of the trails, the hold-your-breath tight turns, and the steep cliffs didn't bother them at all. They made the journey almost every day. Still, it was a bit unnerving to be told the mules were skittish. Arriving at last on the canyon floor, we had some refreshments at Phantom Ranch, a remarkable and still-popular tourist facility.

Exploring the Canyon

For the next three days, my crew and I walked, crawled, and climbed along the entire 13-and-a-half-mile pipeline route. In most cases, that was on or adjacent to the hard-rock Rim-to-Rim trail that had been built in the 1930s.

As we followed white flags the park service people had placed to indicate where the pipe was to be buried, we studied every problem spot, often taking photographs, noting the difficulties and costs, and drafting copious notes for our subsequent bid. We scrutinized every foot of the pipeline route as we progressed, including along Bright Angel Creek, which runs through Bright Angel Canyon from the North Rim to the Colorado River.

The first huge challenge was that the Rim-to-Rim trail rarely followed a straight line. It would bend to the right in one place, then bend to the left in another, plus every few yards, it would tip down or up in what are known as *vertical bends*. Said my estimator, "Elling, this is going to be the most crooked pipeline on earth. There won't be anything else like it!" He was right.

We realized that building a pipeline in the Grand Canyon presented us with at least five challenges so incredibly difficult, each could be called almost impossible.

Seven Impossible Challenges
#1 – The Trench

Park service management wanted as few visible signs of the finished pipeline as possible. Where the pipeline would go up vertical walls, we were required to hide it behind cliffs and in crevasses. Where it was to run on the canyon floor, we had to invent a practical way to dig a 13-and-a-half-mile long trench—from solid rock—that would contain the underground pipe.

Then we needed to invent a way to fill the trench with "select material." That's a construction term for a mixture of sand and "three-quarter-inch-minus" rocks that are no larger in diameter than three-quarters of an inch. The fill material would surround the pipe and protect it in the trench.

This requirement worried me from the time I first read it during the bid process. The trench would be approx.-imately 71,000 feet long, and, on average, three feet wide by three feet deep. That meant we'd need half a million cubic feet of three-quarter-inch-minus fill material.

Eventually, we set up an equipment staging area at Yaqui Point.

We immediately saw there was no available bedding material anywhere along the trail.

But how on earth could we get half a million cubic feet of small rock from the canyon rim down one mile to the canyon floor? As one man in my group said, "If mules are the only way to get crushed rock into the Grand Canyon, we'll be working here for light years."

We racked our brains for a solution to the problem. Could we vacuum or rake up material from the trail and its border? Hauling select fill down from the canyon rim was impractical. In fact, the nearest rock pit was 20 miles away, and once brought to the rim, the rock would still require crushing and screening. The helicopter costs of flying select material down to the canyon floor would be enormous. It simply was not practical.

As we were puzzling the problem, I got a brilliant flash of inspiration. *I was standing on the solution!* We had to create a rock trench anyway to lay the pipeline. We could recycle the dynamited rock to become the select fill we needed. This idea energized my team because it would save both time and money and have the least impact on the canyon itself.

But after that inspired moment, I realized no equipment existed to do such a unique job, especially given the rest of the impossible challenges.

#2 – Trail Restrictions

In its stewardship of the Grand Canyon, the National Park Service imposed a tough rule concerning where vehicles and equipment could operate. For the most part, our construction company was confined to the six-foot-wide right-of-way, or the width of the trail, whichever was least. As we explored the trail and pipeline right-of-way, the significance of the restriction hit us hard and caused other challenges to surface. Where would we store the blasted-rock backfill, since we could not stack it on the canyon floor itself? And how could we travel the narrow pathways on the Rim-to-Rim trail with normal construction equipment? Ouch. We'd been in the Grand Canyon only a few hours, and already we had serious problems. I thought, *Maybe this job is simply not doable.*

#3 – Transporting Personnel

As I planned the job and worked on solving challenges, I realized we would need about 50 construction workers in the canyon almost daily. And I immediately saw that if our construction people had to get down to the job site by mule ride, half their work day would be lost sitting on mules. We needed a better answer than "mule transit." I decided we would solve that issue two ways. First, we'd construct a temporary camp with bunkhouses and a cook house. Our crews would stay in the canyon all week and go home on weekends. Second, we'd transport workers in and out using helicopters, as we did in our earlier mountaintop project overlooking Lake Tahoe.

#4 – Delivering Equipment and Supplies

I realized that another solution we'd invented at Echo Summit would help us move major equipment pieces. We would disassemble the equipment at our staging area above the canyon and then helicopter individual pieces down to the canyon floor, where they would be reassembled. But what about moving supplies? Most water pipe weighs *tons.* How could we ever get 71,000 feet of it down into the canyon? We considered using tethered balloons to lower heavy iron pipes to the job site. Other ideas included an aerial cableway, large helicopters, mule trains, and variations of each idea. This challenge had me thinking every minute about solutions.

#5 – Blasting and Crushing Rock

We had to find practical ways to drill holes in the rock where we would insert explosives for controlled blasting. Then we needed to invent ways to crush the blasted rock to three-quarter-inch-minus on site, all the while keeping the trail open for our workers who would be on foot and using trail scooters.

Self-Manufacturing

All of these conditions meant we had to find special tractors, backhoes, wagons, and rock crushers. Each piece of machinery had to be self-propelled and narrow enough to fit the trail and negotiate tight turns.

As I glumly pondered these obstacles, I suddenly hit upon a solution. I realized that if we couldn't find the unique equipment we needed for this narrow rock trail, we would just have to build it from scratch. I shared the idea with my guys, and they immediately saw the sense of it. We weren't defeated after all.

Workers disassemble equipment to be airlifted to the canyon floor.

That evening I began to rough-sketch each individual piece of equipment we would design and build. First was our own rock-drilling rig. Next was a crawler-tractor backhoe that would fit the confines of the narrow trail. Getting into the groove of this "possibility thinking" over the next several days, I then visualized and sketched a self-propelled screening and rock-crushing machine. My crew was right with me. If the equipment we needed didn't exist, we would manufacture it ourselves.

Naturally, each piece of gear we handmade would have to be capable of navigating the trails adequately with front-and-back steering, while never exceeding 39 inches. As I developed more and more solutions, I became enthusiastic about the potential project that earlier had seemed impossible.

Before submitting our bid proposal, I brought in a very reputable firm, Lent's Mechanical Contractors, out of Bremerton, Washington. They provided me with a piping superintendent to manage my crews who would be bending, placing, and welding the pipe.

Adapting to Project Specifications

The source of water for the pipeline was a forceful stream on the north end of Bright Angel Canyon fed by an underground river. In fact, the stream exits the canyon wall so fast, it's named Roaring Springs. I felt confident I could design and build a reliable dam, along with a penstock using 12-inch pipe down to our eight-inch line.[2]

The federal government's bid specifications also acknowledged there were places where we could *not* follow the trail. In order to follow the flagging, we had to design and build a total of eight bridges. They included seven rigid-frame bridges over Bright Angel Creek and one 640-foot suspension bridge over the Colorado River.

We also had to consider the nature of the Grand Canyon's climate. We peppered the park service people about it. "Can our people work here in comfort and in safety?" We were told summer temperatures soared up to 120 degrees, so all of our workers in the canyon would be

---

[2] The pipeline itself consisted of three diameters of pipe, beginning with 12-inch pipe. As the pressure increased, the pipe reduced to eight inches, and then finally down to six inches. As the diameter changed, the thickness of the pipe walls also increased, according to the amount of water head (pressure). At the bottom of the Canyon, the pipe held about 2,500 pounds of pressure psi (per square inch). Where we delivered the water up to Indian Gardens, the pipe reduced back to eight inches and about 400 psi.

required to carry their own daily water supply. For our camp water system, we piped water from Bright Angel Creek, and then filtered, chlorinated, and stored it in a pressure tank. That gave us good potable water for drinking, cooking, and bathing. Each man carried two gallons of water to work in the mornings. When it got really hot, occasionally someone would also cool off with a dip in Bright Angel Creek.

To offset the hot afternoon weather, we decided to start our construction day much earlier than normal. Work would start at dawn in our race against the Arizona sun.

Given the many, many risks and multiple engineering challenges, I thought it was likely that our company would be the only one to submit a bid on the Grand Canyon job. But when the official bid-opening day arrived, I was quite surprised to learn that two other firms had also submitted bids. I'm certain our ingenious ideas to solve the Grand Canyon problems enabled us to be the low bidder. I suspect the competing contractors submitted far more expensive bids since they likely planned a traditional approach to supplying the select fill material.

It turned out that our low bid initially made the park service people nervous about our young group. They interviewed me and my team before finally awarding us the contract. They later told us that since our quote was so much lower than our competitors, they needed to make sure we knew what we were doing. As we detailed our accomplishments and problem-solving on other challenging jobs, they gained confidence in our abilities.

Curious about the competing bids, I crunched some numbers regarding a more traditional approach: transporting 39,000,000 pounds of select-fill rock and contracting for a medium-lift helicopter to make some 19,000 trips to get the fill rock down to the canyon floor. I figured they'd fly about 6,500 hours at about $1,200 an hour, costing them nearly $8 million, just to move the fill rock.

Given these numbers, I'm convinced their bids were significantly higher than the one we submitted with our completely different plan.

5
OVERCOMING CHALLENGES ON A GRAND SCALE

We were officially awarded the Grand Canyon pipeline contract in late 1963, and we started the project in early 1964. As the reality of the huge job sank in, our excitement faded. We worked day after day to come up with solutions to the five "impossible challenges" we had to solve before construction could even begin.

One of the stickiest challenges concerned the delivery of supplies. I mentioned earlier we considered tethered lighter-than-air balloons, mule trains, an aerial cableway, and other methods of transportation. What we did agree on was that simply transporting pipe, supplies, and workers to the canyon floor didn't solve the problem of how to deliver everything and everyone to 13 and a half miles of different locations all along the pipeline route.

Ultimately, we realized that helicopters, with their proven ability to fly materials into the mile-deep canyon and rapidly deliver everything to specific points, trumped any other approach. But many other tough problems remained to be solved—and quickly. One of my best guys said, "Elling, this project makes the Echo Summit job look easy!"

Doing the Impossible

A lot of my engineering success in designing and making the custom construction equipment resulted from the help of two wizards in nearby Flagstaff, Arizona. In 1964, I'd found one of these men in a machine shop and the other in a welding shop. They became my second family.

We knew the stakes were high. We felt the pressure of the challenges. For several months, this challenge had almost 100 percent of my focus. At night I'd make machinery drawings, and in the morning I'd show up at the machine shop with coffee and my ideas. Doing what others thought was impossible became routine for us. We were cocky. But we were a great team at what we did, and we succeeded in creating machines no one had seen before.

Our pneumatic-powered Stoper rock drill[3] was so heavy, we had to find a machine to mount it on, but at first we couldn't find anything powerful enough that fit our size requirements. Then I happened to come across a picture of a small crawler tractor that would fit our needs perfectly. It was only about two and a half feet high and five feet long. We were able to obtain one, and it worked great. I've never seen anything quite like it since.

We carefully calculated that every 18 inches on the rock trail—a path that covered most of the 13-and-a-half mile pipeline—we'd need to drill a blasting hole 30 inches deep. How many drill holes was that? I still remember: approximately 47,000.

Making the Crushed Rock

The process of manufacturing crushed rock always started with a bang. Our blasting experts, known in the trade as "powder monkeys," set dynamite charges inside the holes we'd just drilled. The brilliant dimension of this idea was in using delayed charges that would break the rock better than any other method known.

Blasting caps are sold with differing delay options: 3 milliseconds, 5 milliseconds, etc. When the powder monkey would push the plunger, a charge of electricity would go to all the caps. Milliseconds after the first explosion was shattering the hard rock around it, a second explosion was triggered, followed a millisecond later by a third. The kinetic energy from each blast would help break up the material in the other blasts detonated just milliseconds apart. In a flash, the three blasts created an instant trench in the rock trail. It also created tons of broken rock to go into the crusher and come out as select three-quarter-inch-minus fill.

---

[3] To operate the drill, we mounted a pair of Swedish-built rotary air compressors on two Athey wagons pulled behind the crawler tractor. Each compressor produced 85 cubic feet per minute at 120 psi, and we knew we needed 160 cubic feet per minute, but happily, when manifolded together, the two compressors produced 170 cubic feet per minute at 120 psi.

Soon after hatching the blasting idea, I focused on the design of a backhoe that would dig the shattered rock, making enough room in the ditch for us to lay in the pipe.

Next, I worked on designing a rock crusher. While dynamite has the power to shatter rock, only a rock crusher has the ability to make larger rock into a specific size. Our rock crusher, like all our other equipment, could be no wider than 39 inches.

Then there was the problem of what to do with the rock after crushing it. We couldn't leave it along the trail, because we had to use the trail for ground transportation until we installed the pipe. I realized I needed to build a conveyor and digging machine that could produce its own crushed-rock trail.

The concept I came up with was a backhoe that would drop the rock into a receiving bin. Then a conveyor would transport the rock up to a four-foot-square shaker screen constructed of crisscrossed steel rods. When the slanted screen shook, rocks small enough to fit into the eight-inch crusher would drop through the screen's six-inch openings. Rocks too large to fall through the screen would continue moving along and fall off the end into the crusher. Any rocks too big for the crusher were thrown off to the side by a worker.

The resulting three-quarter-inch-minus fill would drop onto the conveyor belt below and then be moved to a point several feet in front of the crushing machine. From there, the select fill would fall off the conveyor belt onto the trench, creating a trail, and the crushing machine could continually move forward on the trail it had just created.

There was just one hitch. In building the self-propelled machine, I needed the right jaw crusher. The problem was, I couldn't find one small enough. Everything available was designed for huge machinery, and we needed a Lilliputian machine. I was worried. Many searches turned up nothing, and I was only a few months away from the start date of construction. In fact I thought for a while I would have to design and fabricate a jaw crusher myself—an enormous job.

But one morning I learned of an assayer's jaw crusher, a portable device made for mining prospectors. The unit could be broken down into many small components, and each component could be transported by pack horse to a remote mining site. Once the device was reassembled, a miner could turn the crank, get the flywheel going, and crush small pieces of ore to be packed out and assayed later for minerals, such as iron, copper, or gold.

I realized the eight-inch jaw would suit our needs well, so I purchased it immediately. When we attached it to a 50-horsepower engine, it gave us a lot of crushing power in a small package. Now we had the missing link in the chain of equipment we custom-made to fit our extreme job. That amazing one-of-a-kind machine enabled us to produce a temporarily finished trail where Tote Gote off-road motorcycles could move people, and small tractors with trailers could move supplies on a gravel trail.

Ultimately, each element in the complete system, including the drilling unit, backhoe, crawler tractor, and rock crusher, was pneumatic, hydraulic, or belt-driven, allowing us to run the operation efficiently. Thus, we had an economical solution that was also environmentally sound.

Creating the Pipeline

Our next challenge was deciding what kind of pipe we would select. We could choose from steel, ductile iron, or aluminum. All were acceptable to the government. With ductile iron, we could accommodate vertical and horizontal bends with bolted fittings. Steel or aluminum pipe would have to be bent in the field.

It did not take long for us to conclude that aluminum pipe was best for this job due to its bendable quality and far lighter weight, even though aluminum comes with its own handicaps, especially in its welding. We decided to build a pipe-bending station at Plateau Point, about halfway down into the canyon. Since twists and turns happened about every 12 feet or so along most of the pipeline route, our Plateau Point bending station operated daily. Each twist or turn meant we had to make a vertical or horizontal bend in the pipe. We trained people to measure and then engineer the needed bends in the pipe at least two days in advance of installation in the trench. Each evening, the engineering data would be given to our pipe-bending crews. The next day, they would bend the pipe, and it was later helicoptered to its specific location where it would be laid and welded in the pipeline trench.

To our knowledge, this was the first time a MIG (Metal Inert Gas) welding process was used on a large-scale production in the open air. We were skeptical as to whether the process would be feasible, since the slightest gust could blow gas in the wrong direction, ruining the weld's quality. We were required to have perfect welds, and they were x-rayed every night to be certain there were no flaws. But we built special windshields that clamped around the pipe to protect the area from wind, and we were able to accomplish our goal successfully.

Rising—and Dropping—to the Challenge

Foremost in our minds was the awareness that many of the bent-pipe delivery flights would be hazardous. As we visited the flagged pipeline pathway on our initial inspection trip, we noted the more challenging places our helicopters would have to navigate.

This remarkable construction challenge, set inside one of the most challenging environments in the world, was a bidder-designed job. Therefore we—the low bidder—had the responsibility to design much of how and where the job would be accomplished. For example, the freshwater pipeline would terminate at Indian Gardens, located on a plateau about 2,000 feet below the summit of the South Rim. While 2,000 feet might not sound like much, nevertheless it is a vertical distance of almost half a mile. It was our job to design and build a powerful pumping facility that would push the water up to the top of the parched South Rim. We constructed a pump house about 40 feet square and installed two 600-horsepower positive displacement electric piston pumps. Those pumps could be run one at a time or in tandem, as required.

Another challenge for us was designing and constructing the eight bridges where the pipeline had to cross rivers and streams.

An Aircraft "Lift" for the Company

Almost every day, at every turn, this unique pipeline job presented complications. One of those complications involved the locations our helicopters could not access. So we came up with different methods to cope with the terrain, the cliffs, and the water channels all along the pipeline route. What a challenge that was! I felt we ran every option known to man.

While we always knew we'd need more than just one helicopter on the project, we eventually utilized 10 of them with varying lift capacities. Our fleet included almost every type of helicopter available, which wasn't much at the time. To minimize costs, we used our

Helicopters move equipment and supplies down to the canyon worksite.

light helicopters for everyday operations, and we leased large ones for the heavy lifts. At that time, the Vietnam War had been going on for about five years, making parts difficult to obtain at times. Whenever I had to get parts out of Bell to keep our show going, I told them I was involved in the Grand Canyon War and needed those parts.

In this largest-ever use of helicopters on a single construction site, we logged some 25,000 flying hours. In fact, from project start to project finish, we ended up scheduling approximately 7,400 helicopter flights just to move the pipe lengths to the canyon floor.

At the bottom of the canyon, a worker prepares pipe to be securely welded.

I felt I needed to be on hand full time for the very risky and expensive job, so I moved my family to the area, enrolled our kids in school, and we lived there for two years.

Still, even with all the demands of the Grand Canyon project occupying so much of my time, our company was also working on a number of other construction projects at the same time. Fortunately, the company airplane enabled me to travel up and down the West Coast so I could tend to our various projects under construction.

One of the pilots I hired from time to time was a fellow everyone called Old Mac. One of his hobbies was rock climbing. He recalled some of those busy days:

Elling was cashing in on the school-building boom in California. He had schools going up or coming out of the ground in San Mateo and Redwood City. He also had a major contract with the port authority in his home town. He was so busy, in fact, that he was logging close to 50 hours a month on his Piper Apache, which Elling usually piloted himself from job to job.

The number of hours that Elling spent in the air going from city to city and state to state was nothing compared to the time spent in meetings with architects, engineers, job supers, and in planning and zoning-commission offices. In fact, he made most of his commutes in his twin engine plane at night.

Late one evening, Elling called from the airport to my home in Salem, Oregon. He was bushed, but he had to be in

Redwood City the following morning for a meeting with principals and bankers. He also wanted to stop at San Francisco International on the way down that night to talk to his superintendent on the San Mateo job. He asked if I would fly him down while he caught a few hours of sleep en route.

Of course I said yes. I needed more multi-engine time in my log book. I had slightly more than 500 hours in twins, which was the bare minimum to qualify for insurance and a corporate flying job. Those thousands of hours of military single-engine-jet time in Korea were worthless, and no prospective employer gave a damn about my carrier landings either.

It was a perfect night for flying. Not a cloud in the sky between Salem and San Francisco, and the lights of the cities below us looked like jewels on a necklace laid out on a display counter. It was after midnight when I landed at SFO, and Elling's man met us at the plane when we parked at Butler County's General Aviation Terminal. I was amazed by Elling's ability to wake from a sound sleep and immediately begin looking at blueprints and discussing changes the school board had requested. In less than an hour we were in the air again, heading for the Redwood City airport.

"The runway is under construction," Elling informed me, "and the field is officially closed to traffic. But I've been using the taxiway for a landing strip, and you can too."

"Roger," I said, as I lined up on the parallel lines of blue lights. The landing was smooth as silk. But seeing a six-foot deep canyon next to us where the main runway should have been raised my hackles as the gear kissed the macadam taxiway.

The following morning, after a few hours of sleep in a hotel, we took off into a blanket of fog. We climbed up through the low stratus layer and headed southeast. During our stay in the hotel, Elling had asked me to fly him down to the South Rim of the Grand Canyon where he, plus his wife and kids, were living in a temporary mobile home. I agreed. We refueled the plane and had breakfast in San Jose. I plotted a course for the Peach Springs Omni beacon and filed a VFR flight plan direct.

In the middle of Death Valley, there's a place called Ash Meadows. They have a dirt landing strip beside a Spanish-style hacienda in the shade of a cluster of cottonwood trees. The place served the best chili verde burros this side of my Aunt Rene's joint in "San Berdoo." We dined well, then flew on to the Grand Canyon.

As we landed at the South Rim airport around 2:00 PM, Elling's wife, Barbara, was there to meet us, along with all of their kids. It was a delightful reunion for Elling, who hadn't seen his wife or kids in several weeks. I was surprised, because their home was in Seattle, and thus far Elling had not said a word about our reason for flying to the Grand Canyon. We climbed into the station wagon, and as Barbara drove away from the airport, I wondered, were they living here in their vacation home?

The kids were so excited to see their dad, the commotion in the car made adult conversation impossible. Yet Elling listened to each of them tell about something "super" that he or she had discovered. His twin six-year-olds had seen coyotes, squirrels, and sidewinders. The older boy had trapped a Durango scorpion and kept it at home in a jar.

Barbara drove through the edge of the Kaibab forest of stunted Ponderosa pines to their double-wide mobile home and parked close to the expanse of redwood deck on which stood a wading pool and an assortment of toys. We hardly had time enough for the kids to display all of their "neat stuff" before Elling and I were off again.

This time we were riding with his helicopter pilot, "Little Bob," in a battered pickup truck that hardly had room enough for Bob. Elling and I shoehorned ourselves into the cab. Bob's truck was waved through the gate at the entrance to the monument, and he drove straight to his helicopter pad at Yaqui Point.

During our flight from San Jose, Elling had told me quite a lot about Bob. He'd also told me he had a surprise in store for me that day. I was sure the surprise would be a flight into the canyon, but it turned out to be Elling's question, "Can you climb this cliff? I need someone to mark the right-of-way." That area was the only place where park service people had not staked the path.

Bob climbed into the 47G Bell helicopter's left seat, Elling got in the middle, and I had the small space next to the open door. Yaqui Point's elevation is nearly 7,200 feet above sea level. The Colorado River runs through the gorge about a mile below, and from the Point, it looks like a mere thread.

Bob's takeoff was a climb to three feet, a forward flight out over the drop-off, and then a plunge into the canyon in what felt like a vertical dive-bombing run. It took scant seconds to arrive at a sand bar on the south bank of the river.

Elling knew I was an experienced rock climber, but he still laughed hard when he looked at the green shade of my face. He said, "Bob's going to fly up the face of the gorge. I want you to take a good look at it and tell me whether you think you can climb it."

The lowest part of the Inner Gorge wall is comprised of metamorphic rocks: gneiss, schist and granite. No problem with that. Above the granite are bands of fractured limestone that

Workers install aluminum pipe up the cliffside route marked out by Old Mac.

look like white books placed loosely on shelves. I figured if I could handle that part of the climb, the rest would be a breeze. The upper 300 feet are sandstone- capped with a layer of solid limestone at a place called Plateau Point.

Bob hovered briefly over Plateau Point, giving me another perspective of the whole thing—all 1,800 feet of variegated rock and the river into which one would fall if he peeled. It was awesome . . . and a challenge I couldn't pass up.

Bob zoomed up the Bright Angel where I saw a mule train laboring its way up the trail. As Bob flew us back to Yaqui Point, I told Elling, "I can climb it, but I'd like to try finding a partner."

"Where?" Elling asked.

"There might be some climbers at Northern Arizona University," I said. "When we get back to your trailer, I'll call."

It turned out there were two rock climbers at the school. They were planning to climb Courthouse Rock in Sedona that weekend, and I was invited to come along. Elling sprang for a pair of Pivetta rock-climbing shoes and 200 feet of good Perlon rope. The two kids from the university had a good assortment of pitons, 'biners, and slings, so we went the next day and climbed Courthouse Rock.

The boys were pretty good climbers, but neither wanted to chance the Inner Gorge in the Grand Canyon. So I free-climbed the damned thing solo, with a couple cans of Day-Glo orange spray paint attached to my belt with bits of coat-hanger wire. As I climbed, I marked my route with paint, keeping in mind that a pipeline would be hung from the cliff and had to be kept out of sight from tourists standing on Plateau Point.

Bob was scheduled to pick me up at Plateau Point at 1300 hours. He arrived a bit early and hovered out over the river while I was working my way up a narrow, vertical crack.

"Cracking" is fairly simple. You jam a boot and a hand in the crack and twist them to get a grip. However, I remembered how that morning, just before Bob flew me down to the sandbar to begin my climb, one of Elling's boys had told us about the Durango scorpion he'd captured on their terrace. So every time I had to jam my hand into a blind crack, I was expecting to get stung!

Just as I neared the top of the cliff, something flew out of a crack—and my heart nearly stopped. Attached to the rock by one twisted boot and a fist, I swung my body away from the rock face like a garden gate. It turned out to be nothing but a grasshopper, but it gave me a full shot of adrenalin straight into the pump.

When Bob picked me up on Plateau Point a few minutes later, he said: "I'll swear you ran up the last 300 feet of that there cliff." Bob's voice was high-pitched and nasal, but when he got excited he squeaked. "And how come you did that swinging trick? I thought for sure you was a goner."

"Well, Bob," I retorted. "That was the easy part. I thought you'd get impatient and fly off. I didn't feel like hiking back to the top."

Challenges and More Challenges

Even our top professionals found it a challenge to blast mile after mile of the pipeline trench. The delicate operation required the well-skilled technicians to avoid harming the trail wall. We succeeded however, in preserving the trail's integrity.

The helicopter pipe-laying method often made for very dangerous flying. Many times the six-foot-wide right-of-way areas along the trail were located next to a sheer cliff wall on one side not far from another sheer cliff wall on the other side. That meant our pilot, descending into a box canyon enclosed with straight-up vertical walls, was allowed no errors, either by human or machine. The statistics prove that our pilots were excellent aviators.

Early in 1965, however, we experienced a setback. A group of hippies disregarded the "Trail Closed" signs and hiked down from the North Rim to the bottom of the canyon. As night descended, they built a campfire. At some point their campfire got away from them and turned into a small but destructive forest fire.

The roaring blaze raced up the canyon slope, fed by the crackly-dry juniper and pine trees. Soon, the flames licked at our aluminum penstock pipe that lay above-ground and melted the pipe into liquid.

After we rebuilt the destroyed portion of the pipeline, I kept a foot-long piece of that melted aluminum on my desk as a reminder that in construction everything and anything can—and usually will—go wrong.

By December 1965, all the pipe was in the ground. The construction part of the job was finished, and water filled the entire pipeline. All that remained was to run the final test and finish trimming and dressing the trails for turnover to the government. We were all breathing normally again and feeling very relieved.

But then we encountered a new problem. The federal government was dragging its feet on our billings. The issue was that the Grand Canyon project was a unit-price job. For instance, we were paid per foot of pipe we laid, per foot of pipe-wrap used, per cubic yard of dirt we moved, etc. When we started the project, we knew approximately how many miles long the pipeline would be, but we had no way of knowing how many feet of pipe we'd end up using or how much select fill we'd need. We did our best to be as accurate as possible, but the inspector that was assigned to us turned out to be a very suspicious person. He questioned every measurement and quantity we billed for and disputed most of our claims. He wasn't signing off on the unit-price items, and as a result, our pay estimates were consistently short.

I talked to Hal about the issue, and he recommended an attorney, Pat Sullivan, based in Spokane, Washington, who had a proven specialty in construction matters and had impressed Hal with his legal work.

When I called Pat, I also was impressed with his knowledge and quick response. He came to the canyon to investigate the federal inspector's failure to approve any of the progress payments and change orders. We both knew that unless the situation changed, I would be severely stretched financially.

Well, the situation *did* change, but in a way none of us could have imagined.

Visible from the South Rim is the North Rim of the Grand Canyon, with abundant water.

Our pipeline captures water from "Roaring Springs" on the North Rim and delivers it to the South Rim communities.

THE CANYON WITHIN A CANYON: Angel Creek Canyon

Route of the 13.5-mile-long water pipeline.

South Rim of the Canyon, where water is scarce.

We designed pipes and pumps to lift the water almost a half-mile up to the South Rim.

6
A RAINSTORM NOT SEEN IN 15 CENTURIES

The Grand Canyon rarely receives rain in December, and the rest of the year is pretty dry as well, with a total average annual precipitation of only about 16 inches. Most rain falls during the mid to late summer months with almost daily scattered thunderstorms that usually last from one to one and a half hours at the most.

But around noon on Saturday, December 3, 1965, I was astounded to watch mysterious clouds roll across an eerie-looking sky over the canyon. *It looks like the Devil's in the sky,* I thought to myself.

Although we got some rain on the South Rim, it was over the North Rim that those clouds let loose monsoon-like downpours and drenched a 100-square-mile area for the next 36 hours at the rate of about half an inch per hour. Something like a foot and a half of water funneled directly into Bright Angel Canyon.

Along with others living nearby, I was astonished. And worried. What was this storm doing to our pipeline? Even after the rain stopped, heavy

I investigate flood damage at Phantom Ranch.

clouds still smothered the entire area, so we couldn't fly in to view the damage until the atmosphere cleared on Monday morning, December 5.

At least we'd taken all the crew out on Friday, except for one cook who stayed to watch the camp. I worried about him too. Did he survive? In that pre-cellphone era, no one had heard from him since the storm began. Only one other man was in the Grand Canyon during that time—

an employee of the US Geological Survey. He lived in a cabin on a spit of land between where the Colorado River and Bright Angel Creek converged. His job was to monitor conditions in the area and take regular measurements.

Raging water inundated our equipment and uncovered newly laid pipe.

At daybreak on Monday, my pilot and job superintendent and I took off in a helicopter from Yaqui Point. The destruction we saw below us was far beyond our original fears. The raging torrent down Bright Angel Canyon had taken everything with it, including six of the seven rigid-frame bridges we'd built over Bright Angel Creek. Trails were destroyed. The forest of towering cotton-wood trees had been swept away. Part of Phantom Ranch was washed out.

Many segments of our once-buried pipeline were now merely twisted, crushed pieces of aluminum lying along the canyon floor. Our costly custom-made construction equipment had been smashed and was still lying underwater.

I returned to Yaqui Point with a heavy heart at this huge detour for our project. I had to break news of the destruction to everyone, lay off some 50 strong, sun-bronzed men, and inform them it might be a long time before any of our work could resume—if ever.

The mood of the moment I finished my announcement was awful. Everyone on the job was out of work now, including me. I saw financial ruin coming at me head-on. We still owed bank loans on some of our equipment—machinery that was uninsured. We hadn't bothered purchasing insurance on it because we removed it every night to a point higher than the 100-year flood plain. Another reason was that park service management had completely closed the trail during our construction project, so, with no tourists around, vandalism wasn't a risk. Our resulting loss on remaining bank obligations for equipment alone was half a million dollars.

When I met with park service people, they, like us, were confused and in shock at the magnitude of the storm's damage. We were all trying to make sense of what had just happened.

I immediately return-ed to Bremerton for a meeting with my part-

We still owed money on destroyed machinery.

ners, Lent's Mechanical Contractors. I showed them our photos and provided the initial information that we and the park service had gathered. Then, in Seattle for a few days, I spent considerable time on the telephone with Carl and Hal. Their experience in such calamities helped me a great deal. They were two rocks I could lean on—and did.

One week after the historic flood, I flew back to the canyon with measuring tapes and cameras in order to estimate our losses and figure out how long it would take us to rebuild. I planned to spend whatever time was necessary. So, on December 12, we descended into the canyon again, and our helicopter's fateful encounter with an unseen antenna wire left me critically injured on the rock floor.

As I felt my body grow cold and my life ebb away, it came to me that I hadn't done much for God. I thought about the many promises to him I had broken. That realization brought me to a changing point. I prayed, "God, if you deliver me from this, I will always share my story and my faith whenever I have the opportunity." You might call my experience something of a foxhole rededication.

I immediately began to experience a string of seven miracles. They were all vital to my survival. If any one of them had been left out, or if they'd happened in a different order, I wouldn't have survived. Six spared my physical life, and the seventh rescued me from financial and occupational ruin.

The First Miracle

The first of the seven miracles was that *I crashed in the presence of the only person living in the bottom of that canyon for 277 river miles.* He was the United States Geological Survey employee. Even our camp was vacant. When the USGS guy saw us land on the sandbar and take off again, he began filming us with an eight-millimeter movie camera. He was still shooting when we hit the wire. Seeing our trouble, he didn't wait for us to hit the ground before he stopped recording and ran to his house to telephone topside for help.

After seeing the crashed helicopter's remains, no one believed I could possibly survive.

Another helicopter of ours was running up on Yaqui Point. As soon as my employees learned of the crash, several jumped into the aircraft and came down immediately to be at my side. Some people might think the USGS man's timely presence was a coincidence, but I believe it was a miracle.

The Second Miracle

After the flood, the USGS employee had *the only working telephone in the canyon.* We had clipped telephones to an existing line along the entire pipeline, but the flood took out every phone except the one at the USGS employee's cabin. It was located just 100 yards from where I crashed. If I had gone down around the next curve, the man wouldn't have seen me, and we would have had no way to communicate my urgent medical needs.

Some might call the working telephone a mere coincidence, but I believe it was the second miracle.

The Third Miracle

The fact that *I remained conscious and mentally alert*, in spite of my grave condition, was the third miracle. It enabled me to recognize that I was drowning in my own blood. When those around me were too afraid to help me turn so the blood could drain, God gave me the strength to perform that life-saving act myself. My mental alertness also helped me recognize, even though no one around me did, that something was terribly wrong with my lungs and I needed oxygen immediately.

Some people might call my mental alertness a coincidence, but I believe it was a miracle.

The Fourth Miracle

When I gasped out, "I need oxygen!" the request was sent out over the park service radio system: "Anyone near Yaqui Point who has a resuscitator, Elling Halvorson is in need of it at the bottom of the canyon where he has just crashed."

A National Park ranger "just happened" to be driving by our helispot on Yaqui Point at that moment, and *he "just happened" to have a resuscitator in his vehicle.* He was able to pull into the turnaround on the point—an area closed off to the public—and hand the resuscitator over to our helicopter crew. Within a few precious minutes, I had the breathing assistance I needed. Some might call the provision of the resuscitator a coincidence, but I believe it was the fourth miracle.

The Fifth Miracle

The fifth miracle concerns *how quickly I received medical attention.* I knew the local doctor well, Dr. Rafael Garbayo. A Basque from the Spanish province of Navarra, he had interned in New York and studied surgery in Denver, where he also met his wife. He enjoyed the wilderness area, so he had his office at Grand Canyon Village, as well as a little two-bed hospital that included an operating room. But if anyone down in the canyon needed a doctor, he never flew to them. He always said, "Bring them to me."

Knowing I was too injured to be moved without emergency medical attention first, I prayed, "Lord, have someone tell him it's Elling. Maybe he'll come for me." Then I learned that Dr. Garbayo wasn't even in the area. He'd gone to Flagstaff on a brief trip. My heart sank.

But in his place was a young Dr. Thomas who'd served a residency with Dr. Garbayo the year before. We knew each other pretty well and had even played softball together. When he heard about the accident, he grabbed the medical satchel, came to the heliport immediately, and was at my side within some 15 to 20 minutes after the accident.

I still remember Dr. Thomas taking my pulse, shaking his head, and giving orders for the other injured men to be taken out by helicopter. He later told me my blood pressure had dropped to 40 over zero.

Then I remember him cutting off my shirt and stabbing a hypodermic needle into my heart to administer a stimulant, and he inserted another one, filled with morphine, into my veins. After the second shot, I drifted in and out of consciousness.

The doctor left me on the cold ground for about a half an hour until he started getting a minimum blood-pressure reading. Then he had the pilot and other crew members help him place a sleeping bag under me, carefully lift me into the cargo basket on the outside of the helicopter, and strap me down.

Being December, it was very cold, especially at 7,000 feet in altitude and with all the rotor-blade downwash blowing on me. However, the freezing weather probably slowed my metabolism and was helpful at the time. Drowsy from the drugs, I dozed off and then woke up at some point during flight, vaguely realizing that something good was happening. The USGS man had grabbed his movie camera again and shot footage of us flying up to the rim.

At Yaqui Point, I was transferred to a ranger's station wagon that was made up to be an ambulance. I remember bumping my head when they rolled me in. Moments later, they unloaded me outside the tiny hospital. I was still in a fog of shock, pain, and drugs. But I grinned when I saw my personal buddy, Dr. Garbayo, waiting for me in the operating room. He had rushed back from Flagstaff to attend to me.

Also in that small operating room was what seemed to be almost everyone else in the village. I'd never seen anything like it. My construction superintendent, workmen, the two doctors, the nurses, the park superintendent, park rangers—something like 15 people were all in there with me, even when x-rays were taken. Nobody would leave.

At first it didn't look as if I would survive. My entire chest cavity had collapsed around my heart. When Dr. Garbayo studied the x-rays, he saw immediately that I had 18 breaks in my ribs, a punctured lung, a fractured leg, and lacerations all over my body. He told me that my heart was bruised and that potentially lethal bone fragments were floating in my body.

Dr. Garbayo then approached me with a device that looked like a long tube with a sharp, needle-like point on the end. He climbed up above me, aimed the point at my bare chest, and used the weight of his body to puncture my chest wall and push the tube into the pleural cavity that surrounded my lungs. I still bear the scar of that puncture to this day.

The park service superintendent later told me, "Elling, when Dr. Garbayo was pushing that tube through your chest wall, you made the understatement of all time. You said, 'Oh, that hurts,' in a soft, quiet voice, just as polite as could be."

In the operating room, I continued to drift in and out of consciousness. I had been connected to a device that helped my lungs expand and heal more quickly.[4]

A nurse was constantly at my side during those first few nights. At some point, not completely aware what I was doing, I felt the rubber seal and thought it was something like chewing gum. I closed my fingers around the tube and pulled it. Then I held it up, and said, "What is this?"

---

[4] The tube from my chest went into a sealed water bottle using a one-way valve system that allowed air to escape but not reenter my body. As air was gently pulled from my pleural cavity, water in that bottle was siphoned through a tube that drained into a second bottle below it. I assume the bottles of water enabled the system to work on the principle of negative pressure.

The nurse nearly had a heart attack. She immediately ran to the telephone and told Dr. Garbayo what had happened. He came to the hospital around 3:00 AM and put a new intercostal tube into the pleural cavity.

The next day, Carl and Hal flew into town. In a moment of consciousness, I asked Dr. Garbayo about Barbara and our children. He said Barbara and the family were praying for me. He didn't mention that he'd told Barbara I had no chance of making it. Other people had given the same grim message to my children, who were being watched by friends while Barbara was at the hospital. I learned later that Brenda (11), Kent (10), Lon (eight), and the twins, Randy and Rod (seven), had been taken out of school and told I'd been in a terrible helicopter accident.

In spite of his doubts about my survival, Dr. Garbayo worked to get me to a larger hospital. An ambulance was ordered to transport me from his tiny emergency facility to a regional hospital in Flagstaff. Barbara had arranged with friends to have our kids lined up along the highway in front of Moqui Lodge where the ambulance would pass by. She and my brothers would be in a car following the ambulance. In spite of having heard that I probably wouldn't live, all the kids knew about the extent of my injuries was that I had a broken leg and was being transferred to the Flagstaff hospital.

It turned out that no ambulance was available. Instead, a hearse, bearing the name "Flagstaff Mortuary" on the back, was sent to transport me. My oldest son, Kent, recalls that day.

> We were expecting a bit of a motorcade with Dad's two older brothers plus our mom in one car and then, in front of them would be the ambulance, carrying our dad. All of us kids were standing by the side of the highway, in front of Moqui Lodge, ready to wave to Dad as he went by. We waved to Mom and our uncles driving by. But Dad was in a flipping hearse! Now even when you're only 10 years old, you still know the difference between a hearse and an ambulance!

For an hour and 20 minutes, Carl, Hal, and Barbara followed the hearse to Flagstaff. Nobody said a word the entire time. No one thought I would live.

When I reached the hospital, all the doctors, nurses, and medical attendants were ultra-careful about not moving me an inch, not even to take me off the dirty sleeping bag I ended up lying on for three days. They knew from Dr. Garbayo's x-rays about the fractured bone segments inside my body, each as sharp as a knife, with the potential to go off with the slightest touch, almost like land mines. As soon as they had me settled, the doctors ordered new x-rays, which also showed loose, jagged bone fragments all around my heart and lungs, confirming the need to keep me absolutely still.

The room I was in seemed quite dark. I soon came to realize I was inside a special room in the intensive care unit (ICU) as I hovered at the edge of death. I had received many blood transfusions. My gentle and careful nurse would come by at intervals to give me treatments from a "bird respirator," a common term in those days for medical ventilators.[5] In my almost out-of-body state, still receiving morphine for the pain, I thought my nurse looked like an angel. I came to feel as if even her gentle touch was angelic.

It felt good to have my two brothers with me at the hospital, and I had Barbara's visits to keep me informed about our family. For a time, the doctors insisted that we keep my kids away, but soon they were able to visit me in intensive care.

Brenda remembers that visit. "When we kids were finally allowed to go into Dad's room to see him, he broke down and cried. So did I. Tears were running down my cheeks, and they were running down Dad's cheeks too. All I could think was, *Oh, my God, you are still alive!*"

"Dad's head was swollen to the size of a pillow in width," Kent recalls. "You couldn't even tell it was him. The rest of his body seemed like a bag of bones. He was so hurt, it was terrifying to me." Kent then referred to another recent medical crisis in our family and added, "It was

---

[5] After I was released from the hospital, we purchased a medical ventilator and donated it to the little hospital at Grand Canyon Village.

a terrible time in all of our lives. Mom was so wounded and was just trying to cope."

Lon remembers my head as a basketball instead of a pillow. "Honestly," he says, "we only really understood how serious the situation was when we saw Dad for the first time about two weeks after his accident. He is lucky to be alive."

Some people might say that all the immediate medical attention I received was a coincidence, but I believe it was a miracle.

The Sixth Miracle

The sixth miracle concerns *my rapid recovery*. At first I was so beat up, people couldn't even recognize me. But I survived that. I improved. Once I got out of intensive care, I healed so quickly, it seemed like a miraculous touch from God. Within two weeks, I was on my feet, and by mid January, I had healed quite well. Even the dangerous bone fragments, now secured by scar tissue, were no longer a threat. I felt in reasonably good health.

During my recovery, I had a lot of time to contemplate the preceding few months. I came to appreciate the terrific physical shape I had been in as a result of putting in very long days of vigorous construction work. I was only 33 years old, had walked many miles on that job every day, and had even been walking up cliff walls with the help of a rope I used for pulling myself along, hand over hand. Being at the peak of my health and age helped me survive and recover from the crash.

The doctor at the Flagstaff hospital told me it was the fastest recovery he had ever seen in his profession. Some people might call that—including my being in great physical shape to begin with—a coincidence, but I believe it was a miracle.

The Seventh Miracle

The seventh miracle is almost more incredible than any of the others. It has to do with the way God rescued me from complete financial and vocational ruin. But first, I need to tell you how I was plunged into yet another serious detour before my situation started to improve.

7
THE FIGHT OF MY LIFE

When the park superintendent and others first came to see me at the hospital, they said, "Elling we're going to do everything we can to help you."

I appreciated that. They issued a one-year stop-work order on the job because there were penalties for not completing on time. The stop-work order gave us a chance to sort out what needed to be done. I realized that the standard clause in all government contracts—giving them the authority to make this decision—was working in our favor.

But after I was able to be up and walking again, it was a different story. Regional directors and government attorneys from Denver got involved. They took the position that because the flood was an act of God, it was the responsibility of the contractor—me—to replace the pipeline at no cost to the government.

My position was that, although the rainstorm had been an act of God, the resulting destruction had not been. The park service people had staked where the pipe should go, and they had staked it too low.

Life looked pretty bleak. A major part of the pipeline we'd worked so hard to construct had been destroyed, along with all of my equipment. Now a squadron of federal lawyers was headed my way, determined to make me pay for everything.

Soon after I was finally discharged from the Flagstaff hospital, Barbara and I decided to drive to Seattle with no kids, no doctors, no stress. It'd be just the two of us. I was not exactly a picture of health yet as I hobbled around on crutches and still had a full cast on my left leg. But off we went, eager to leave the pain and worry behind. What I couldn't share with Barbara right then was how low I was mentally because of the losses and the certain battles ahead. Our long drive gave us the time we needed to talk it all out. So often those types of exchanges are the most valuable, intimate moments in our life together.

One topic was the idea of building a home, from the ground up, that would be big enough to hold our growing family. We are both social people, so we also wanted a home nice enough to attract our friends and family.

I'd been told I'd need to wear the full cast on my leg for at least six months, and our short stay in Seattle gave me time to get more accustomed to crutches. Then, oddly, after enjoying a time of rapid recovery, I began feeling not quite right. In fact, I felt worse each day.

I complained to my wife and friends. Barbara said, "Your body experienced a lot of damage. You're still healing. This is just part of your recovery." Our friends agreed. So the next day, Barbara and I loaded up our car and headed south to rejoin our kids at the Grand Canyon.

But even though I looked forward to seeing our herd, I continued to feel a decline in my well-being. Despite what everyone was saying, I felt sure I was somehow seriously sick. In fact, Barbara finally realized that something was wrong when I continued to get weaker each day. Arriving at last at Grand Canyon Village, before we even went home to see our kids, we stopped at Dr. Garbayo's office.

He took one look at me and said, "My God, Elling, you have serum hepatitis!" He explained I'd likely gotten it through a blood transfusion. I was in shock. Now what? Dr. Garbayo moved closer to me, peering into my eyes and adding that serum hepatitis is the worst form you can get.

I mumbled, "Are you sure I have it? How can you tell so fast?"

He looked at me soberly. "I'm sure. Your eyes are like yellow cue balls."

I didn't know how to react. I had no idea what hepatitis was. All I could think of was spinal meningitis. Struck with fear, I asked, "Am I going to die then?"

Dr. Garbayo grinned. "Actually, Elling, I haven't had one hepatitis patient die yet. But you could be my first if you like!"

That made me feel better. But then Dr. Garbayo put his hand on my shoulder and said quietly, "However, you're going to have to check into our hospital for treatments, which will probably last thirty days or so."

I started to complain about the 30-day sentence of hospital time, but my doctor friend, who had already saved my life a month earlier, became stern with me. "Elling, this is very serious. It's hospitalization for you, starting right now, today. " I was put into isolation. All visitors were required to wear masks.

Kent remembers how the news affected all my kids.

> I'll never forget when we finally felt confident Dad was going to live. And then, boom! He ended up with hepatitis. Got it from a blood transfusion. I clearly remember him in the Grand Canyon hospital, fighting hepatitis. He was as yellow as could be. But his spirits were good. He was amazing. However, while we said nothing to Dad, we heard around our small town he might not survive the hepatitis. So all over again, we had our worst fears and stress over losing our dad.

The hospital was located near the school, so every day at noontime, my kids walked over and communicated to me through my hospital window. After school they did that again while waiting for the bus. It was really nice to see them every day.

Flat on my back in the hospital for a month, I felt like I was serving another indefinite sentence in medical prison. I wasn't allowed to get up at all, not even to use the bathroom. I had to lie absolutely still. Being immobile bugged me so much, I developed a renewed dislike for bedpans. I continually groused, always asking if I could just get up and go use a real bathroom. The answer from my wise doctor and friend was always "No!"

After about two weeks of that restriction, I dreamed up a scheme. I asked a dear friend who lived next to the small hospital to bring in a bunch of plumbing pipes while Dr. Garbayo was away. Some of my construction guys helped.

THE FIGHT OF MY LIFE

Brenda, a co-conspirator in my mad scheme, ordered a fake plastic urinal she'd seen in a magazine ad. The day it arrived, my friends attached the fake urinal to the wall just two feet from my bedside. To add more realism, they scattered a few pieces of real pipe and some sawdust on the floor nearby. The artificial system looked authentic.

I couldn't wait for Dr. Garbayo to come in the next morning. I counted the minutes until his arrival. When he walked in and saw the newly installed urinal, he stopped in his tracks and stared, bug-eyed, without a word.

I said, "Doctor, I had some of the men who work for me come in and install this right next to my bed for me to use since you won't let me get up."

A few very tense seconds of silence ticked by before the doctor realized it was fake, and he began to laugh.

That was an amusing moment during a difficult time. Another lighthearted moment was when, after learning I'd acquired hepatitis from blood transfusions, I accused my wife of buying me cheap blood.[6]

When my 30-day hospital stay was up, I was released to return home. I felt more than ready for life again. But while I was still receiving supportive words from people I knew in the park service, the federal government itself was taking a tough stance on who was responsible to clean up the mess created by that historic rainstorm.

Astonishing Discovery

When we received the one-year stop-work order from the federal government, I wasn't alarmed. That was a normal procedure whenever a calamity, like a fire or flood, hit a construction project.

---

[6] After researchers discovered and identified the Hepatitis C virus in the late 1980s, I learned that the "cheap blood" I'd received had infected me with that type too. I was told it was incurable and could lead to cirrhosis or liver cancer. Fortunately, it seemed to remain dormant in my body, so I was able to carry on in relative good health until it reactivated in 2015. Then a couple of years ago, a direct-acting antiviral became available, and my doctor prescribed it. Within weeks, all traces of the virus were gone from my blood in what's called sustained virologic response (SVR). I am very blessed indeed.

Soon, independent scientists and scholars were studying the storm's scope and nature, just like forensic police specialists analyze evidence at a crime scene. In their investigation, they reviewed existing maps and photographs of Native American village ruins that dated back some 1,500 years. They compared those maps and photos to the flood-damaged area and found that the ruins had been almost totally swept away.

That meant the natural disaster we'd just experienced had not happened in *1,500 years*. When these findings were released, the nation's press descended on the canyon.

Hung Out to Dry

We were encouraged by the independent scientists' discovery. But the federal government saw it all quite differently.

The fight of my life with the government began in a lopsided way. The Feds had many more lawyers on the case than I could ever assemble or afford. Amazingly, though, my one lawyer, Pat Sullivan, truly was up to the challenge. And the more I worked with Pat, the more I appreciated how talented he was. He showed rare savvy in both law and in a fight.

As I mentioned earlier, Pat had flown down to the canyon a few months before the flood to help me do battle concerning the Feds' slow pay with us. I had been deeply impressed as I watched Pat quickly and expertly assemble a complete fact portfolio detailing our 13 months of continuous construction.

Now, as we engaged in this new and quite different battle, Pat told me it would take federal government lawyers two to three months to prepare their case against us.

When those lawyers called for a meeting at their regional headquarters in San Francisco, I was still in my full-leg cast and couldn't fly our private plane there. Even after the cast was removed, my body had to relearn how to walk. So Pat and I went by commercial airline.

At that first meeting, the government reiterated their position that the 1,500-year flood was an act of God. And therefore, according to the government contract, standard form 23A, acts of God are the responsibility of the contractor. When they concluded their arguments, it looked as if I was a dead-broke dead duck.

Pat Sullivan and I returned home and revised our strategy for the second meeting in San Francisco scheduled about one month later. However, at that subsequent meeting we were told once again that the federal government wouldn't pay us anything.

At the third meeting, Pat and I showed a photo of how the 1,500-year flood had pulled the aluminum water pipes right out their rock beds, leaving them twisted and shredded. We stated that the financial losses were the federal government's responsibility since park service people had laid out the right-of-way where each foot of the pipeline was to go. Our argument was that because the government had made a design error, it should bear full liability for the flood damage and repairs.

But the government lawyers wouldn't buy that and stuck to their position. We met regularly for months, always at bitter odds. Pat and I knew they were confident they could beat us down. After all, I didn't have unlimited supplies of money to continue the fight. I was financially destitute. My only income at the time was state workers' compensation. In what the federal lawyers thought was a "war of attrition," I looked like a certain loser.

An Ace up My Sleeve

I had purchased a bond that would have finished the job, but the bonding company wouldn't do anything unless I said, "It's my loss." And I knew deep in my heart it truly wasn't my loss.

A secret I hadn't told another soul about was that right after my company had been awarded the original contract for the Grand Canyon pipeline, I'd purchased a comprehensive, all-risk Builders Risk Policy from Lloyd's of London. Immediately after the December 1965 flood, I notified Lloyd's about the loss. And while I felt I had coverage from them, I couldn't know what position they would take. However, they must have felt they had a lot of exposure, since in February 1966, an independent adjuster on contract to Lloyd's, Marshall Miller, traveled to

London to talk with them about my case. I knew nothing about it, but Marshall seemed to be aware that my father, my two brothers, and I were all in construction. He also knew a lot about me personally. I don't know how he obtained his information, but in London he used what he'd learned to convince the insurance company I was a good risk.

When he returned to the States, he telephoned me. "Elling," he said, "I'd like to come to your home and talk about your loss with you." I was pleased to hear from him and extended an invitation. Sometime in April or May, we sat down in the living room of the new family home I'd built in Redmond, near Seattle.

As we talked about the loss, he surprised me by saying, "We know your income from the project is cut off and that financially, this has destroyed you. We want to do something helpful about that." And almost like you'd see in a television drama, he handed me a check for $100,000. That sum would be like three-quarters of a million dollars in today's economy.

What a phenomenal gesture by Lloyd's of London! I stopped breathing for a moment. As I was coming out of shock, I heard Marshall say, "Elling, sign this promissory note stating you owe one hundred thousand dollars to Lloyd's of London. If you prevail in this battle and you are able to pay it back, fine. If you lose and you can't pay it, we'll tear up the promissory note. We want you to negotiate out of a position of financial strength."

Never in my life had I heard of anything like that before—nor have I heard anything like it since. Nobody I've talked to has. The check was such an encouragement to me, I had a hard time keeping it a secret. Only Pat and Barbara knew about it. That remarkable boost from Lloyd's gave my brilliant lawyer and me the strength to endure the federal legal team's relentless negotiating strategy that followed.

Dealing from a Position of Strength

One of the first things I did with the Lloyd's of London money was to buy a new, high-quality suit. And then, even though I gulped at the price, I also snapped up one of the first-ever hand-held electronic calculators on the market. It was a Sharp model with integrated circuits (ICs). At the time, nearly everyone in business used Marchant mechanical calculators that weighed some 30 pounds, so this device's small size, lightning speed, and quiet operation made it a sensation.

During the next set of negotiations at the attorneys' boardroom in San Francisco, I strolled into the room wearing my expensive suit. In my hand was the innovative calculator. No one there had seen anything like it before. They clustered around and asked me to do sample math problems. I demonstrated all kinds of fancy calculations. They were amazed.

When Pat and I staged this, we believed that the handsome suit and expensive new calculator would suggest an aura of affluence and communicate the unspoken message that, contrary to what government lawyers had been led to believe, I was doing quite well financially. We hoped our playacting would prompt the attorneys to conclude I *could* afford a long legal fight and that they could no longer depend on financial starvation to make me agree to their tough terms. Pat and I could barely remain patient at that meeting, watching for the one best moment to reveal yet another aggressive dimension to our strategy.

The right moment did not come at that meeting, however, so we returned to San Francisco in early fall for the next meeting where government lawyers again repeated their contention that what happened was an act of God and I, as the contractor, was liable for damages.

When it was my turn to respond, I felt like a soldier about to throw a grenade into the enemy's cave. I tossed it. "Well, Gentlemen," I said, "you win. We will put the pipeline back at no cost to the government. I have the wherewithal to do so because I have two financial resources: I have the payment and performance bond I provided at the beginning of the project. And . . ." I paused for effect, "I have a Lloyd's of London Builders Risk policy that will pay the full cost of the replacement."

Oh, the jubilation that erupted in the room! "Elling, we knew you'd see it our way eventually," they said, shaking hands and patting me on the back and practically doing high-fives.

When it all quieted down, I said, "I have just one favor to ask of you folks, if you'd be so kind."

"Oh, sure," they responded, "We'll do anything to help. What do you need?"

I knew I had them hooked. "You need to put the Grand Canyon back the way it was when I bid the job."

Stunned silence. They lost their glow immediately. We had them right where it hurt. They couldn't possibly restore the Grand Canyon to the way it was when they approved my bid because the 1,500-year flood had wiped out trails, huge stands of trees, and entire cliff faces, not to mention the Native American ruins. Even riverbeds had changed. Mile after mile, the canyon landscape had been transformed in hundreds of ways.

Floodwaters turned bridges into waterfalls, leaving them twisted off their foundations.

The attorneys were also aware that Lloyd's of London was one of the strongest financial firms on the planet. With Lloyd's as my insurance partner, we could afford to fight the government for decades if they wanted to drag it on that long.

Over the years I did a lot of business with Lloyd's. Eventually, my aviation insurance broker, Anthony Cowan, who used to work for Lloyd's, arranged a private audience with the chairman of the board. Anthony, Kent, Lon, Brenda, and I flew to London for the meeting. I told the chairman about the $100,000 check and asked if he had ever heard the story before. He had not—nor had he heard of anything like that happening with anyone else.

Restoration Work in the Changed Canyon

But of course, the government had to win something. So Pat and I gave them the backfill my company had crushed on the spot when we first built the pipeline.

The result: Uncle Sam wrote me a change order of $4.6 million, an amount that today would compare to about $32 million. The change order meant our company agreed to build new trails in areas where the original Rim-to-Rim trail had been swept away, and we would undercut the trail in many areas, making it safer and more stable for future hikers. We would also replace the six pipeline bridges across Bright Angel Creek the storm had swept away.

Of course, the new contract also required our firm to replace any and all pipe that had been destroyed. Five and a half miles of the original pipeline we laid had actually survived, since it wasn't in the flood zone. That left approximately eight and a half miles of thoroughly trashed pipe that had to be replaced in completely new trenches with new select fill.

What a difference that record-breaking deluge made in almost every way imaginable! The famous Rim-to-Rim trail had been so savagely damaged, most of it no longer even existed. So, since there was no longer a historic trail, we no longer needed a skinny rock crusher to fit it. Instead, we could scoop our three-quarter-inch-minus select fill right out of the streambeds. We were also now able to use regular construction trucks and large crawler tractors on the canyon floor itself. In fact, during this new and often different construction phase, we realized we needed a Caterpillar D7 bulldozer that weighed many tons. But how could we get it down to the canyon floor?

A good stroke of fortune during the reconstruction was that we were able to take advantage of some new helicopters recently brought to market. They had more lifting power than ever before, which meant we were able to fly in major components of Caterpillar tractors, trucks, backhoes, and drills, in record time. Those helicopters handled bridge-replacement components too. So, to move the D7 into place, all we had to do was disassemble it, lift each piece with the more powerful helicopter, and reassemble the tractor at its destination.

In this new and more cooperative phase of the rebuilding project, we restrung the primary electrical power cables that had been damaged or severed. The operators of Phantom Ranch were delighted to get electrical service restored once again.

So that our workers could have a weekend away to themselves, we'd typically helicopter all of them, about 30 to 35 workers total, out of the Grand Canyon every Friday after work. Normally, those Friday flights meant that only one employee, our camp cook, was left behind at the construction camp to perform the uncomplicated weekend job of watching over the empty buildings. The trouble was, as we learned way too late, he was a secret drinker.

At some point, a fire broke out in the camp kitchen. Normally, such a fire would have stopped after burning down the cook shack. The Grand Canyon is, after all, mostly rock, so the original fire would not have reached outlying buildings that included cabins with bunk beds, various machinery shops, warehouses, and other temporary wood structures.

Unfortunately however, our little Western town had boardwalks connecting the buildings, just like you see in Western movies. The crew living there during the week used to say, "Everything here either stings you or bites you or pokes you!" So we built wooden sidewalks to save our workers from sharp rocks, critters, and other nasty things that litter the canyon floor.

When the cook shack caught fire, those wooden walkways provided an easy path for the flames to spread everywhere, quickly consuming all of our buildings. Unable to stop the conflagration, our cook climbed a hill and watched it all burn, probably with a bottle of hooch as his companion. The camp that had survived a 1,500-year flood couldn't withstand a careless cook's fire.

We were at least halfway through the pipeline rebuild when the camp burned down. Rather than rebuild it all, we decided to bite an expense bullet and fly our construction workers down into the canyon every day.

Of course, that created an additional major flying job. And unintentionally, all those in-and-out flights over the course of the project put our company into aviation record books. Once done, our construction project was recognized worldwide for what was called "The largest helicopter job yet done in the United States with some 25,000 total hours of helicopter flying time!" Since then, no other single peacetime construction job using helicopters—at least that we know of—has reached that level.

Part of our reconstruction project was relocating the Bright Angel Creek streamed in certain places, as well as doing what we could to prevent constant bank erosion where the rapidly flowing water passed by Phantom Ranch. We would use Gabion baskets to prevent erosion.

Gabion baskets are containers made from Italian wire mesh. Once filled onsite with stone, they work well in preventing erosion. Unfortunately, the baskets are also expensive. So, naturally, I decided to save money by figuring out how to make our own. The wire mesh part wasn't difficult. But I needed to come up with a durable connector for fastening the ends of the wire mesh. Eventually, I found that number 8 hog rings, the heaviest available, worked well, so I made a trip to Phoenix to look for a large supply. On a shelf in the first tack store I entered, I found a small box of the rings. I asked the proprietor if he had more.

"How many do you need?"

"About eighteen thousand," I said.

He gave me a strange look. "I don't know where you could find that many here in Phoenix. You'd have to contact the manufacturer."

I thanked him and then decided to make an unrelated impulse purchase.

As I was going out of the store, he called after me, "Good luck with your hogs, Mister!"

To fill the Gabion baskets with enough rocks, we needed a mechanical rock picker. Those machines have tongs, set at specified widths, that go under the dirt and sift out the size of rock required. The machine I purchased was painted red and pulled by a tractor. I was so proud of my new machine. I didn't know anyone else who had a big red rock-picker.

We lined the stream's critical banks near Phantom Ranch with our custom-built Gabion baskets. They worked well to stop most erosion and, I understand, are still in service to this day. I'm proud of our work. I also believe that park visitors continue to benefit from our accomplishments in a practical way even now, more than half a century later.

One thing is for certain; the two contracts together—for the pipeline installation and for the reconstruction project after the flood—comprised the largest construction contract in the history of the United States National Park Service. In fact, Congress had to pass a special appropriation bill to finance the reconstruction project.

Not long after the bill was presented to Congress, Secretary of the Interior Stewart Udall, who lived in Tucson, Arizona, called our house. "Barbara," he said, "congratulations! The president had just signed the bill. That's great for the country, great for the canyon, and great for our park service!"

Some people might say that coming through such a catastrophic detour to find my footing once again was a mere coincidence. But I am convinced it was a miracle.

PART II: THE IMPORTANCE OF FAMILY ROOTS

✦ ✦ ✦ ✦ ✦

8
INHERITING A SOLUTION MINDSET

Family is at the heart of almost everything in life, and the family we're born into has a very important role in how we turn out. A child welcomed into a stable home and reared by a loving father and mother has a much better opportunity for a successful life.

I had the distinct benefit of being born to a loving Christian family that was closely tied to the church and many friends. The extended families of both my parents were connected by marriages and relationships to hundreds of additional family members—cousins, aunts, uncles, grandparents. As I grew up in that wide family circle, I was made to feel welcome and loved. To me, that's the finest gift a child could possibly be given.

I was born in Saint Paul, Minnesota, on January 2, 1932, when my mother was 42 years young. I was the last of a brood of four. Being the "caboose kid" seldom bothered me. In fact, I probably got a lot more attention than kids do when they're in the "chain gang."

My father, Elling Halvorson Sr., had emigrated from Norway, and my mother, Beda Karin (pronounced *Carn*) Larsson, had emigrated from Sweden. They first met in 1914 at a Saint Paul trolley stop. Each experienced such a powerful emotion, they became engaged one week later. The new couple's first photos show a beautiful, gracious young woman and a handsome, well-dressed young man. About a year after their trolley-stop meeting, they married and would spend the rest of their married lives very happy together.

The year they met, however, was full of turmoil. World War I broke out in 1914 and transformed the Atlantic Ocean into a bloody battlefield. Elling and Beda read daily newspaper stories of millions of people dying and freighters and passenger ships being torpedoed at an ever-growing rate. Many of those who survived battles bore lasting wounds, particularly when poisoned by the recently invented mustard gas. Then there was the spectacular sinking of the British passenger ship, *Lusitania*.

The ship left New York Harbor on May 1, 1915, headed for Liverpool, England. Just before the ship left, the German embassy in Washington, DC, purchased newspaper ads advising Americans not to sail on *Lusitania*. The warning was cheerfully ignored. However, unbeknownst to the passengers—and even officials at the Port of New York—the ship's cargo included munitions.

As the ship approached the Irish Coast on May 7, the captain received a telegram warning of U-boat activity in the area. He put his ship on alert but didn't know he was already in the crosshairs of Captain Walther Schwieger's German Navy U-boat. When *Lusitania* abruptly changed course, Schwieger fired his first torpedo. It exploded just below *Lusitania*'s bridge. An internal explosion followed.

Lusitania sank so fast, the crew trying to untie lifeboats found themselves floundering in the freezing Irish Sea surrounded by terrified passengers. Realizing they had no chance of rescue, most began to pray.

More people died from hypothermia than from the actual ship sinking. Those who died—1,195 men, women and children—perished in minutes. Most were Americans. The only cruise-ship disaster that took more lives was the sinking of *Titanic* three years earlier. The attack on *Lusitania* caused a storm of protest in the US and influenced the country's decision two years later, in 1917, to declare war on Germany and its allies, thus making Atlantic travel even riskier.

In spite of travel risks, Elling and Beda were homesick. They missed their families, friends, familiar places, and traditions in Norway and Sweden. Eventually, they longed so much to return that they were willing to risk their lives to visit their homelands once again. So they worked hard and saved every penny they could to purchase steamship tickets. When they achieved their goal, they bought passage to Norway.

The war still raged. Even though Norway and Sweden were strictly neutral countries, danger was constant because both the British and German navies mined the approaches to North Sea ports. But the ship my parents sailed on delivered them safely to their destination.

Since Dad had not yet obtained his American citizenship and was still a Norwegian citizen, he, like all young men there, was drafted into the Norwegian Army. His conscription meant they could not return to the United States until after March 1921, when his service term ended. But at least they were safe, since Norway was neutral and Dad didn't have to fight.

They settled into Sele (pronounced *say-la*), a small fishing village on the island of Øygarden, which was just about the last in a chain of inhabited North Sea islands. Today, in oil-wealthy Norway, a series of modern bridges lets travelers drive to Sele from Bergen on the mainland coast without ever pulling an oar or manning a sail. But back then, reaching Sele 40 miles across the water required an all-day sailboat trip.

My parents moved into a vacant house that had ceilings about six and a half feet high. The doors were so small, adults had to stoop to walk through them. It was the house where Dad had been born and reared, just like his father and grandfather before him. Since the house was set on Sele's highest hill, Mom and Dad flew the Norwegian flag every day. Today, the 300-year old structure is a national historical building.

Dad always was a high-energy person, so in no time he built a salt house for making salt herring. Both Mom and Dad were industrious people, a trait that mattered, since life during wartime wasn't at all easy. Norway and Sweden were relatively poor nations. The war throughout Europe meant that commodities such as diesel oil, gasoline, and lamp oil were scarce and costly. Nights indoors were dark and often chilly—the perfect set-up for a baby boom.

Family Additions and Moves

Extending the legacy of Halvorson sons being born at the historic family home in Sele, my eldest brother, Carl, arrived there on October 3, 1916. However, my mother's memories of her childhood years in Sweden were very strong. So, when Carl was about six months old, my father asked for and received permission to move to a farm in Sweden called Deserud, near the village of Ed, while he remained on call with the Norwegian military. Mom and Dad's second child, Halvor, was born there on March 4, 1919.

Eventually, deciding that Scandinavia wasn't as they remembered it and also anticipating the end of Dad's military service, my parents saved money for steamship tickets back to America. Of course, instead of needing two tickets, they now needed four. It took sacrifice and thrift to afford passage for the voyage. Since ships sailed from Bergen, Norway, the family returned to Sele to await the opportunity to leave.

On October 1, 1921, Elling and Beda, plus little Carl and Halvor, boarded *SS Bergensfjord* at Bergen. The ship advertised 100 first-class staterooms, 250 second class and 850 third class. It was a bittersweet moment when the Halvorsons waved goodbye to family and friends. Many at the dock they would never see again, including their parents.

In third-class staterooms, they made the best of an 11-day Atlantic crossing. Their ship sailed past New York's Statue of Liberty to dock at Ellis Island on October 10, 1921. I have microfilm records of their arrival at US Customs. The information states that Mother was 31, Dad was 29, Carl was four, and Halvor was two.

The family boarded a train bound for Saint Paul. Less than a year after their arrival, child number three, my sister Evelyn, was born on August 19, 1922.

Upon his return, Dad set his sights high. He went right to work for a very successful Minnesota firm, the Lovering-Longbothum Construction Company. In his spare time, Dad built a home at 1029 Hawthorne Street in Saint Paul for his growing family. Always looking for more spare-time challenges, he also built a duplex that he rented out for extra family income. In a speed and manner that happened often for the rest of his life, Dad went up the ranks of the company, ultimately becoming its general manager.

The timing was excellent. The war was over, the economy boomed, and new buildings were going up from coast to coast. And thanks to Henry Ford's new and very affordable gasoline-powered motorcars, in just a decade the entire nation switched from horses to autos. That meant streets, highways, and bridges had to be built all over the nation. In what turned out to be a wild decade, America was having a party called the Roaring Twenties. My dad and all of America prospered. But the prosperity couldn't—and didn't—last.

On October 29, 1929, the economic boom suddenly crashed with the total collapse of stock-market prices. In just moments, $100 stocks were worth 10 cents. For weeks, newspaper headlines reported people who'd lost fortunes committing suicide in every way imaginable, from walking off piers, to jumping from bridges, to leaping from tall buildings. To this day, the calamity still holds the record for the most devastating stock market crash in US history. In the Great Depression that followed, most construction work simply vanished.

The Halvorson family in the 1930s.
Back row: Evelyn, Carl, Halvor.
Front row: Beda, Elling Jr., Elling Sr.

But we contractors are accustomed to radical ups and downs. No job lasts forever. There is no gold watch waiting at retirement. Each construction project has a start date and a completion date, so a contractor must always be alert for the next opportunity.

That's why my father and his company took note of a city where boom times had not succumbed to the Depression. Dad quickly moved our family to Butte, Montana, at the time named the most prosperous town in America. Butte was alive with companies mining gold, silver, and copper. Nearby, the Anaconda Copper Mining Company had a copper-refining smelter. At that time, the company was the fourth largest firm in the world. It was later purchased by Atlantic Richfield Company (ARCO) in 1977.

Copper wire and cable was used to bring electricity to every home in every state in the nation. Copper also went into every bullet in every gun Americans fired in World War I and later World War II. No wonder Butte was booming.

When our family arrived in Butte in 1935, I was three years old. Dad's firm had a contract to construct a new Butte High School. Later, he won a contract to construct a building at the School of Mines in the foothills of Big Butte, the mountain adjacent to the city. Our home at 1020 Waukesha Street was positioned on those same foothills.

The personal achievement Dad was most proud of was raising funds and soliciting donated building materials to construct a new church for Gold Hill Lutheran in Butte. It's still there today. Our family appreciated the sense of community we felt in raising the church and valued the lasting friendships we made with families such as the Orrestads, the Kwassheims and Hoilands.

When Dad's construction jobs were completed, we returned to Saint Paul, Minnesota, although we wouldn't stay there long.

The Move to Billings

In 1939, while America was still in the grip of the Great Depression, Dad and Carl made the astute choice to start up a construction company of their own in a more prosperous place: Billings, Montana. As the only city in a 400-mile-wide region and the largest city in the state, its retail and business districts were healthier than most. The city benefited from tourist traffic, since it was located not far from Yellowstone Park and close to where the 1876 Battle of the Little Bighorn—better known as Custer's Last Stand—had been fought.

Dad bought a new two-ton Diamond T truck to move us to our new home. He and my two brothers packed our belongings as tightly as they could, but there still wasn't room for everything. Although those construction guys should have known better, their solution was to build a little addition to the back of the truck.

At first, everything looked perfect. But when they started to drive away, the truck was so backloaded, its front wheels came off the ground and the truck reared up like a frightened horse. The sight struck me, a six-year-old, as so hilarious, I rolled on the ground with laughter, much to everyone's annoyance. Finally, Carl, Halvor, and Dad counterbalanced the truck by adjusting the load and hanging sandbags on the front bumper. Then off our gang went, like a movie comedy, heading for Billings. Carl and Hal took turns driving the truck, while the rest of us rode with Dad in his Whippet automobile.

Looking back, and grinning every time I remember that moment, I realize I was surrounded by family members who believed there always was a solution to virtually *any* problem. Nothing was impossible. You simply had to keep working on it. As they used to say to me, "No job is too big, Elling. It's just tools that are too small." So? Build bigger tools! This problem-solving creed would help me overcome enormous challenges throughout my life. I'm forever indebted to my father and brothers. And I'd give absolutely anything to see that big Diamond T truck rear up like a scared horse again and embarrass the devil out of Carl, Halvor, and Dad.

Dad and Carl recruited my sister Evelyn as office manager and hired my brother Hal as a construction-manager trainee. So for a time, Halvorson Construction Company was strictly a family affair.

Given Dad's credentials, Carl and Hal's smarts, and Evelyn's knack for detail, their new outfit landed many contracts to build everything from schools to housing developments. They had the winning bid to construct Billing's beautiful new Fox Movie Theater that delighted everyone, including kids like me. And theirs was the winning bid to put up the Clark Grocery Superstore, the first place in town with automatic electric doors.

Whispers of Romance

Although Dad's frequent moves to take advantage of new construction opportunities meant always changing our family's town and home, attending new schools and adapting to new classes seemed normal to me. While we lived in Billings, I attended second grade and part of third, and during that time a first-ever romance fluttered into my innocent life. I was eight, and so was a girl who lived two doors away from our home. We were both certain we were in love. Solemnly, secretly, we agreed on marriage, though with no time or place selected.

Quite smitten with romantic thoughts, I bicycled to the Woolworth dime store[7] to look at rings. Entering the door, I felt six feet tall. Clueless that the rings were nothing more than cheap costume jewelry, I soon found one I liked, put it in my pocket, and headed for the exit as innocently as I could. The store manager confronted me there. He seemed to be extremely tall, and suddenly I felt way smaller than I had felt when I'd come in.

The man looked down at me and asked for the ring back. With shaking hands, I returned it. Then he delivered his power blow. "Do you think I should call your folks?"

My blood stopped circulating. I grew dizzy. My throat was so dry, I could barely squeak out, "No, sir." I must have looked totally pathetic because he let me go without calling my parents. As I madly pedaled away on my bike, I decided I would never do that again. Subsequently, my romance with the neighbor girl faded as fast as eight-year-olds change their minds.

But I wasn't the only one who'd been thinking of marriage. On the afternoon of March 4, 1940, Hal planned to marry Rodella "Mickey"

---

[7] *Dime store* was what many people used to call a variety store. The concept was largely pioneered in the early twentieth century by the F. W. Woolworth Company.

Mikelsen. Hal was the first of Mom and Dad's offspring to get married. The bridal couple was thrilled, nervous, and worried about everything.

Dad had the honor of driving the bride across town to the American Lutheran Church in Billings. But on their way, they were stopped at a railroad crossing where a yard engine was creeping back and forth, adding one boxcar after another to make up a train. Dad and his about-to-be-daughter-in-law became increasingly frantic at the delay.

Meanwhile at the church, all the waiting guests began whispering to each other. One hundred pairs of eyes watched Hal stand awkwardly at the altar with his uncomfortable best man Carl and the equally uncomfortable minister. Had the bride changed her mind? In those days, there was no quick way of finding out the reason for the bride's absence.

Hal kept shifting his weight from leg to leg, exchanging frequent glances with Carl. When he reached into his tuxedo pocket, pulled out his pocket watch, and checked it, the nervous move produced giggles throughout the room. The merriment grew until some people began laughing hysterically, which broke the tension. After an agonizing delay of about 20 minutes, Dad arrived with the missing bride, and the wedding ceremony began.

Thank you, Lord!

Admirable Siblings

As young as I was while we lived in Billings, I developed a terrific admiration for my brothers and sister. They were the kind of siblings most kids could only wish they had. Certainly, they shaped me as much as my parents did.

Carl, considered the brightest guy around, startled people with his photographic memory. Hal, a couple of years younger than Carl, was sharp, liked for his people skills, and always seemed to be watching out for me. Evelyn was a person of true grace—and incidentally, the first licensed woman contractor in the state of Montana. She was a devout Christian and always full of concern for me.

Now that I'm in my eighties, I deeply regret not spending more time with Evelyn, a real-life angel. I so wish I had told her how much I looked up to her. In any family storm, she was a rock. In any need, she found a way to help. In a family of mostly men, she never lost her charm, patience, humor, or femininity. While strangers might initially have seen Evelyn as a very quiet or even shy person, I knew better. My sister was always self-assured but never self-centered.

Deeply religious, she expressed her faith in deeds. She was always donating her time to the underprivileged, to youth ministries, to Native peoples, and others in the community.

Evelyn's husband, Herman, worked for my father as project manager on some jobs, and Evelyn served as clerk of the works. During the construction of a new highway from Anchorage to Seward, they lived in Alaska. After that, Herm and Evelyn moved to Idaho, where they raised potatoes and sugar beets. Later, they built a home on a lake in Smithers, British Columbia, about 700 miles north of Vancouver.

The year that Evelyn died of a heart attack, Herm also died as the result of an unfortunate airplane accident involving their float plane. Eventually, pieces of the plane were found in a remote lake, but the bodies of Herm and his young passenger were never found.

The deaths of Evelyn and Herm within the space of seven months left their son and two daughters—in their late teens and early twenties by then—without parents. Nevertheless, my nieces and nephew later grew to be as active as Evelyn had been in church and community work.

Today, I find it hard to remember my real-life angel without a tear or two.

9
DISTANT GUNS

While Dad's family-based Halvorson Construction Company was doing well in Billings, Germany declared war on Poland. Britain and France soon honored their treaties and joined Poland's fight. Newspapers and radio broadcasts warned of worldwide war.

In March 1940, 900 miles west of Billings in the vast rangelands near Corvallis, Oregon, some mysterious events were going on. Word of the mystery flew across the state via telephone party lines.[8]

To add fuel to the mystery, residents spotted dozens of strangers popping up everywhere, working hard from sunrise to sunset as they surveyed different parcels of land and took soil-core samples. From the party-line phones to gossip in coffee shops and gas stations, locals tried to solve the mystery. Maybe oil had been found! Maybe those topsoil cores contained gold! The newly arrived strangers couldn't tell anyone that their work was part of the federal government's hush-hush, all-out effort to prepare the nation for war.

Our nation's leaders were in shock at what was happening so swiftly in Europe. Two months later, on May 10, Germany attacked the British expeditionary and French armies, and in less than six weeks, defeated them both.

American military analysts noted that the equipment used by French and British forces, left over from World War I, was mostly obsolete. During the Great Depression of the 1930s, Britain and France had been

---

[8] A party line was one telephone line shared by several homes. Each home on a party line had a different set of rings. Six rings meant it was a call for, say, the Peterson family. Two shorts and a long meant the call was for the Littlejohn ranch, while just two rings meant a call for Widow Abigail Smith. Sharing one telephone line resulted in many people often quietly picking up their phone and listening in on conversations. After all, with no television or Internet in those days, eavesdropping was cheap entertainment in the remoteness of Oregon's sprawling ranchlands.

unable to provide sufficient funding for their military. As a result, both nations were 10 to 20 years behind the times in weaponry, tanks, aircraft, and ships. They were being out-flown, out-gunned and out-fought. What had been two of the most powerful armies on earth a decade earlier were now being crushed in just weeks. Most of the European continent was suddenly under Nazi control. That would soon include Norway.

The cost of being poorly prepared was vividly clear to our nation. In Washington DC, the administration launched a massive effort to fully modernize all the armed forces, adding funding for research and development of new radar systems, rockets, weapons, planes, ships, and tanks. And with its new Selective Training and Service Act of 1940, Washington now had the names and signatures of more than a million young men who qualified for the draft. The names included Carl and Hal.

The government's urgency to modernize and prepare is why the newly arrived surveyors and engineers were working fast in Oregon's countryside to identify the best sites for airports, short landing strips, Army training camps, tank practice battlegrounds and—literally—mile upon mile of military barracks.

Back in Montana, Dad and Carl were reading newly issued government bid requests that called for a high-speed job building a military training camp near Corvallis. It would be the Army's 57,000-acre Camp Adair, home to the 69th Infantry Division, a famous unit with many achievements. The completion deadline was January 1943 or earlier.

Since there was usually extra profit when a customer wanted extra speed, wild horses couldn't stop Dad from bidding the job. But Dad never let his ego get in the way of his common sense. He felt he needed a construction partner with more strength and depth than just his own firm. He called executives he knew at his former employer in Saint Paul, the Lovering-Longbothum Construction Company. Quickly, he and his new partner put together a joint-venture firm called Halvorson-Lovering to bid the War Department's urgent new task. They won the contract, and once again, our family packed everything we had, including our company's construction tools, onto several larger Diamond T trucks, with me hoping for a replay of the "leaping stallion." But Dad and my brothers made extra sure I'd have no reason to roll on the ground with laughter this time. Escorting the trucks in a large new Hudson automobile, Mom, Dad, Evelyn, and I got underway, headed to new places and new adventures.

On the Oregon Trail

Motoring west and south out of Montana on our two-day journey, we drove along the legendary Oregon Trail. A century earlier, thousands of pioneers had come that way, many in wagon trains, searching for an opportunity to acquire affordable land that would allow each pioneer to build a better life. Corvallis itself was the Eden that pioneers looked forward to seeing at the end of their long Oregon-Trail journey.

I realize now that as Dad drove deeper into Oregon state, he had to be troubled about what lay ahead. Yes, the growing threat of war was creating welcome new construction contracts, yet he was also painfully aware, as were the rest of us, that Carl and Hal's signatures on military draft cards meant their lives could soon be in danger.

As our caravan entered Oregon's lush Willamette Valley, we saw miles of ranchland and wilderness, with the white peaks of Oregon's Cascade Mountains and Coast Range to the west, plus winding rivers, and the town of Corvallis itself set on a broad plateau a mile and a half across. Corvallis and later, the nearby town of Salem, would be home to some of the happiest moments I would know.

Boyhood Memories

I was about eight years old when we settled into Corvallis. Looking back, I think the years of eight to 10 are likely the best time period in a boy's life. I remember having a vivid imagination, mostly unrestricted by rules or facts. My buddies and I dreamed our dreams. We read Superman comics, staged sword fights with sticks, and bicycled everywhere daily.

Even as we were having fun, families continued to cope with the effects of the Great Depression. Everyone saved in every possible way. Kids got their hair cut at the kitchen table, not downtown. Wet clothes were hung on clotheslines stretched between trees or poles in backyards. The term *hand-me-down* was an everyday expression. Socks with holes weren't tossed out; they were darned to be used again and again. And no one owned a purebred dog. I can't recall even hearing the word *purebred*. When Dad filled up at the gas station, attendants cleaned the windshield, checked the oil, and looked at tire pressure without a charge. Service mattered in that tough, difficult economy.

In spite of the difficult economic times in Corvallis, few folks had to worry about safety like they do now. Mothers could let kids play outside the entire day without an ounce of fear. No one was ever missing, no predators hung out at schools. Houses were rarely locked. No bicycle I can remember ever had a padlock.

On a typical Saturday morning back then, you could hear the sound of push lawnmowers nearby. A mom would call for her boy: "Charlie! You get home! I mean *now*, Charlie!" Kids on their bikes flew along neighborhood streets.

Saturday's paper, thrown perfectly by a paperboy who was already peddling to the next home on his route, whizzed through the air and landed on our front steps. Our screen door squeaked open as Dad swooped down in a well-practiced move to retrieve his paper. As the door spring slapped the screen door shut behind Dad, I was heading to the driveway with the garden hose to wash his car. I didn't have to ask Dad for the keys, because they were always in the ignition, and the car doors were never locked anyway. Why on earth would they be?

Hearing my noisy buddies down the block bicycling toward me, I'd soap, rub, and rinse as fast as I could. Dad would open the screen door and toss me a dime. Catching it, I'd jump onto my bike, pumping the pedals like crazy to meet up with my buds. We wanted to be first at the baseball field. We were playing scratch baseball, a good practice for our Little League games all summer long. When we weren't chasing fly balls and stealing bases, we talked about heading down to the river where we were building a raft. We played to the max on Saturdays, the one day of the week where we owned our world and our own time.

Sundays, by contrast, were the Lord's Day. Even most stores were closed. We kids dressed up, not down. We attended Sunday school, and, when we were old enough, worship services also. There, too, we were surrounded by friends and family. When I look at how hard we played and how hard we worked all week, I realize Sunday was a restoration day, both physically and spiritually.

My personal faith has deep roots in those Oregon years. Dad and Mom were devout Christians, yet they never wore their faith on their sleeve, nor can I think of a moment when they questioned their faith. The most valuable gift they gave me was faith—the deep, powerful, and loving force that has guided Barbara and me so well for so long.

Our noisy, industrious family liked living in Corvallis, four blocks from Oregon State College (now University). And thanks to the growing number of military projects, Dad and my brothers were working long hours and earning welcome incomes from the new construction. Not to be outdone, I earned a little income of my own, serving beverages to the Camp Adair construction workers as they came into town after their shifts.

The first bus stop where workers got off was only a block from our house. So I set up my little business there. When they stepped off the bus, those bone-tired and thirsty workers would immediately see my display of cold glasses of Kool-Aid and lemonade. Since there was no such thing as bottled water then, I prospered.

In the background of all this prosperity was my mother, always with such a caring spirit, helping and teaching me how to take after my parents' example and be industrious in life.

Evelyn managed Dad's construction office at the Camp Adair project, handling payroll, billing, and payables. As the pace of construction increased, she became swamped. Soon, she invited her good friend from Minnesota, Katherine "Kay" Boyer, to come out to Oregon to help in the office. That proved to be serendipitous. Kay eventually married my brother Carl before he was called to war.

Seeing Action on Two Fronts

The first week in December 1941 proved to be a good time for Dad and Mom, along with me, to visit friends and relatives we'd left behind in Billings. We made the Corvallis-to-Billings drive in good time, arriving on Sunday morning, December 7.

While we were visiting friends in their living room, the radio was playing in the background. Suddenly, an announcer interrupted the program. Pearl Harbor in Honolulu, Hawaii, had just been attacked! Our families spent the rest of the day listening to the barrage of alarming news bulletins and praying for the servicemen under attack.

Years later, I read about what happened that same day to two brothers from Oregon who were stationed at Pearl Harbor. Del Pitzer was a Marine at the Navy barracks, and Dallas Pitzer served on the *USS San Francisco*. Since December 7 was Dallas's 21st birthday, they planned a breakfast, then a round of golf, and more celebrations later.

A few minutes before 8:00 AM, as the brothers were finishing breakfast at an outdoor café, the first of about 300 Japanese war planes flew over with a great roar. Del Spitzer later said, "The enemy planes were headed over the harbor toward the seven ships docked at Battleship Row. Before we knew it, there were explosions, and smoke began pouring from the ships."

Dallas rushed to a small dinghy bound for his ship while Del scurried with other men at his barracks to find ammunition and any kind of weapon they could use to defend their area.

Although the brothers survived the surprise Japanese air assault, thousands more servicemen were not so blessed. Japan's attack at Pearl Harbor killed 2,400 military personnel and wounded 1,100 more. Twenty major ships were sunk or damaged, and 169 aircraft destroyed.

Life seemed to stop in America. In the 11 seconds it took for each bomb to drop from a Japanese plane onto an American ship in Pearl

Harbor, our country's era of peace shattered. The next day, the president was on the radio making a formal declaration of war. As young as I was, I realized that nothing would be the same again.

Everywhere, from the War Department in our nation's capital to Oregon on the opposite coast, America was kicking into high gear, producing aircraft, ships, and weapons—plus building camps to house and train new soldiers by the millions.

Up in Seattle, the Boeing Company was on its way to producing 16 B-17 bombers per day, while near Detroit, the Ford Motor Company was making 14 B-24s a day. Construction contracts were issued at high speed and demanded high-speed completions. As a result of the speed-up, Dad was signing up more construction work, and much of it was near the state capital. So our family moved 40 miles north from Corvallis to Salem. Dad rented a house on Winter Street, just a block from Leslie Junior High School.

One of Dad's contracts in the area was to build a bomber base at Redmond for the United States Army Air Forces. In that all-out wartime effort, it wasn't a question of *whether* you got a government contract; it was a question of *which one* you got. It was all military, all the time.

On a darker side, Mom and Dad's concern for their oldest sons grew as World War II intensified. Mom was grateful that, for a brief time, Hal and Carl were officially deferred from military service since they were key men in military construction projects.

But all too soon, Hal went into the Army, training to become a forward observer for the field artillery. I suspect the job description for a Forward Observer could scare a ghost. I think it might have read something like this:

Each day, carrying an Army field telephone (the type you crank to generate a bit of electricity to power your call), you will carefully make your way to the front lines. You will take along a helper or two to carry heavy spools of phone wire and to string that line of wire back to the officer directing the fire of the artillery guns.

As you approach the front lines, crawl on your belly, getting as close as you can to enemy lines without being seen, heard, or shot. If you are still alive, pop your head up for a second to locate good enemy targets. Keep in mind that the enemy knows you're there somewhere, because they also have artillery and forward observers, so they're looking for you as you are looking for them.

Once you've stuck your head up long enough to identify a target, duck back down to phone the artillery officer who is as much as a half mile behind you. Give him the compass coordinates that will bring a large exploding shell onto the enemy spot you identified.

Hal landed on France's Normandy beaches in June 1944 and was, thereafter, on the front lines as the Allies pushed German forces steadily back, foot by foot, field by field, death by death. The fighting was always ferocious as Hal and hell were together on the front lines.

For the initial six months of the invasion, the Germans were forced steadily to retreat. Then, in a moment, everything changed. On December 16, 1944, Germany launched a huge surprise counterattack in the area of Ardennes, Belgium, forcing American troops into immediate retreat and causing them to suffer huge losses. The entire world held its breath.

Germany had prepared the offensive with great secrecy. They moved troops and equipment only at night and kept radio traffic to a minimum. That attack produced total surprise among the Allied forces. Germany's generals hoped they could split and surround the British and American Allied line, possibly forcing the US and Britain to agree to a peace treaty favorable to Germany.

Hal, always where the action was, got swept up in the first phase of the German attack. Despite a snowstorm and freezing temperatures, the previously hidden German forces quickly swarmed over the outnumbered American troops to a depth of five miles or more. On the front line in the forest at that moment, Hal and two other soldiers had been handling the telephone wires running to artillery guns behind their position. Both of Hal's companions were killed in the attack.

Hal went into hiding, staying on the move, aware he was now behind enemy lines. At one point, he met courageous people in the Underground resistance movement who hid him from the German forces. Experts in hiding spies and agents, the Underground agents moved my brother around until Lt. Gen. George S. Patton Jr. led his Third US Army in counterattacking the Germans, causing them eventually to lose all the ground they had gained. American forces fully recaptured the territory. That pivotal event has come to be known as the Battle of the Bulge.

Of the 600,000 American troops engaged, almost 20,000 were killed, another 20,000 captured, and 40,000 wounded. The battle Hal survived was the largest, bloodiest battle that American forces experienced in all of World War II. God bless the civilian volunteers of the Underground who risked their lives to save my brother.

One year after Hal had joined the Army, Carl was drafted and specifically trained for the much-feared invasion of Japan, in a vast plan secretly called Operation Downfall, composed of two coordinating thrusts: Operation Olympic and Operation Coronet. Not made public until half a century later, the secret American invasion plan called for using the entire Marine Corps, every vessel in the Pacific Navy, and key elements of the Seventh Army Air Force, the Eighth Air Force, and much more.

From their battles with the Japanese Army on islands from Guadalcanal to Iwo Jima, US military planners knew how fiercely the Japanese fought—almost always to the last man. With that experience, the planners of Operation Downfall forecast millions of dead and wounded when mainland Japan was invaded in what would have been the largest amphibious operation in history. In fact, Navy Department planners estimated total casualties to America would range between two to four million men, with 400,000 to 800,000 dead. The Navy also estimated up to 10 million Japanese casualties.

No wonder President Truman chose an option no one knew he had—dropping two atomic bombs on Hiroshima and Nagasaki as a demonstration of power, hoping the Japanese government would end their fight. After Japan didn't respond to warnings by the United States, the Air Force carried out the attack. The initial blasts and aftereffects killed an estimated quarter of a million people. Overwhelmed, and with no weapon to match the atomic bomb, Japan surrendered on September 2, 1945. Historians now recognize that Truman's decision likely saved some eight million American and Japanese lives.

Japan's surrender meant that Carl, instead of fighting the Japanese, spent his time *helping* them. He was part of a most unusual US occupation Army in Japan, an enlightened and mostly friendly endeavor devoted to building the first Asian democracy along with a robust industrial and business sector. It succeeded beyond anyone's imaginings. All of us, especially Carl's wife, Kay, and their child, were greatly relieved that Carl escaped invasion combat. He was in occupied Japan for three long years, but at least his life was never at risk. Once home again, Carl soon launched a construction firm later known for major accomplishments.

10
COMING OF AGE IN THE WAR YEARS

During the war years, life changed for almost everyone. Our nation's all-out effort at grass-roots support of the war sparked the popularity of "victory gardens" where families would grow much of their food in their own backyards.

In addition to our home victory garden, Dad purchased a small conventional farm just outside of Salem. The Goertzen family operated it for Dad and produced fruit, vegetables, and grain. I worked there every summer throughout the war years and became good friends with Don Goertzen, who was my age. Our row crops included beans and strawberries. Most of our crops were bought by the two major vegetable and fruit packing companies in Salem—Del Monte, and Kelley, Farquhar & Company.

The Whizzer

When Dad's company was building the Army Air Forces' bomber base in Redmond, around 130 miles southeast of Salem, he had to be at the build site much of the time. He would drive through Santiam Pass where the North Santiam Highway crossed over the Cascade Range. The route was difficult back then—an unpaved dirt road that was mostly just a single lane with turnouts.

All that driving put a lot of wear and tear on our family car, and it wasn't like we could just run down to a dealership and order a new one. The war effort had diverted many materials for the manufacture of military supplies. However, since Dad was building highly important defense projects, he was given priority to purchase a second car. He bought the last Oldsmobile available for sale in Salem. It was gunmetal gray—as were all the cars produced during that time.

Gas rationing was also in effect during the war. "A stickers" were issued to people with the lowest priority and allowed them only three to four gallons of gas per week. B stickers allowed military workers up to eight gallons per week. And C stickers were granted to people deemed essential to the war effort. Dad had a C sticker, allowing him as much fuel as he needed.

Because Dad was gone from home so much, I didn't have access to enough gasoline to get me to the farm as often as necessary. Then a light went on in my mind. Maybe I could persuade Dad to buy me a Whizzer bicycle engine to turn my bicycle into a motorbike! Comic books carried ads for them all the time, and every boy my age wanted one. The Whizzer kit included a belt drive and a small gas engine of a little over one horsepower.

Somehow I talked Dad into the perfect logic of it all, although I suspect that he, like most males, was a sucker for any new piece of machinery. Whatever it was that persuaded him, he spent $54.95 to get me the kit. Thanks to the Whizzer, I worked at the farm more often, doing a little bit of everything, from picking strawberries to cultivating.

We had tractors and trucks and other machinery at the farm, so I learned to drive pretty much every different vehicle there. As my confidence rose and as Dad was out of town more often, I would even drive the family car around a block or two and then stealthily put it back.

A Memorable Lesson

When I was in sixth or seventh grade, a boy who lived a half block down the street asked if I knew how to drive a car. Well, thanks to my work on Dad's row-crop farm, I replied that I had, indeed, driven before. My friend's next question was, "Do you think you could drive my dad's car?"

I said, "Sure, I could do that."

He grinned and said, "Let's go start it."

His folks were at work, and my friend had the keys to the car, so we closed the garage doors to keep from being noticed by anyone. Then I started the car, and the two of us sat there, clueless, in a cloud of poisonous carbon monoxide. It's amazing we didn't kill ourselves.

Fortunately, it wasn't long before my buddy said, "Think you can back it out of here?" I nodded. So he opened the garage door, and I backed the car out. With that achievement behind us, off we went in his dad's car looking for kids we knew. Within five or 10 minutes, our car was full of kids.

I was savvy enough not to drive recklessly or show off. But I did drive all over Salem. I went past Leslie Junior High School and then out to the airport. I drove us all over town for maybe 45 minutes. Finally about midday, I returned the car to the garage. We had plenty of time left to play some baseball and chase. By the end of the day, I had already forgotten about our excursion.

As I came home and walked up our sidewalk, I saw Dad standing outside our house. Instead of saying hello, he asked, "Did you do anything wrong today?"

At age 14, I had already developed an interest in aviation.

I looked my dad square in the eyes and said in all honesty, "No."

Dad waited a moment. Then, returning my direct gaze he asked, "Did you drive Mr. Davidson's car?"

The question shook me. I hadn't even thought of the morning's earlier drive, probably because it had been without incident. But at Dad's words, I crumbled and nodded.

Dad said, "Go to your room, and take your pants down." I did as he directed and sat there with my pants down for what seemed like forever. The waiting was awful. When Dad came upstairs, he said, "You're not getting this licking so much for what you did, but because you lied to me." And that hurt way more than the licking did.

Looking back at those summer days in Salem, when I was having all kinds of fun with my good friends, I realize I was at a stage in life where an event like the car caper was just one of a dozen different things we'd do in a typical day. As soon as I turned off my friend's car, I probably shouted, "Hey, let's go play some ball!" A buddy would have responded, "Race you there!" We'd all be off, pedaling our bikes like crazy. What car ride?

The thing was, I admired Dad so much, I would never even *consider* lying to him on purpose. But with great sorrow, I realized I had ended up lying anyway. Whenever I got a chance during the subsequent weeks, I'd say "Dad, when you questioned me, I didn't lie to you. I answered so quickly, I hadn't reviewed my entire day yet, and that memory hadn't flashed into my mind when I replied."

The incident still nags me to this day, decades later.

More Fun and Games—and Confessions

In those years, baseball was a passion for me and my buddies. I played on Mayor Robert (Bob) Elfstrom's team. The Elfstroms were family friends. One afternoon, just after my buddy Don Goertzen and I had finished a game on the baseball field adjacent to the community swimming pool, some excited boys came over to whisper to us about a just-discovered peephole into the girls' shower room. We were enthusiastically told that the peephole would let us see the whole shower area! Nothing, not even an atomic blast, could have kept us boys from visiting that peephole.

That same large playing field was also where traveling circuses set up. The circus was a giant magnet for us kids. With no enforced child-labor laws, many of my buddies and I would offer to work there, helping with the hotdog stand or caramel-corn kiosk. When circus workers set up the big show tents, I'd help carry items for the men. They would give me a free show pass and a few pennies for my work.

One evening, after seeing a circus show with friends, I headed for home. Behind the big tent was where the animals, including quite a few elephants, were kept. As I ran along the open field behind the tent, I came to an empty cardboard box and started kicking it. I would kick the box ahead of me, then run, then kick the box again, and then run.

I didn't mean any harm, but that activity totally spooked the elephants. They started trumpeting and moving around restlessly. I was stunned and stopped kicking the box. Circus people ran out of their tents, trailers, and wagons, trying to discover what was going on. I was scared to death I'd started a stampede, slowly realizing, as only kids can do, that elephant stampedes couldn't be a good thing. I took off running through the darkening night, straight for home. The next day I learned with huge relief that no stampede had taken place. For years afterward, I kept my moment of stupidity all to myself.

One winter, as Christmastime approached, I announced to Dad and Mom that I would go to the woods and find a nice Christmas tree. We lived near the school at that time.

After searching a nearby forest all day in vain, I began to realize that all the good trees had already been taken. What was left was either too large or too scrawny. Toward dusk, I headed home empty-handed and defeated.

Then, out of the corner of my eye, I suddenly saw *the perfect tree*. It was in a row of trees that formed a tall hedge at the graveyard. Without the tiniest hesitation, I sawed down the tree and happily lugged it home. That outstanding tree earned me many compliments from my parents, siblings, neighbors, and friends.

Fortunately, dead people tell no tales.

Sharing the Radio Experience

Many of us who remember the 1930s and '40s share memories of listening to war news on our radios. Radio sets back then were the high-tech devices of the day, the focal point of every living room. Typically, larger sets were from three to five feet high, two or three feet wide, and each had a huge glowing dial. They could pick up local stations as well as some far away. At night in Corvallis or Salem, we could pick up broadcasts as far away as Salt Lake City, San Francisco, and Denver. It seemed magical.

Each city had only one or two stations. In addition, there were several coast-to-coast networks. So when President Roosevelt gave radio talks, which he did often, virtually everyone in the nation tuned in and shared the same listening experience. Recently I heard a man recall how, in the summer of 1939, he walked from his Chicago home to his best friend's house half a mile away. On that warm evening, all the neighbors were on their front verandas listening to their radios. During his entire walk, the young man never missed a word of Roosevelt's speech.

When the president gave his radio address right after the attack on Pearl Harbor in 1941, virtually everyone in the country heard his radio speech. The next day, December 8, everyone talked with each other about what the president said. That shared experience brought us together. We felt we were part of a nation, not just part of an "interest group."

America experienced that feeling of unity again when President John F. Kennedy was assassinated in 1963, as well as when Neil Armstrong took "one small step for a man, a giant leap for mankind" on the moon in 1969.

We also felt it on September 11, 2001. As everyone watched the terrorist attacks take place, we felt like a national family reunited. We flew flags and enjoyed the feeling of complete unity.

The Effects of War

In 1940, when we all listened to the same news programs, we learned together about the spreading World War in Europe. By September of that year, we were hearing live newscasts from London with stories of a completely new kind of war—nearly continuous, day-and-night bombings of London by the German Air Force.

Nothing quite like this had happened in known history. It seemed to be the first time when, instead of soldier killing soldier, a group of maybe

200 military pilots dropped bombs to try to kill as many civilians as possible: babies, children, adults, seniors, everyone.

War is so vivid and shocking, hearing about it creates never-forgotten memories. Suddenly, every American was listening to programs about aerial war and hearing announcements about government programs designed to help us defend ourselves.

In 1940 and 1941, practice blackouts and dimouts became law. A blackout involved blacking out all lights across entire cities and regions so overhead enemy bombers couldn't find their targets. A dimout greatly limited the amount of light that could be used after dark. Government-ordered blackouts took place up and down the Atlantic and Pacific Coasts.

Oregon's Civil Defense Association was a leader in these drills and staged a major practice in October 1941. Volunteers were trained how to be air-raid wardens. The Portland area counted 8,000 "lady air-raid wardens" and 10,000 male wardens who patrolled streets at night. They were given specific neighborhoods to cover in search of anyone who still had a light on.

For a while, our home town of Salem staged a blackout every night. Ultimately, blackout drills were mandatory everywhere, even in towns far from the coast.

On June 21, 1942, radio reports brought more news that scared everyone in the Pacific Northwest. At night, a Japanese submarine surfaced at the mouth of the Columbia River and fired its deck cannon at Fort Stevens. Since Fort Stevens was a Civil-War-era military fort with a set of obsolete cannons, the shelling accomplished nothing except giving Oregonians the jitters. Would Japan actually invade? Would their submarines or ships come farther up the Columbia River?

Two months after the scary submarine event, a Japanese seaplane dropped two 180-pound incendiary bombs near the Oregon town of Brookings in an attempt to start a forest fire. The scheme fizzled. Still, radio news announced that it was the only aerial bombing of mainland America by a foreign power.

Even though the war was not being fought in our homeland, it still became quite personal for most of us. From time to time, I would see US service flags in the front windows of different homes around Salem. Each flag that had a blue-edged gold star in the center indicated a home that had lost a family member in action. As the war progressed, we saw more and more gold-star service flags. They made me think about the grief inside those homes.

Back to Scandinavia

World War II touched everyone, everywhere, and gave all of us cause for fear and worry. That was especially true for Mom and Dad, with two sons in the military and dozens of relatives and longtime friends back in their homelands of Norway and Sweden.

My parents had no way of receiving reassurance about the fate of their loved ones overseas. Few letters, if any, came through, and certainly no phone calls. All my parents knew was that Norway was enduring a brutal five-year occupation by the Germans, and that, while Sweden managed to maintain its 200-year tradition of neutrality, it was nevertheless blockaded by the British and German Navies. Because of those blockades, food and fuel became scarce and costly.

After the war ended in September 1945, my parents decided to travel to Norway and Sweden to find out how family and friends were doing. It had been almost a quarter-century since they'd been in their home countries. But their plans had to wait for passenger ships and airplanes to resume services in Northern Europe.

Meanwhile, Dad continued his construction business as best he could, although it was not always easy getting materials. During the war, no new motels or hotels had been built, and immediately after the war ended in September 1945, there was a need for more guest lodging. So my father built the Rose Garden Motel in Salem in 1946. Then he and Mom invited Sigvart and Martha Hoiland, good friends of theirs from Anaconda, Montana, to manage it. They had become friends when our family had lived in Butte.

In 1947, when travel to Scandinavia was finally possible again, Dad, Mom, Evelyn, and I—15 years old by then—took a train from Portland, Oregon, to New York City where we planned to board a passenger ship to England. From there we would take a smaller ship to Norway to spend the summer. But when we stepped off the train in New York, we learned that New York's longshoremen were out on strike. That meant no ships were arriving, and none would be leaving.

But Dad wasn't about to give up. After all, he lived his strong belief that all problems can be solved, and all obstacles can be conquered. Moreover, he and Mom had been praying for and dreaming about this trip for years. So Dad decided that instead of taking a boat, we'd take an airplane, even if we had to leave our steamer trunks behind. Without delay, Dad and Evelyn began working the telephones like racetrack bookies, calling and calling until they found seats on KLM Royal Dutch Airlines.

Then our elation at the good news faded. The reality was, not a lot of people flew across the Atlantic in 1947. The flight took 23 hours due to three separate refueling stops along the way. Worse, most passenger planes in that era had unpressurized cabins, forcing them to fly at lower altitudes where conditions were bumpy and uncomfortable. Dad, Mom, and Evelyn deliberated and debated. Should our family take the flight? Wasn't it foolish to take so many of us on one airplane across a huge ocean? Since we were putting our family at risk, Dad held a serious prayer meeting in our hotel room. In the end, we all decided to go for it.

Perhaps in answer to our prayers, our airplane turned out to be a new four-motor Lockheed Constellation propeller-driven airliner with cabin pressurization. That allowed us to cruise above most storms on our hopscotch journey that involved refueling stops in Newfoundland, Greenland, and Ireland before we finally landed in Amsterdam.

Before flying on to Bergen, Norway, we spent three days in the Netherlands. We took a riverboat tour, and we rode the train to the coastal town of Volendam, a little north of Amsterdam. The town's citizens wore traditional garb, including wooden shoes. It was like stepping back in time.

We learned that the New York longshoremen's strike had ended, allowing our steamer trunks to be shipped to Norway. Steamer trunks, by the way, were quite large, typically three feet across, and two feet deep by two feet high. We filled them with items we knew our family and friends could not get during wartime—chewing gum, dolls, games, soccer balls, and clothing for the children, along with real coffee for the adults.

Dad and Mom were thrilled to be returning after so many years away. As our great three-month adventure got underway, I was probably embarrassing people. I couldn't help staring at the kids. They wore wooden shoes too. Leather had become scarce in Norway during the war—a result of the blockades.

A Place of the Heart

On our first night, Dad and Mom put me into a rickety, old van filled with my uncle and a host of other strangers headed to my cousin's house someplace out in the country. Nervously, I watched my parents wave cheerful goodbyes to me, and by the time I arrived at my cousin's home, real fear set in. In this strange house full of strange people, no one else knew a word of English. I panicked. Who *were* all these people? What were they going to do with me?

Until that jarring night when Mom and Dad suddenly dropped me into an unknown world, I had been happily secure in my close-knit family. Now I was surrounded by strangers who, I concluded, didn't even know how to talk.

I spent the first night, along with my uncle, trying to sleep on the floor of my cousin's house. When the strangers woke me in the morning with smiles and food, I relaxed and soon began to enjoy my surroundings.

We developed a plan. I would teach them English, and they would teach me Norwegian, a good bargain for both sides. I finally discovered what Dad and Mom knew all along—I had a whole other family who seemed to love me just as much as my original gang did.

My summer in Norway and Sweden was idyllic. All around me was the magnificent countryside, along with warm, likeable, fun-loving people. At one point, I visited my great-grandmother's abandoned home in Sweden near the Norwegian border. The small, humble, one-story home, sitting by itself in the country, had stunning views of the lake it sat next to and of the mountains beyond. Mother told me that when the nearby lake froze over in winter, she used to skate across it to her village school on the other side.

Somehow I felt that this crumbling home, where my mother and her mother and many generations before them had grown up, was a place of the heart. In different ways, at different moments, the empty, deteriorating house held attractions for me.

After I explored the first floor, I worked up courage to investigate the attic. At first, its damp, dark interior was intimidating. In one corner, I noticed a light but quickly realized it was where a bit of the roof had fallen in. Would the attic floor give way too?

Soon I lost my fears and became captivated by family heirlooms left behind. I touched a spinning wheel that surely my grandmother and maybe great-grandmother had used, perhaps even to spin wool for my mother's first clothing. I uncovered some large, hand-carved wooden spoons up to almost 12 inches across. Somehow, mysteriously, those simple but finely carved pieces of wood evoked a feeling of kinship in me. I felt a tie with unknown family members of yesteryear who had shaped my mother's birth and life and were now shaping my own.

I was startled to feel tears in my eyes and was grateful no one could see me. Something moved me to save many of those abandoned family treasures. I carefully packed each piece into a large shipping box to send home to Oregon. Dad, Mom, and Evelyn thought I was foolish to bother with them. I understood their feelings but, without knowing why, I wanted them with me.

However, once back home, my good intentions of restoring the lovely old heirlooms lost out to my day-to-day life. The treasure box remained closed for decades. Recently, I've been visiting those heirlooms, feeling the same powerful emotions I felt as a kid back in 1947 when I first discovered them.

Our Grand Swedish Tour

While I appreciated getting to know my Scandinavian family and learning Norwegian and Swedish, I was excited when Dad took Mom, Evelyn, and me on a great auto trip through Sweden. Boy, were we traveling in style! Dad hired a big prewar touring car, complete with a chauffeur. It was the perfect choice for our grand tour of Sweden as we caught up on 25 years of family news and events.

Later, Evelyn told me she sometimes felt awkward to be with Dad in certain situations because he was the most enthusiastic American anyone could imagine, with his positive, over-the-top outlook about his new country. While thousands of Norwegians and Swedes had been emigrating from Scandinavia to the United States for decades, Dad was the only one in his family to do so. He was excited and amazed about the opportunities his adopted country offered to so many people, including him.

When our wonderful three-month vacation came to an end, we sailed for home on a passenger ship. I remember seeing the White Cliffs of Dover as we made our first stop in England. Even though we were there a year and a half after the war's end, the week we spent in London left an indelible impression on my mind. The city had been pounded to the ground. Bombs had decimated the city's northeast side, and as far as the eye could see, everything had been leveled.

When we set sail for America, each of us was grateful for the risks we took and the precious time we'd spent among so many old-country family and friends. We regretted that the summer of 1947 was ending.

11
OFF TO BOARDING SCHOOL

At Saint Paul's Norwegian Lutheran church, my parents found their faith and became members. I was baptized there as an infant, and my entire life was built on the foundation of a family of faith who had devotions and went to church and Sunday school regularly.

In about the sixth grade I attended a Youth for Christ rally where Billy Graham, a young budding evangelist, gave a dynamic message. Although many around me went forward to accept Christ that night, I didn't go with them. I felt in my heart that I already belonged to God, but I prayed the salvation prayer on my own anyway. From that time forward, I became more active as a young Christian because my greater sense of peace with God increased my confidence. My decision at that rally significantly changed the rest of my life.

Arriving in Fergus Falls

My parents decided to send me to boarding school for my high-school education. They carefully handpicked what they felt was an excellent school, and I didn't doubt their choice. Home or away, I felt blessed to have them as parents. So, when we landed in New York after our summer in Scandinavia, Dad, Mom, and Evelyn headed for home in Salem, and I took the train to Minnesota.

My destination was the small town of Fergus Falls, about 150 miles west of the Twin Cities. Fergus, with its waterfalls and ringed by 1,000 lakes, was home to Hillcrest Lutheran Academy. The Christian-based boarding school had, and continues to have, a strong scholastic reputation. When I arrived, I was a 15-year-old sophomore, eager to meet and make new friends.

But at first, I got off to an awkward start. I'd been told Hillcrest was quite formal, so I put on the only suit I owned, complete with vest, in order to make a great first impression.

Within the first few seconds of my arrival at Hillcrest, I realized that wearing a suit to school was way over the top. Instead of smiles I got giggles. I was desperate to change into something casual. However, all my other clothes, packed in my luggage returning from our Norway adventure, failed to arrive on time. So for three of the longest days of my teenage life, I was condemned to social death. Overnight, I became the dork of the school. "Who is this guy, straight from Norway, who doesn't have any regular clothes? Do you think he's going to wear that suit all year?"

Barbara was a freshman at Hillcrest that year. She remembers noticing "that guy in a suit." She told me later she couldn't believe her eyes, and, although she didn't say anything to anyone, she thought, *That guy is really different.* Fortunately, as soon as my steamer trunk arrived and I could dress appropriately again, she decided I had "turned normal."

Despite my painful first few days, Hillcrest Academy turned out to be a great school for me. It was alive with special times and full of people who would become lasting friends.

By today's standards, Hillcrest was excessively strict. Yet back then, its rules were not uncommon. We couldn't leave the campus after dinner. No student could own a car. Girls could not wear lipstick. Girls walked along one side of the hall, guys on the other side. Seating in chapel was similarly segregated. Dating was strictly forbidden.

Out on a Ledge

Even though Hillcrest was a Christian academy, my friends and I did not always act like angels. Occasionally, we would bend a rule or two. We guys figured out how to get down the fire escape at night without a sound and then go to a corner store, about five blocks away, for dessert. We were good kids, but we didn't see anything wrong with a little nightcap of ice cream and cookies. The region's cold winters never bothered Minnesotans and never bothered us. We'd walk to town no matter what the temperature was. When streets were packed with snow, we'd often catch the rear bumper of a car at a stop sign and ski on our shoes to wherever we wanted to go. It was little dangerous, but great fun.

During my first year there, I noticed a very sweet girl who became the object of my first real romantic crush—if you don't count my second-grade fling with the neighborhood girl for whom I tried to swipe a dime-store ring. Up until this point, girls had been playmates and buddies. The girl who caught my attention now was named Elgie, and she apparently had a similar crush on me. We got along very well and saw each other as often as possible in places where we wouldn't be noticed. We had some fun outings with another couple, Milt and Norma Lou (who went by the name of Betsy). Milt lived on the fourth floor in the men's dorm. I lived on the third floor.

One evening, Milt and I crafted a daring plan that Elgie and Betsy later agreed to. We boys would make our way along the building's ledge, a distance of about 50 feet, to the first room in the girl's dorm. Then we'd rendezvous with Elgie and Betsy.

Elgie's room was the first girl's room on the fourth floor, at the opposite side of the building from the fourth-floor men's dorm. But now, as with most amateur plots, our simple idea quickly sprouted arms and legs and all kinds of complications. Elgie's roommate would have to move out to make room for Milt's hot date, Betsy. So the girls did some adroit swapping of rooms. Betsy would be Elgie's temporary overnight guest during the evening of the great ledge-walk. In an odd twist of fate, Barbara, who hadn't caught my eye yet, allowed Elgie's temporarily homeless roommate to stay overnight with her.

On the designated evening, we two guys dressed in the least noticeable clothing we could find and quietly waited in a fourth-floor storage room until we were sure everyone else was asleep. Then slowly, silently, as nervous as bank safecrackers, we opened our window.

Milt stepped out first and began the clandestine "ledge journey" some 50 feet above the lawn far below. A second later, I slipped out the window and got my footing on the narrow ledge that looked a lot narrower to me now than it had previously. I followed Milt and edged along in a sort of step-shuffle-shuffle, step shuffle-shuffle system. The entire way, we spread-eagled our arms so we could grasp the grout joints with our fingertips as best we could. The tension was incredible. There was no going back. My heart pounded as we inched closer and closer toward the girl's dorm.

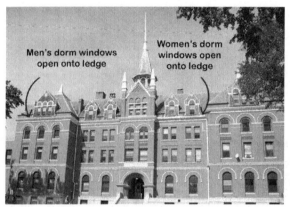

When Milt and I arrived at the right window, he softly tapped on the glass. Finally we heard a little tap back. Elgie slowly opened the window, and Milt and I climbed through.

Those moments are burned into my memory. After the constant fear of getting caught, plus the greater fear of falling 50 feet to our certain death, our visit with the girls was an intense thrill, although I never once even tried to kiss Elgie. The four of us whispered and giggled and flirted until the sky began to lighten. Milt and I then realized we had to crawl back to our dorm before anyone woke up. So, we stepped out onto the ledge again and began our scary step-shuffle-shuffle gait all the way back to the open window of the storage room. Back inside our dorm, we were both amazed we had pulled off our escapade.

Once we had caught a couple of hours of sleep, we talked about it over and over, although we never seriously considered the dangers. Did we realize all of us would have been kicked out of school if we'd been caught? *No.* Did we recognize we would have been killed if we'd slipped? Well, yeah, but we were just 16 years old, the age of teen immortality, and we didn't figure such a thing would happen to *us.*

Today, the exterior of Hillcrest Academy looks much as it did when I was a student there. One can readily see a thin white ledge running from one side of the dorm to the other at the fourth floor level. After being in construction for many years, I'm fairly confident that as they were completing the building, the contractor told the architect, "I wouldn't put a ledge up there if I were you. Some idiot kid will get out on that thing and probably fall to his death. That little ledge is trouble waiting to happen."

The architect probably said something like, "Sam, you builders haven't got a clue about what good design means. That white ledge-work gives the building its distinction. And besides, no kids would be crazy enough to crawl out on that tiny ledge!"

No one except me and my buddy, Milt.

A Life-Changing Date

Elgie didn't return to Hillcrest the following year, and she disappeared from my life. Eventually I began to notice another girl who looked prettier every time I saw her. I had to ask around casually without letting anyone know I cared. Discretion matters in a boarding-school environment, where gossip travels at twice the speed of light. But I managed—with some stealth—to learn quietly that she was Barbara Tweed, a second-year student from Iowa.

By the time Barbara started to take an interest in me, however, she was a sophomore. She later told me that what drew her eye was when all the guys on the basketball court got into an argument and several wanted to fight, I would just stand back and let it happen. When I never got into it, she thought, *That guy's a neat kid. He really has sportsmanship.*

In my third year, I again happily broke Hillcrest's rule about students dating each other. Surreptitiously through a friend, I invited Barbara to go with me to a basketball game at another high school. Barbara's message back was, "I'd love to," so I and another guy rendezvoused at a set location near Hillcrest with Barbara and another girl, and we all went to the game together.

Barbara looked prettier every time I saw her.

So help me, I can't remember one second of what happened in the game. All I remember is how good it felt being with Barbara, how one of her smiles would give me a brain freeze, and above all, the moment when we were walking back up to Hillcrest and I got the courage to hold her hand for the first time. The thrill of that moment is as vivid in my memory today as it was all those years ago.

Of course, our first date didn't immediately lead to marriage. Yet, in those few moments of walking, talking, and our hands touching, I felt we were married in our hearts, without a word spoken, without a vow given.

Even though Hillcrest was tough about its rules, we kids loved it there. I especially liked athletics and intramural games. Hillcrest was beginning to play other schools and needed a school team name. We all tried to come up with a great one. I suggested *Hillcrest Comets*, explaining to my fellow teammates that comets were both fast and hot. My buddies loved that. So everyone agreed on the name, and to this day Hillcrest's mascot is the Mighty Comet, and its sports teams are the Comets.

Clacking Pants and the Hupmobile

In schools and colleges everywhere, there's an economic truth as strong as the law of gravity: Students are either almost broke or completely broke. For a short time, I was one of the almost-broke students. Although Dad and Mom could have afforded to give me a good allowance, they'd decided to limit what they gave me so I would be inspired to become still more industrious.

It worked. I landed an after-school job at the Ford dealership in town. My duty was to wash cars every night. It was hard to tell which of us received more water—the cars or me. After work, I'd walk up the long, long hill to Hillcrest. In winter it was sometimes 20 degrees below zero, or even colder. In those kinds of temperatures, my wet pants froze solid and made a clacking sound with every step I took. Clacking frozen pants aren't fun, so I was soon looking for an alternative to walking. So was a Hillcrest buddy of mine, Art Pederson, who likewise found an after-school job. He delivered laundry.

We decided to go in together and buy a cheap car. But there was a problem. While each of us had a driver's license, we were not old enough to *own* a car. In 1948 in the state of Minnesota, the age limit for car ownership was 18. That meant we'd have to find an affordable car offered for sale by an individual, *not* by a dealer. We soon found such a car, a two-door 1928 Hupmobile coupe. Perfect!

Art and I were both at the age when cars took over a young man's life. And when a car means everything to you, you can make a lot of bad decisions with enthusiasm and energy in order to maximize the time you have in your automobile.

As quickly as we could count out $35 into the hand of the car's seller, we became underage owners of an unregistered-to-us Hupmobile. Although the whole thing had to be an undercover affair, we didn't care. What laws were in existence concerning licensing and insurance were rarely enforced. We were thrilled to our socks by this car *we actually owned!* That 1928 Hupmobile seemed awesome with its big six-cylinder engine, pull-down window shades, and even a large rumble seat in back. It definitely beat walking up to Hillcrest Academy in clacking pants.

When we weren't in school or working our after-school jobs, Art and I drove the Hupmobile all over the place. When we parked it away from school, we were always careful to do so on a downward slope because the car's ancient battery couldn't hold an electrical charge. The only way to start the car was to get it rolling downhill. Saving money for a new battery became our highest priority. Soon enough, we were able to purchase the battery we needed.

We pulled the old battery from under the car's floorboards and installed the new one. While the battery cost almost 20 percent of what we'd paid for the entire car, we didn't mind. We loved the feeling of having our own car.

Soon the vehicle had more problems. The starter needed to be overhauled. But after we paid to have that work performed, the Hup worked fine.

One beautiful spring day, we took two female friends with us and drove 60 miles to Fargo, North Dakota. It was a great trip for us neophytes. I drove one way, with Art and a girl riding in the rumble seat, and we swapped places on the return trip. Soon, we were driving all over the place. We put every penny we could into the mechanical love of our life—the razzle-dazzle Hupmobile.

Then not long after our great roundtrip to Fargo, we were driving in downtown Fergus Falls when the spindle on the right front axle suddenly broke. The tire went sideways, and our Hupmobile lurched like a woozy drunk. I put the Hup in low gear and got it to the curb. With the car safely parked, my buddy and I walked home, quite depressed. The new freedom and open roads we'd just discovered had come to an abrupt end. We knew the odds of finding a spindle for that axle were beyond bad. We'd probably need a machine shop to custom-build a spindle, which we couldn't possibly afford.

Two days later, we returned to the car in something of an act of homage since we still had no recovery plan. But to our astonishment, the Hupmobile had vanished!

As the shock of its disappearance wore off, we realized we'd left it in front of the courthouse. How clueless can 16-year-old teenagers be at times? Of course, it didn't take long for us to figure out where the Hup might have gone. We walked to the police station nearby and spotted the Hup in the fenced impound lot behind the building. We realized we were getting deeper and deeper into trouble. We couldn't ever tell anyone we owned the car.

Walking back to Hillcrest, we thought about the expensive battery we'd just installed and what a waste of money that had turned out to be. The realization prompted us to come up with a seriously bad idea. We would climb the fence into the police impound lot, remove the battery, and sneak back out with our new battery in hand. Who would know? Who would care? What could possibly go wrong?

At about two the next morning, we sneaked down the fire escape at Hillcrest Academy and descended the hill to the police station, carrying a few tools we'd need. We constantly looked around to see if anyone was watching. It was all clear. God bless small towns where almost everyone is in bed by 10:00 PM.

Noiselessly, I climbed up and over the chain-link fence and tiptoed to the Hupmobile. Opening the car's door, I quickly lifted out the new battery. Taking a nervous look around, Art and I saw nothing, so I climbed the chain-link fence again, trying not to set off any alarms or wake any sleeping dogs.

Tiptoeing away from the police station, we didn't dare talk. We just continued walking, taking turns packing the battery, which somehow got heavier and heavier. I was sure that *someone* had to be noticing us, trudging through town at 3:00 AM with a car battery. But fairly soon, we were climbing the steep road to Hillcrest Academy in the dark, realizing we were pulling off the whole thing. Soon we were in our dorm beds safe and sound.

We later sold the battery and recouped most of our money, thus minimizing the loss of our investment in the Hupmobile.

For the Love of Music

Hillcrest Academy not only provided me with an excellent education, but it also opened the doors of my mind and heart to music. As soon as I had enrolled as a sophomore in the fall of 1947, I was swept up in the many music programs. That's not surprising. I believe the love of music is inherent in all of us and is an important part of the human experience, especially for teens.

Hillcrest's excellent music programs were augmented by two other institutions located on opposite sides of town from each other. They were a seminary and a Bible school, both owned by the church that had founded Hillcrest. When our outstanding choir director, Professor William Windahl, held tryouts for the *a cappella* choir, he was able to select the best voices from among students at all three schools. Immersed in this rich environment, my fellow students and I developed our musical skills, including learning methods of singing and performing music. Eager to increase my musical abilities, I enrolled in a number of Professor Windahl's classes.

During my senior year at Hillcrest, from 1949 to 1950, I was the student body president and also the assistant dean in charge of the men's dormitory. For a guy who didn't always follow 100 percent of the rules— and who had begun his academic career as the school dork by wearing a dress suit three days in a row—I had come a long way.

Gospel-Team Adventures

My love for the gorgeous Barbara Tweed continued to grow. Each of us had dated others, yet when we started seeing each other, it became impossible to imagine dating anyone else. We were a natural pair.

However, Barbara and I realized that we would soon be pulled apart. I was 17, graduating from high school, and looking forward to summer break at Mom and Dad's home in Salem. After that, I planned to go to college but didn't know yet where that would be.

Barbara was 15. She would return to Hillcrest as a senior. We each knew the bond between us was strong. In fact, it was probably stronger than either of us thought. But then it wasn't exactly made of steel, either. As teenage sweethearts often do, we promised we would write each other.

After my Hillcrest Academy graduation and tearful farewells, I was happy to be home again in Salem and excited about getting together with longtime friends. Most of those friends loved music as much as I did. We had a committed gang, bonded by music and our faith, made up of people such as Maynard Nelson, Charlie Dahlen, and Mervin Brockie. We also had the Vettrus twins—Dean and Dennis—plus their older brother, Paul. On the female side, our group included Anna-Marie, Irma, and Alice Rundstrum, plus Herdis Michelson, Anna Hoiland, Jo Ann Blunt, Helen Melby, and Janice Olsen.

It was one of those oh-so-rare instances where different people, sharing a common faith, create an atmosphere of mutual enjoyment of each another as well as of the music. The only thing we loved more than our music was to perform our music.

Not willing to wait to be asked to join a group, we formed a group ourselves and named it the Central Lutheran Gospel Team. It was amazing to see what a common interest could do. Our gospel team consisted of 16 or 17 teenagers, with no fights, no rivalries, no complaints or politics, just everyone working long, long hours together and loving it. When we weren't performing, we were practicing, so we became quite good, thriving as a team and proud of the applause our performances earned. The gospel team produced deep, personal friendships which have lasted for decades.

One team member, Maynard Nelson, later became pastor of one of the largest Lutheran churches in Minneapolis, with some 6,000 members. During one year at Hillcrest, he was one of my best friends. But unlike me, he didn't go ledge-walking or sneaking out for treats. He was the good boy, and I was the mischievous one.

Rule number one in the gospel team was that if someone provided a place and an audience, we would be there. Skid row in Portland was one example. Ole Barnes, a down-to-earth street evangelist who connected with the men on their level, arranged for us to do a concert in the area where he ministered.

As I drove a group of us to that event, with the rest of our gang following in a second car, our red-hot piano player, Anna Marie Rundstrum, was wedged between me on one side and another singer on her right. She turned out to be hotter than any of us imagined. We were making good time, but I noticed Anna Marie kept twisting and squirming a lot. Each time I looked over, her squirming got worse. I was baffled. I'd never seen her do that before.

When I finally screwed up the courage to ask what the squirming was all about, smoke began to billow from under the front seat. Instantly, I pulled to the side of the road, and everyone jumped out. The seat cushion, right where Anna Marie had been sitting, was on fire!

Someone wisely pulled the burning cushion out of the car. Spotting a house about half a block away, I figured I would find water there, so I ran toward it, dragging the flaming seat cushion along. As I ran through a field, the burning cushion started a fire, but others in our group instantly stomped it out. When I got the cushion to the house, I found water and poured it on the bottom of the cushion, dousing the flames.

We later learned that the muffler had been hit and shoved up against the floorboards. Lying on top of the floorboards, under the seat, were a few pieces of scratch paper. The heat caused the papers to burst into flame, which spread to the underside of the cushion. Fortunately, after dousing the small fire, we were able to put the cushion back in the car, lay something over it for Anna Marie to sit on, and continue on our way.

In spite of the mishap, we made it to our Portland destination on time and had great success with our gospel team program. Anna Marie performed as if nothing had happened, even though part of her leg suffered some light burns and her nylons had been scorched and ruined.

Meanwhile, as I was having a great summer, Barbara was experiencing doubts about our relationship. She remembers those days:

> After Elling graduated from Hillcrest Academy and headed to his parent's home in Salem, I not only missed him, but I also found myself worrying and becoming pessimistic for the two of us. Just the physical distance between us was now some 1,600 miles.

In his letters, Elling said he was having the best summer of his life singing and traveling with the gospel team. I loved to sing as much as Elling did, so his well-intentioned letters were making me wish even more that I was there, sharing the fun.

But that was 1950, and there was no such thing as hopping on a cheap flight to go somewhere. One bought plane tickets only for major events, such as reunions, weddings, or funerals.

Phones weren't used much either. First, they were bulky and tethered in place by a phone cord, so they wouldn't fit into a pocket or purse. Second, they didn't work in cars or airplanes. Third, they cost a small fortune to use. Placing just one call from a phone booth to someone in the same town was quite pricy. And a long-distance call to a faraway friend cost what the average family paid for a week of groceries. Therefore, few people made long-distance calls. If the phone rang in the middle of the night, it usually frightened everyone because it often meant bad news, such as a loved one's illness or death.

So, with no real means of communicating with Elling except for writing letters, I was forced to try to stay positive about our long-distance relationship. It wasn't easy.

12
FAREWELL TO THE COCOON

On June 1, 1950, the Mauna Loa volcano in Hawaii started erupting and scaring everyone. Three weeks later, North Korean troops invaded South Korea, putting Uncle Sam's Army back into war. Around that same time, a new cartoon strip called *Peanuts* appeared in the funny papers.

While these events were going on, Odvin Haggen, the music director at Waldorf College in Forest City, Iowa, came out to Salem on a visit. When he happened to hear our gospel team, he asked me to sing some solos for him. Then he convinced me to come to Waldorf, enroll in the pre-engineering program, and become a member of the school's well-known *a cappella* choir. I jumped at the offer for two good reasons: (1) I would have the chance to sing in a superb choir, and (2) Barbara's parents lived near the college. Early in August, I scrambled to fill out the enrollment forms. My Pre-Engineering major included studies in math, chemistry, and other sciences.

I enjoyed my first year at college and made dozens of new friends. At one point I was asked to run for student body president. Since I'd already served as student body president at Hillcrest, I didn't hesitate taking a shot at running for the position at Waldorf. My campaign manager and I hatched a "Big Idea" that's still remembered with laughter and the shaking of heads by Waldorf College alumni to this day.

Our awesome idea was to have a big "Yelling for Elling" rally and end it with a giant surprise. Excited about our scheme, and blind—if not entirely *numb*—to the potential negative effects of the surprise, my campaign manager and I, along with some volunteers, drove out to Barbara's parents' farm where her dad let us kidnap pigeons in his barn. As our group clambered around the barn's top rafters, one person would aim a flashlight to a pigeon's eyes. While the bird was mesmerized by the ray of light, a helper would grab the pigeon and put it into a gunny sack. We caught a lot of pigeons.

Next we tied a small banner that read "Vote for Elling" on one leg of each lucky pigeon. With superior tunnel vision, we ignored how spooked the birds were becoming in their gunny-sack jail.

The following day, our exciting Yelling for Elling rally got underway at 12:00 noon in the college auditorium. Our volunteers went all over campus urging more students to head for the big event. After my short speech, we let our pigeons loose. Yes, *loose* is the correct verb.

The second we released the scared-to-death pigeons, they flew wildly all over the place, pooping, and dive-bombing everyone. We watched in astonishment as pigeon pandemonium reigned. We'd never seen people clear out of the auditorium so fast.

With a sinking stomach, I realized that all those who were washing their hair or cleaning their shoes or taking their sweaters to the drycleaners had already decided to vote for anyone *but* me. They weren't Yelling *for* Elling; they were Yelling *at* Elling. That's why I was shocked to learn I'd placed second out of three candidates. I later realized that those not unfortunate enough to have been in the auditorium during the pigeons' antics probably considered the whole thing to be hilarious.

Music to My Ears

The phrase "music to my ears" is the best description I can give of my time spent as a member of the Waldorf College *a cappella* choir. My three-octave range allowed the director to use me wherever he needed me. I mostly sang baritone, but if he needed a bass or a tenor on a certain piece, he'd plug me into that part. The other members were top-notch, and I felt honored to be part of them.

In addition to enhancing my skills as a performer, Professor Haggen also taught me how to direct and improve choirs—almost an art form in itself. The fact is, a choir director interprets music just as a piano player interprets music. In this case, *the choir itself is the instrument,* and the choir director adds expression to the song and gives it animation and life.

Using his arms, hands, and facial expressions, the choir director transmits to the singers his musical interpretation. A choir is very capable of responding by changing tempo, feeling, and tone.

Professor Haggen showed me many methods of getting a choir to put more expression into a performance. When I directed choirs, this is how I explained the process to them:

> When I give a sign to you to soften, then soften. When I give a sign to you to boom out, then sing loud. When I signal to slow down the tempo, slow down with me. I will talk to you with my hands and body language. Sometimes we almost whisper, and sometimes we are a *double forte* of loudness. Sometimes we *retard*. Sometimes we're *up tempo*. When I direct you today, we'll express this music as I interpret it. You'll recognize my points of emphasis and my rhythm style as you watch my body language and facial expressions.

The techniques of a choir director, from guiding timing and pacing to softness and loudness, can improve the music and its performance. To this day, I love passing on what I learned at Waldorf.

Meanwhile, as I was learning how to sing and direct choirs, Barbara was still struggling with our physical separation:

> I was back in school at Hillcrest Academy in Minnesota, still missing Elling, and there he was, far, far away at Waldorf College. The school sounded really appealing, especially with its *a cappella* choir. In the lowest of my low moments, I couldn't shake the feeling I'd never see Elling again.
>
> Writing me from college, he mentioned he'd taken a few girls out on dates. I didn't tell him I already knew that. Since my parent's home near Forest City, Iowa, was only 14 miles from Waldorf College, the lowdown on Elling's dates was

transmitted to me at the speed of gossip, thanks to my hometown's girlfriend network.

Long Trips in the DeSoto

Despite being tagged "the pigeon guy," a lot of good things happened for me at Waldorf. For instance, I played right tackle on the football team, and I also took advantage of the DeSoto that Dad lent me for college. Several times that year, I drove out to see Barbara at Hillcrest. The drive was a little over 500 miles round trip. When you're young and in love, 500 miles is a zero problem. Maybe affording gasoline for a 500-mile trip is a problem. But the time and effort themselves do not matter. Love conquers all.

Those visits meant a lot to Barbara too:

> When Elling would drive up to Hillcrest Academy in the DeSoto to visit me, my perpetual worries about us surviving as a couple disappeared into thin air like a magician's silk hankie. Two or three times during the 1950–1951 school term, Elling drove the 250-mile-long route between Waldorf College and Hillcrest Academy, just to take me on a date.

Barbara Graduates

When Barbara graduated from Hillcrest, I was glad I could drive out to see her get her diploma. Both sets of our parents attended. Barbara and I felt honored to have them there.

Barbara's sister Kay, an eighth-grader at the time, also attended Barbara's graduation. She was quite impressed when she met my family. Here's the story in her words:

> I idolized my older sister Barb, so I thought, *Since Barb can have any boy she likes, this boyfriend of hers, this Elling guy, must be pretty special.* When I met him, I realized what Barbara saw in him.

Elling's dad turned out to be one of the funniest men I'd ever met. After we were introduced, talked a bit, and he realized I was Barbara's sister, he said, "I wish you'd come to Norway and live with us." I was both flattered and shocked for a moment until he continued. "My wife, she needs somebody to reach under the bed and get rid of those white things that are floating around there."

The house Dad built a century ago in Saint Paul is still standing today. So also is the house next door, despite my mischievous pranks.

At that point, I was thinking, *This guy's totally nuts.* But his pretty wife, Beda, just stood there and smiled. Later I came to realize that Elling's mother was a spotless housekeeper and that his dad was known for humor and hijinks.

No doubt his sense of humor had rubbed off on Elling. I'd heard that when Elling was three years old, he became infamous in his neighborhood for feeding a garden hose into the open window of a neighbor's bedroom, then turning the tap on full blast.

Reserve Officer Training Corps

Every time our nation is suddenly called to war, the first and most difficult task is to find bright, educated people to train quickly to be officers. With even the best candidates, officer training takes several years. Having seen so many thousands of lives needlessly lost when badly trained Civil War officers made poor decisions, Congress passed the Morrill Act in 1862. This bill established land-grant colleges and required them to include military-tactics training as a mandatory part of every curriculum, forming what became known as the Reserve Officers Training Corps (ROTC).

The concept worked, ensuring that America would have an ample number of trained officers ready on a moment's notice. ROTC training included classes on leadership, problem-solving, and strategic planning. Soon the ROTC was providing 40 percent of all active duty officers for the nation.

Since Waldorf College was not a land-grant institution, the legislation did not affect me. However, for my second year of college, the 1951–1952 term, I decided to transfer to the University of Idaho in Moscow, Idaho. I was drawn by their well-regarded engineering school. The university then had some 4,000 students. It has almost three times that number today.

The construction company my brother Hal owned, H. Halvorson Inc., was located in Spokane, Washington, only 84 miles from the U-Idaho campus. His company had built the University of Idaho's engineering center, their home economics building, and a women's dormitory. When I enrolled at the university, Hal's firm was at work on another campus structure, so I was counting on Hal giving me some part-time construction work each week.

On the day I enrolled, I likewise signed up in the Army ROTC program as required by law. A little over one year prior, I had left the cozy, happy cocoon of Hillcrest Academy. Dorm life at Waldorf College had also been rather sheltered. But now, my enrollment in ROTC was a major part of my powerful introduction to "Real Life 101." My warm cocoon was truly gone, my rent payment was entirely real, and my car was always out of gas. I had been launched into real life, leaving me with little or no dignity.

As for employment, Hal didn't let me down. Over the winter, I was hired to tend "salamanders," which are kerosene-fueled heaters that contractors use to keep concrete warm enough at night to cure properly. I was expected to make sure the salamander heaters ran okay and always had ample fuel.

On weekends, I did general cleanup work at the construction site, so I was able to make some real money. Overnight, I became a rare form of a college person, one of just a handful of students with three or four gallons of fuel in his car's gas tank. The rest of the students' cars ran mostly on fumes.

Even though I appreciated having a bit of income, my work schedule, along with a heavier academic load, brought an end to my trips to see Barbara. This sudden absence of contact hit both of us hard.

Also, adjusting to college life at the University of Idaho was a challenge. It was such a radical change from the small, friendly Christian environment I'd recently left. At U-Idaho, I felt like one tiny, confused ant lost among 4,000 other ants all scrambling in a crazy panic, each of us trying to look as if we knew where we were going and acting as if we knew the answers to the perpetual questions of "Who am I?" and "What do I want to be?"

When I think back, I'm amazed at how innocent I was then about the ways of the world. At age 18, I was perhaps more naïve than a 10-year-old boy is today. I believe it's because my boyhood took place just before the early 1950s when television changed the nation and changed how young children come to view the world.

Few inventions have been accepted by society as quickly as television was. In spite of its popularity, I have come to believe that TV makes kids grow up a lot sooner than they used to. Kids' natural excitement and curiosity used to result in the satisfaction of discovering things independently. Now, knowledge and life are displayed right on television and computer screens, so kids are often denied the thrill of personal discovery. They don't have to think through concepts or do any investigative work themselves to find out about life. In my opinion, we lost something valuable with the arrival of TV. We lost the necessity to discover life on our own and deal personally with the world around us.

Barbara Gets "Engaged"

Back home in Iowa, Barbara continued to feel the effects of our separation:

Elling and I did write one another, but our letters were somehow making me feel more lonely, not less so. It felt like we were drifting apart. But being just 17 in the fall of 1951, I was so, so young. I kept having "heart attacks"—not the kind that would kill me, but the kind that made me feel awful, all day.

So, when a fellow I'd met at Hillcrest began asking me out on dates, I went along. He really was a nice guy and a lot of fun. But he didn't have the best sense of timing. After just a few dates, he asked me to accept an engagement ring he'd bought for me. I was dumbfounded. Our relationship hadn't even reached the kissing stage yet. I remember blurting out words I'm sure he didn't want to hear. I said, "I wouldn't think of it. I haven't gotten over Elling yet."

Not willing to give up, the young man said, "Well, maybe the ring will help you get over Elling." That struck a chord with me. I was continually lovesick over Elling, a condition made worse since we so rarely saw each other anymore. All we had left were our letters.

"Just try it on," the fellow insisted.

Troubled, confused, and a bit scared, I did as he asked. To this day, I'm not sure why I went along with it. But as we were looking at the ring on my finger, I said, "We can't call this an engagement ring, or I can't wear it." My eager young man agreed.

While schools teach us math, geography, and other skills, they offer no insight concerning matters of the heart and how to deal with love gained and love lost. Here I was, almost 18 years old, struggling to understand what was happening to me.

Thoughts of Elling were coming and going with no rhyme or reason. Mom would be talking to me, and my thoughts would pop over to Elling. Mom would say, "Barbara, are you listening to me?" Looking back, I realize Mom could read me like a book. She must have known how smitten and heartsick I was.

But slowly, gaining a bit of maturity in baby steps, I began to appreciate what I had not realized before. Elling wasn't just the kid I really liked a lot or the guy I liked singing with or just a fun date. Elling was the man I had fallen in love with.

From the moment of that realization on, I felt older than my age—perhaps not yet fully mature but definitely no longer a teenager. I was a young woman with a new sense of self. I realized I'd never get over Elling if we just kept writing.

I knew what I had to do but, for a week or so, found lots of ways to avoid doing it. Finally, when I gathered the courage I needed, I wrote a short note to Elling at the University of Idaho suggesting that we break off our relationship. I told him I was engaged, which I suppose that in some odd way I was.

I finished writing the letter, but I didn't send it immediately. I needed additional courage in order to actually send it. Finally, I was ready. I stood nervously in front of the post office drop box, opened the hinged metal door, and let my slim letter slide into a dark place, with my heart sliding with it. Immediately I was full of regret, so wishing I hadn't done it. I felt *awful*.

A few days later, the telephone rang. It was Elling. I can't remember his exact words, but as he talked, tears began to roll down my cheeks. I do remember him saying something along the lines of, "I'll be out to see you soon. Do not do anything! *We are going to have a future together.*"

I twisted the non-engagement ring off, looked at it for one moment, then put it in a drawer forever.

Barbara came to her decision about the ring just before Christmas 1951. On Christmas Day she and her family were having a holiday dinner at the home of close friends two miles away when they received a phone call that their house was on fire. By the time the volunteer fire department arrived from their small town several miles away, the country house could not be saved. The drawer holding the ring burned in the blaze.

The family lost everything except what they were wearing at the time of the fire. Later, an uncle, looking for anything he could salvage for the family, found the ring and returned it to the young man.

Detoured by the Tunnel to Hell

In June 1952, the month for final exams at the University of Idaho, I was halfway through my last calculus test on the last day of classes when I received word that my father was critically ill in a Saint Paul hospital. The news shook me to the core. I had already planned to meet up with Dad very soon—but in Fargo, North Dakota, not in Saint Paul. In fact, I was already packed, ready to leave right after finals.

My father, Elling Halvorson Sr., had been the single biggest influence in my life. I loved him, thought highly of his intelligence, stood in awe of his business savvy, laughed at his humor, respected his character, felt his deep faith, and revered his courage in leaving everything behind in Norway to emigrate to the unknown land of the United States.

One of Dad's character qualities that I admired the most was his unshakable belief that every problem had a solution. But on a nightmarish project in California, he finally met a challenge where his "can-do" spirit didn't seem to be enough.

In a joint venture, Carl, Hal, and Dad were boring the seven-foot diameter, 6.4-mile-long Tecolote Tunnel to carry a pipeline from Lake Cachuma to the Pacific coast through the Santa Ynez Mountains. Workers encountered such appalling work conditions that the dreadful and dangerous project came to be known as the "Tunnel to Hell" and was featured on the cover of *Life* magazine and in many other publications.

The difficulty began when the US Army Corps of Engineers (USACE) withheld critical information from Dad and my brothers. The bidding documents never revealed that the tunnel would cross right through the infamous San Andreas Fault. Soon workers seemed to be drilling into the fires of hell itself.

In January 1951, a methane explosion had sent 11 miners to the hospital. Fortunately the workers weren't seriously injured. Eventually summer air temperatures would rise to 112 degrees in the tunnel, and water temperatures would eventually reach 117 degrees.

My father and brothers and their teams had to come up with a way to keep workers alive while also making forward progress. Ultimately, they invented a practical system in which workers were moved in and out of the tunnel while riding in mining cars filled with tepid water. This allowed the overheated workers to chill themselves by sitting, fully clothed, up to their necks in cool water. But they still could accomplish only a small amount of work and then had to be quickly removed and given time to cool off again.

To compound the misery, rock would shift unpredictably, crushing support beams and damaging areas of the tunnel already completed.

Tortured by this tunnel to hell and by the deceits of the Army Corps of Engineers, my dad sent a surprise announcement to the Corps in 1952 that he would not complete the project. The Corps threatened all manner of lawsuits, but he wouldn't budge. Dad told them he had devoted himself to a week of constant prayer, going over every issue in the project. He concluded he could not honestly invite men to come work in a project that could take their lives in a flash.[9]

---

[9] Although Elling Sr. pulled out of the project, Hal and Carl continued to move it forward. But after submitting claims for increased costs due to the unsafe and difficult work conditions, on July 21, 1953, they suspended tunneling operations for the year. After it came to light that the Army Corp of Engineers had known about the San Andreas Fault detail but had deliberately left it out of bidding documents, Hal and Carl entered months of laborious negotiations with the USACE. In January 1954, they finally settled the dispute and got a new contract for construction at 10 times the original payment. They negotiated to subcontract the remainder of tunnel work to two other companies, Coker Construction Company and Peter Kiewit &

Dad's long-held belief that *all* problems can be solved was shattered by what turned out to be his final project.

Meanwhile, to celebrate what Dad had been able to accomplish in his career despite overwhelming odds, old friends and construction-industry associates in Saint Paul planned a picnic in his honor to be held a few weeks later. Dad made arrangements to fly to Saint Paul for the event and stay with good family friends, the Rasmussens. Then he would head to Fargo, where I was scheduled to meet him.

It turned out that the morning of the picnic, Dad woke up with severe chest pains, and around noon, an ambulance rushed him to the hospital.

I knew something serious was going on when the message of an important phone call interrupted my calculus exam. On the other end of the line, Dick Rasmussen told me that Dad had suffered a heart attack. He urged me to come right away. I explained that I was still taking my calculus final and that I would leave for the Spokane airport as soon as I was finished.

Dick replied, "There's only one plane leaving from Spokane that goes to Saint Paul today. A reservation has already been made for you, and you've still got time to catch it, but only if you leave right now!"

I hurried back to class to explain the crisis to my professor. Although he excused me, I didn't know what kind of grade I would end up receiving.

Every member of our family desperately tried to reach our dying father before it was too late. But not everyone succeeded. Evelyn wasn't able to get a flight connection from her home in Alaska's northlands. Hal, still managing the Tecolote Tunnel project near Santa Barbara, also couldn't get a connection soon enough.

I was more fortunate. Already packed for my trip to Fargo, I drove at high speed from the Moscow campus to the Spokane airport and arrived just in time to catch the flight to Saint Paul.

Sons. The subcontractors also encountered nearly impossible work conditions, including torrents of water that eventually reached a maximum flow of 9,000 gpm. For more info, see "Cachuma Project" written by Thomas A. Latousek, published by the US Department of the Interior, Bureau of Reclamation, in 1995: https://on.doi.gov/2RsVQkb.

When I boarded that Stratocruiser plane, I was startled and pleased to see Mother and Carl on board. They'd flown in hours earlier from Portland. So the three of us were together, praying and hoping with all of our hearts that Dad would survive his heart attack. I knew the chances of his survival weren't good, but I was probably in denial. I truly expected to see him. Dad just *couldn't* die! My mind simply would not accept anything else.

Our flight left around 8:00 or 9:00 that night, and with a layover in Billings, it took about seven hours. When we landed at the Minneapolis/Saint Paul airport two time zones away, it was about 6:00 in the morning. Dick Rasmussen was already at the bottom of the ramp to meet us as we deplaned. He gently told us that Dad had died in the night.

I was struck with horror at the realization of how fragile life could actually be. This simply couldn't be true! Dad was only 60 years old. He was my very world. I was crushed and dumbfounded.

Of course in 1952, it wasn't like today where they could open up Dad's heart and get things working again. Back then, medicine could do little to keep a person from dying from the consequences of a heart attack, so caregivers simply worked to make their patients comfortable.

We learned later that in the hospital, when he sensed he was slipping away, Dad had asked for a secretary to take dictation. His request revealed the remarkable kind of guy he was—thinking of his family even on his deathbed, always motivated by his Christian faith.

The only secretary in the building was Alma Clausen, the personal assistant for the hospital administrator. When the message came from ICU that a man had requested a secretary so he could dictate some letters, she responded.

Knowing that my sister Evelyn had not been able to reach an airport in time to say goodbye to our father, Alma later wrote her a letter to describe Dad's passing. In it, she said:

> I was called to your father's room sometime in the afternoon between 3:00 and 3:30 last Wednesday in answer to his call for someone to take a few letters. As I entered his room, his

condition had been considerably weakened, and although it must have been a discomfort for him to dictate, there seemed to be a guiding hand strengthening and sustaining him in his last wishes.

His only thoughts were for those of his loved ones. As he expressed himself so very beautifully in his letters, so too was the spirit that remained with him to the very last. As I left his room, I could not forget his noble resignation and his seeming lack of concern for the material things so many find difficult to relinquish at such a time. I thought of his words, "You know that I am living with God." How tranquil and simple were his meditations in the lonely hours that confronted him.

When I inquired of the Head Nurse on the floor and was told that she had notified the Nurses Registry for a special nurse but did not know how soon one would arrive, I told her that I would like to stay with your father. She instructed me in what to do to help him and so, when I finished my work at 5:00, I went upstairs to be with him.

As I came near his bed, he looked at me with a surprised expression. I told him I would like to remain with him until his special nurse arrived. He reached out to touch my hand and said: "God bless you." From that moment on, we were a team.

He hemorrhaged occasionally, but as the evening wore on, the episodes became more frequent. He evidenced a great interest in the Kleenex as I wiped his mouth and would try to turn it and look at it for any discoloration. I noted his apprehension and, after a time, quickly folded the Kleenex so that he would not be alarmed. He asked several times if I thought he would make it, and with a quick pat of my hand, I would rearrange the towels on his shoulders, stroke his forehead and try to comfort him. He never failed to appreciate my gestures, and as night drew near, he would open his eyes and say; "Are you still with me?"

The letter Alma wrote to Evelyn, and a second one to my mother, Beda, were remarkable acts of kindness. We learned later that after taking dictation from our father, she returned to her desk. At 5:00 PM, she put on her coat and headed for her car. As a single mother, she was concerned about getting home to her children. But then she thought about Dad dying alone in his room, so she went back inside to stay with him until his nurse arrived.

While Dad was slowly passing into another life, Alma also composed a poem to send to Evelyn and my mother.

How can I say what I feel in my heart,
For how does a stranger share
The sorrow that comes like a thief in the night
On the wings of a loved one's prayer?
While the candle of life was burning low
And the Angel of Death drew near,
The Master's voice was calm and sweet
As He bent to His Servant's ear.
"Lo, I am with you always,"
Came the gentle, sweet refrain,
And the blessed assurance, saved by Grace,
Freed the body wracked with pain.

Due to unfortunate circumstances after Dad's death, his company lost significant money over the next few years, and his estate dwindled. However, even though he left us little in the way of an estate, he left us everything in the way of dealing with life. For me, he symbolized character, that quality so essential in business and in everyday life. His devotion to the combination of engineering and futuristic thinking allowed the companies he ran to be very successful in their field. His belief in innovation and sound engineering allowed the construction careers of all three of his sons to be successful.

Dad's sudden death hit everyone in our family hard. We had so much love and so much respect for him. He had a warm and generous sense of humor and loved a good laugh. All of us kids were modeling our lives and behaviors after him. His sensitivities to different people and his appreciation for them were visible in how he managed construction work. For instance, while he was a construction expert in many areas, he never lectured anyone. He became known as a team-builder and an exceptional manager of people. Certainly, I owe him a great debt for teaching those techniques and habits to me.

Although he was just 60 when he died, he had already retired twice. In fact, for the previous five years or so, Dad and Mom enjoyed trying out different locations and cities as retirement getaways. They concluded they liked Southern California, settling on a view lot overlooking Palm Springs. But after Dad passed away, mother sold the property. Dad had made a great choice of building site, and because of its spectacular view, the property was swiftly snapped up by a movie star.

As Carl, my mother, and I sat through the memorial service in Saint Paul, and later, the formal funeral in our home town of Salem with all our family present, I slowly came out of shock to realize I had lost the man who was the center of my world. Before the heart attack had struck him down, Dad and I had made plans to spend the summer working together in Salem. Dad had purchased a backhoe tractor for the two of us to use doing work for others and for a small project at our family home.

Looking back, I realize Dad was going from a successful and significant construction company to the smallest of outfits—just Dad and me, "Elling and Elling." I understand now, years later, that improving the house and doing other small contract jobs was our announced goal, but spending time together was our real one.

It Has Been a Great Pleasure to Love You

This is the letter that Dad wrote to my siblings and me when he was very aware he was slipping away:

Dear Carl, Halvor, Evelyn, and Elling,

It has been a great pleasure to love you. And I appreciate your love for me so much.

Be very considerate of Mother. Do what you can to make her happy. She needs your assistance. And I just love that she will be happy and not sorrowful after I have passed away.

I am so glad that Jesus is in my heart, and I want each and every one of you to seek him more and more. I have no fright in my heart whatsoever.

If God wants to take me now, there is nothing that hinders me from leaving. I would love to see all of you in heaven. May God so bless all of you.

With my love,

Dad

The words in the opening sentence of Dad's letter meant a great deal to me then, and they mean even more to me today.

Carl, Hal, Evelyn, and I talked at length about how we could support Mother, as Dad had asked us to do in his deathbed letter. Eventually, I agreed with my siblings that for my third year of college, I should transfer from the University of Idaho to Willamette University in Salem. Dad and Mom had just built a new home high on a bluff overlooking the Willamette Valley. It was one of the more prestigious homes around.

As it turned out, my decision to move to Salem to support Mom was only part of the story of how my life was radically—and *quickly*—detoured, once again.

PART III: A FAMILY OF MY OWN

✦ ✦ ✦ ✦ ✦

13
FROM "ME" TO "US"

To fulfill my promise to help Mom after Dad's sudden death, I transferred to Willamette University in Salem for the 1952–1953 term. It turned out that well-respected Willamette, founded in 1842 and the oldest university west of the Mississippi River, had little to offer me in my pursuit of an engineering degree. However, it was a great business school, so I enrolled in business classes. The knowledge I gained proved extremely valuable in future years.

Some months after Dad's passing, the University of Idaho wrote to let me know that my calculus professor had given me a good grade, and I had passed the course. Meanwhile, after Barbara graduated from Hillcrest Academy, she moved back home to Mason City, Iowa, and went to work for Standard Oil.

While friends have often referred to me as a gambler in business, they'll likely also tell you I rarely gamble in my personal life. That explains why, before Willamette University's fall term began, I decided to spend the summer in Mason City. I wanted to be as close as possible to the woman to whom I was about to propose.

When I arrived, people warned me, "You'll never find a job, Elling." I understood their gloomy outlook. A deep national recession was being felt everywhere, including Iowa. But before the first day of searching ended, I had three jobs lined up. None of them would be considered flashy. One was at a rendering plant! But the job I chose was with a terrazzo contractor.

Terrazzo workers create walkways, floors, patios, and panels using small pieces of marble or granite set in mortar and finished with a high polish. It's visually impressive. My job involved carrying cement, sand,

and marble up way too many steps, then mixing the terrazzo. That done, I'd head back down stairs to get more cement, sand, and marble. It was tough work, but I survived it. At that job, I wasn't hired for my brains or college studies. What they wanted was youth, stamina, and muscles. I was a young mule, cheap to hire, happy to have the work.

My most important achievement that summer of 1952 was the slow and steady building of trust and friendship with Barbara's mom and dad.

Barbara had been enrolled in Waldorf College at the time of her family's Christmas-Day house fire in 1951. Since her parents were not well-to-do, she dropped out of college and found a job at Standard Oil running a comptometer—a key-driven mechanical calculator.

After Barbara's father got to know me, I asked him if he would allow Barbara to move to Salem in September, where I would be attending Willamette College. He said he would be comfortable with the idea.

Working in cahoots with me, Barbara asked the same question of her Mom: "Okay if I move to Salem, Mom?"

Her mother replied, quite accurately, "You're already there." She and Barbara's father knew, maybe before Barbara and I did, that we were planning our future together.

Once in Salem, Oregon's state capital, Barbara found a good position working for the Secretary of State in the Capitol building, right across the street from Willamette University.

The Proposal

When I found the nearly perfect moment, I went down on one knee to ask Barbara for her hand in marriage. We planned to get married the following June, as early in the month as possible after Willamette University classes ended.

Barbara tells the story from her perspective:

> Recently, some of our friends were talking about how their husbands handled their proposal of marriage. I told them Elling was a pro. We were sitting on a sofa and he had one

knee down. Very old-fashioned. He told me how much he loved me and asked if I would marry him and be the mother of his children. It was just beautiful. My *yes* was genuine because I had already learned so much about Elling—and about myself for that matter. We have similar backgrounds, beginning with the same deep faith.

Elling is a man with probably the best temperament of anyone I've ever known. He rarely, rarely gets mad. And if he does, I've often caused it. Another side of Elling is his generosity. And always, he is a great father, as was his own father.

But the icing on the cake is Elling's happy, mischievous spirit. Like his dad, he has a crazy sense of humor and enjoys adding fun to almost any event. So, I ask you, how could a woman say no to a rare individual like that?

That year at Willamette University was stimulating. I sang in the university's *a cappella* choir and kept busy, from studies to singing. Plus, our original Central Lutheran Gospel Team was still together, and I was able to add Barbara to our group. She has a great deep, rich alto voice. So it was a tremendous year, though I don't know how we got through it all.

During the day, I was at the university, and then I was with Barbara every evening. She had a little apartment not far from school, which made seeing her very convenient. We also did a lot of socializing with our mates in the gospel team. We loved everyone in the group and built lifelong friendships.

We planned to get married as early in June as possible, right after Willamette University classes ended, so several times each week we worked on plans for the wedding and beyond. During our planning, we learned that Sigvart and Martha Hoiland would be leaving on a long trip to Norway and needed someone to manage the Rose Garden motel while they were gone. Barbara and I applied for the position and were accepted.

In that era, engaged couples were supposed to be celibate before their marriage, meaning couples were trusted to postpone sex until after the wedding ceremony. That requirement was a trial for us. The common advice was, "Wait until you are properly married." Today, the question is "Why on earth wait?"

The Big Day

Somehow we two lovebirds survived to the day of our wedding on June 18, 1953, held at the Lutheran church in Joice, Iowa, near the home of Barbara's parents. With Mother and my angel of a sister, Evelyn, as passengers, I drove Mother's car to Iowa for the wedding. After the event, Evelyn and Mom planned to take the train home to Salem, leaving Mom's car for Barbara and me to use to drive to Salem as Mister and Missus. I wished over and over that Dad could have been with us. It's hard to describe how deeply I missed him on that significant life occasion.

Even meteorologists agreed that our wedding was one of the hottest events of 1953.

At the wedding, I was surprised and delighted to see so many of the students I'd gone to high school with at Hillcrest Academy. In effect, that added the element of a class reunion to our happy nuptials. The trouble was, I'd forgotten how so many of my classmates were always full of tricks.

Just before the service began, I, with my best man, Carl, along with the pastor and the rest of the groomsmen, lined up at the altar like penguins. Next, the bridesmaids came down the aisle. Then, as Barbara stood at the back of the church, I sang to her the love song, "Because."

I'd worried about performing the song well enough, but the gamble paid off, and I did okay. The song emotionally touched my bride and our friends and families in the church. Later, dozens of "Halvorson hot stuff" jokes were made on that hottest day of the Iowa summer. The candles, bent over like drooping lilies, dripped hot wax on the carpeted floor, causing a cleaning challenge for many volunteers the next day. The family legend is that our wedding produced the hottest night of the year.

Given the stifling heat, everyone hurried downstairs to the church's slightly cooler lower level where our reception was held. I enjoyed catching up with friends I hadn't seen in a while, and I liked being able to meet Barbara's extended family. But as my bride and I were "meeting and greeting" at the reception, a number of our Hillcrest classmates were transforming Mom's car into a land anchor.

Our Getaway

Carl pulled me aside and whispered, "Elling, I've been hearing rumors about too many pranks being done to your car, so I think you'd better plan on using a different car for going away." I quickly chatted with Barbara's dad. He grinned and slipped me the keys to his vehicle, giving us a getaway backup plan.

After Barbara and I changed into our traveling clothes, we went out to Mom's car where we'd left it parked. We could hardly believe our eyes. The wheels had been removed and stacked on the roof. The car itself was covered with graffiti.

All around us we could hear snickers and laughing. Then we heard barking. Our classmates had locked a dog in the trunk. When he wasn't yipping, he was tearing out the taillight wiring. Someone opened the hood to show us a big brick of cheese lashed to the engine.

We immediately resorted to Plan B.

That plan included a secret reservation I'd made for us a week or two before the wedding at a new motel in Mason City, Iowa, about 25 miles from the church. During my conversation with the manager, I mentioned that Barbara and I would be managing a motel in Salem that summer. I handed the manager a Rose Garden business card and asked him for motel-management tips.

But leaving the card behind proved to be a bad move. One of the men invited to our wedding was painting at the motel and noticed the business card with the Salem address. He asked the manager who the business card belonged to. The manager replied, "Oh, some guy from Salem who's having his first wedding night here. Elling Halvorson."

At our wedding reception, we'd been toasted. Once we left the church, we were just toast. Our friends knew exactly where to find us on our wedding night. As I drove away in my father-in-law's Chevy, a bunch of our friends jumped into their cars and followed us. It looked like a comedy movie. Kids jammed into half a dozen or so cars, honking their horns and raising hell as they chased us.

I thought, *Okay, wise guys, I can out-drive you.* I shouted to Barbara, "*Hold on!*" I shoved the gas pedal to the floor, and away we flew, up gravel roads, sliding around every corner and raising dust everywhere. Finally, they stopped chasing us, and we were pumped. "We got rid of them!"

I slowed down and headed for our night's secret lodging, the Bell Motel. Barbara cuddled up a little closer as we drove on, knowing we had a great night ahead of us.

But as we drove up to the motel, we saw at least 20 cheering, laughing, giggling people waiting for us. They quickly surrounded our car. I rolled my window down about an inch to talk to them. And then someone started to open the Chevy's hood, so I put the car in gear and began to move forward.

They harassed us for maybe another 15 minutes and finally were nice enough to leave. I was still on edge, not sure what would happen next. But as the noise and torment faded away, the memory of it dissolved out of our minds and soon, it was just us—in love, in the magic, in the moment. Never was an evening so thrilling, so passionate, so often remembered.

As the sun rose, we awoke in the warmth of the morning-after glow— two lovers, now fully committed to one another and to a future together. We were both changed. More adult. More in love. Closer than either of us imagined two people could be.

Later that morning, Barbara and I dreamily went back to her parent's house and spent a day opening wedding presents and loading up my mother's car, which friends had restored back to normal, including the taillight wiring. We were rather in a hurry to get back to Salem, since we had to begin managing the motel within a few days.

The bliss that wafts over lovers lasted well into our future. We were so engrossed in our new life together, I suspect that even if a herd of elephants had been alongside the highway, we wouldn't have noticed.

We stayed overnight in Sioux Falls, Iowa. As I slept the sleep of a deeply satisfied man, my lover slipped away in the morning with her total personal money stash of about $8.00. She returned just as quietly with her gift for me. Since every shirt I had packed was an uncomfortable white dress shirt, she bought two sport shirts for me to wear on our enchanted drive home.

Could you ever bottle up the euphoria shared by newlywed lovers? How could one possibly capture the flavors, the feelings, the unspoken speech, the talking eyes, the fleeting touch, the loving trust? I don't think we really drove to Salem on our honeymoon trip. We floated there.

The optimism of newlyweds is often a high-energy, totally positive, what-could-possibly-go-wrong view of life. That was Barbara and me, looking out at the world we'd just inherited. One month earlier, we were anonymous, barely recognized teenaged students. But the moment our marriage vows were announced in front of God, family, and friends, we were certified by society as new and important. Wow! It was heady stuff.

In the time it took for each of us to say "I do," I morphed from being addressed as, "Hey, Kid!" to "Mr. Elling Halvorson." At the same moment, a beauty called "Hey, Barb," was transformed into Mrs. Barbara Halvorson. To have society suddenly regard us former nobodies in such flattering ways boosted our egos. As a brand-new couple, we were impressed with how, after a simple wedding, society solemnly conferred upon us the power to take on large debts, to acquire a home, to sign up for a car, to vote, to fight and die in military battles, to procreate, regenerate, and consume, consume, consume!

Our First Home—in a Motel

The day after we arrived in Salem, Barbara returned to her job in the state government building, and I became interim manager of the Rose Garden Motel. While the Hoilands were in Europe, we were invited to stay in their home, a two-bedroom house about 1,200 square feet in size.

The job added to our small income and provided a comfortable place to live. When Sigvart and Martha returned from Europe, we moved into what used to be called an "efficiency unit." It had a small living room, a mini-kitchen, and a bedroom.

Of course, still living in a happy honeymoon fog, we didn't see the "efficiency" itself. We saw the *Halvorson Residence*, complete with a few wedding-gift items and a new, poorly built rocker we bought from a Gypsy who knocked at our door. While we couldn't really afford the few dollars the Gypsy wanted, we also couldn't resist the delicious pleasure of being "us," which meant the chair was *our* chair, for *our* place, bought with *our* money after *our* decision was made.

Being "us," is an emotion in the depth of the human heart. It's what may well be the *invisible* dimension of love. It rarely involves words or even eye contact. It's unseen, unspoken. And when you don't have this invisible thing, you miss it. The sense of being "us" may well be the glue that keeps people like Barbara and me together in marriage for more than 65 years.

Having a mini-home with a mini-kitchen was a major benefit for us, the former nobodies who measured money not in dollars, but in pennies, nickels, and dimes. Another benefit was the deer I shot with hunter friends in Oregon's back country. We paid a butcher to cut it into ribs, roasts, steaks, and more, then paid a small fee to have it kept in a cold-storage locker. Barbara or I would drop by the unit whenever we needed meat. It saved us a small fortune during our first winter together.

For evening entertainment, we had a little table radio. In 1953 we listened to such programs such the *Bing Crosby Show*, *Arthur Godfrey's Talent Scouts*, and a police drama called *Dragnet*. Of course, the hottest thing in entertainment that year was the new medium of television. But the cost of a TV set was way beyond our means and dreams. We would see a set only through the appliance-store window—occasionally with a crowd of people in front of it.

We didn't feel shortchanged, however, since we continued to have the pleasure and reward of performing with our great friends in the Central Lutheran Gospel Team. They meant *everything* to us, made us laugh, gave good advice, were patient listeners, and fine teachers. They were the purest and best of friends.

Of all the valuable possessions one can have, I believe friendship is the greatest. Starting out in married life, it was a huge benefit to have our loyal and caring gospel team friends. For instance, when Barbara and I were puzzled because she couldn't shake the stomach flu, the girls in our choir group realized that Barbara was pregnant. But they stayed quiet about it. To be fair to us newlyweds, with Barbara's teenager-flat stomach, she wasn't showing at all. Still, clueless us!

During all this, we were pleased and relieved at how well Mom was coping with the loss of Dad. We could see how much it helped her to have so many friends at church. She was also close to Sigvart and Martha. She and Dad had been very good friends with the Hoilands for some 50 years, so Mom was comfortable and in the best of hands.

Back in Sales

That naïve blindness of newlyweds prevented us from paying much attention to the economy. Shopping around for work, I soon felt the effects of a recession our nation had sunk into. It meant that young, unskilled guys like me couldn't find work anywhere. So, at 22, I wound up doing what so many young guys did in tough times—I became a door-to-door salesman for Watkins Incorporated, selling spices and household products.

The job had little or no prestige, and what each salesperson earned was totally up to that individual. What's more, one couldn't blame the product for any lack of sales, since Watkins products were respected. The company pioneered the first soaps that didn't use animal fats and had created organic products in an era when almost no one was overly concerned about chemicals.

Going door to door, I came to know all the dogs in my sales territory, the whole noisy gang—yappers and barkers, biters and growlers, runners and bluffers, leapers and sneakers, nippers and cuddlers. And while I was learning how to handle different dogs, I also learned how to make sales.

Saying "Hello, want some?" didn't cut it. I forced myself to make quick, interesting presentations, an ability that's helped me over a lifetime.

The job was tough. But I *had* to succeed with my front-door presentations because Watkins commissions were the *only* income the newlywed Halvorson couple had. Barbara had found it necessary to resign her job at the state capitol due to the severe morning sickness she suffered throughout her entire pregnancy with Brenda. Could we have turned to Mom for financial help? I'm sure she would have helped out. But the belief in our family was never to ask but instead to rely on ourselves entirely. And so we did.

While I was selling Watkins products, I decided to enroll in the Air Force Reserve Officers Training Corps in Salem. It was part of a scheme I was hatching. I've mentioned earlier that I'd decided to try out for Officers' Candidate School and learn to be a pilot at no expense to me. However, during my junior year, the Korean conflict was going on and the Air Force decided to train pilots only. So, when I couldn't pass the mandatory eye test without my glasses, that knocked me out of Air Force pilot training, as well as out of the ROTC itself.

The outbreak of the Korean conflict led to an extension of the Selective Service Act, which lowered the draft age from 19 to 18 and a half. As a result, the war was in full swing when my Selective Service draft status changed overnight for the worse. I was now 1-A, meaning I could be shipped away on a moment's notice at any time, to anywhere. I received orders to take a new physical—and I passed it, which meant I was "good-to-go" for the infantry.

Fortunately, the act allowed for a draft deferment test that college students could opt to take. Passing the test with a good grade allowed deferment until college graduation, but then the student risked being eligible for the draft until age 42. Still, it meant I could enroll for two more years at the university without being called away to service. I took the test and passed.

14
GROWING THE HALVORSON HERD

Our first year of marriage had many "firsts." They were part of the fun of our new life together, of being "us." Not only did we have our first "made-at-home" meal, our first new chair, our first radio, and our first dishes, but then, most thrilling of all, our first child, Brenda, was born! Barbara and I remember every moment of that miracle arriving in our lives. We fell head over heels in love with that tiny person, and simultaneously we bonded even more with one another in our newly shared love for our child.

Moderating our joy just a teeny bit was the fact diapers in 1953 were *not* disposable. And we didn't have a washing machine. That meant we washed and recycled many diapers by hand or borrowed the use of someone else's washer. Whenever we had the money, we used a Laundromat. But many times, we couldn't afford that luxury.

In early 1954, while still attending college by day, I got a new job working in a Sears warehouse at night. One night in the warehouse, I spotted a washer and dryer. The side of each had been dented so badly, I wondered if they'd fallen off a truck. Sears certainly couldn't sell them in the store.

Then I got an idea and tested it on the spot. I tried putting the two dented machines side by side to see if the dents would be visible. They weren't. Quickly, I separated the two machines back to the position they'd been in, and when I felt the time was right, I made a ridiculously cheap offer for them. My boss accepted the offer, and we had three additional new "firsts" in our marriage: (1) We had our own Sears washer, (2) we had our own Sears dryer, and (3) we no longer washed any diapers by hand. Thank you, Lord!

But over at Willamette University, I was deep in a different "brown stuff" problem. For an economics class in my fourth and final university year, I was required to write a full research paper, complete with bibliography, each and every week. It became the toughest challenge of my college experience. It took me a while to realize that I hadn't developed a good system for getting the work done, and consequently, I was flailing around, receiving failing grades week after week. I ran the risk of being last in my class for that first semester. Despite working nights at Sears and going to college by day, I knew I absolutely *had* to solve the problem.

Ultimately, I put my engineer's mind into gear and analyzed each step of what I needed to do. I allocated set times to go to the library every week to get a tall stack of the required books. Then I budgeted additional time to read through them all. Next, I developed a way to create a complete bibliography, along with a way not to miss citing footnotes and references.

After completing my shift at Sears each night, I would read the particular books that pertained to my research-report topic for that week, then make handwritten notes of quotes, excerpts, and other information I planned to use. I'd write portions of my report for as long as I could stay awake. After I collapsed into bed, Barbara would get out of bed and type up everything I had written that night. So between the two of us, we created a system that looked like it was going to work.

Did it ever! In the first week of the second semester, I got the highest mark in class. I repeated that accomplishment the following week. In week three, I received the second-highest mark and repeated that in week four. The following week I again earned the highest score.

It wasn't long before the professor called me into his office. "Elling," he said, "who is writing your papers for you?"

I replied, "I am writing them—honest!"

He peered at me closely, scowling.

I felt compelled to add, "You've got to believe me."

After he interrogated me some more and I explained in detail the approach I'd come up with, he finally did believe me, and I progressed from having nearly the worst score in class the first semester, to having the top score in class in the second. Best of all, that performance put me over the hump to allow me membership in the Pi Gamma Mu International Honor Society in Social Sciences. I was fiercely proud of my membership. It was hard-earned—by me and by my bride who was again having the "stomach flu" a lot.

The first week of February 1955, I awoke one morning in a slow, dreamy way, vaguely aware that something good was happening that day. What was it? I was still pretty foggy, coming out of a deep sleep. In her corner of our bedroom, baby Brenda made a little gurgle. The sound brought me a bit closer to consciousness. I felt Barbara stirring next to me. What was going on? Why was I feeling so good? Then my brain clicked and put it all together.

It was graduation day! I wasn't a student anymore. For the first time in four years, I didn't have academic work to turn in—not a research assignment, not an essay, not even a report due.

But it wouldn't be long before my wife was due to have our second child.

I smiled over at Barbara as she blinked her eyes open. I loved Willamette University, but now I couldn't wait to leave it. I got ready for my day, and just before going out the door, I gave Barbara my biggest, longest hug and my widest smile. A passage was happening, and I was very grateful to have her in my life.

Moving to the Emerald City

Graduation meant I was about to reenter the labor market. But this time, the economy was improving tremendously, and I would have a college degree in Economics with the equivalent of a minor in Engineering, plus knowledge gained from other valuable courses in business. I'd been raised in a family of self-made engineers, so the lingo of engineering had been my second language from birth. I definitely had enough engineering knowledge to be conversant and analytical in the field.

Very early that year, a few weeks before I was scheduled to graduate, Hal had called our motel mini-home to congratulate me on graduating with honors. Then he offered me a job with his construction firm. I thanked him and said yes as quickly as I could without sounding pathetically desperate. Hal said he needed me real soon. I said I'd be on the job in Seattle as soon after graduation as I could rent a house and move my family.

Barbara and I packed our suitcases on the evening of graduation day to allow us to leave for Seattle more quickly the following morning to look for a place to live. We located an 850-square-foot house in the Richmond Beach area of north Seattle and made rental arrangements.

When we returned to Salem for the actual move, I rented a trailer and loaded it with our belongings. It helped to be newlyweds with just one baby. We didn't have all that much to pack. I loaded our matching dented washer and dryer to take with us. Mother also gave us a used bedroom set and a hide-a-bed. Once in Seattle, we purchased a table, chairs, lamps, and a few other accessories on time payments.

As the newest Halvorson clan—Barbara, baby Brenda, and me—squeezed into our packed car, the sun was coming up in Salem. We headed north to Seattle toward a new life in the far larger city. We were pumped up by it all. This was life-changing stuff! With our tiny daughter sleeping soundly in the back, Barbara and I kept our talking to a quiet minimum for the long drive.

Eventually, we glimpsed the city's dramatic bayside skyline. Then, about 15 minutes north of the downtown area, we arrived at the small house we'd rented. After looking around more closely, we fell in love with the peaceful, sheltered neighborhood. Our house was a short distance from a waterfront park that ran at least a mile along the shoreline. There, we had panoramic views of Puget Sound, some of the San Juan Islands, and the towering Olympic mountain range dominating the western horizon. Together we simultaneously said, "What a great place to raise our children."

As the sun went down behind the Olympic mountain range, we settled into our first-ever "real" house in less than an hour. We got rooms laid out and drawers filled, and we climbed into our new bed where we pillow-talked late into the night about our amazing, new life.

The morning after we moved into our Seattle home, I headed for Hal's current job site, the construction at the new Shoreline High School, not far from our rental. I had no fears about my new adventure. My attitude was, *Look out, world. Here I come, a new player in the competitive fields of business and life.* Where did my confidence come from? I was born with it. I'd inherited it from the amazing people I had the good fortune to share life with, the family that raised me.

This school-construction job, as you may remember, was where I developed the plan of using an eight-pound sledge hammer to hit each roofing spike just once and drive it completely in with a single, powerful stroke. That resulted in my hands turning extremely red, swollen, and painful.

"Elling was really trying to impress the world," Barbara recalls. "He came home from his first day of face-nailing the roof with his hands so sore and puffed out, I wanted to cry. And his second day's work made his hands even worse. He was in agony. Fortunately, it was a Friday, and he had a four-day weekend. But, you know, the never-say-die aspect of Elling was one of the qualities that attracted me to him in the first place."

Some new joy came along about a month later—our second child, Elling Kent. He thoughtfully presented himself March 22, 1955, at Ballard General Hospital, not far from our tiny home in Richmond Beach. Now we had a perfect balance: one girl, one boy.

After living in Richmond Beach for less than a year, we moved to a little 1,100-square foot house near Highway 99 in the rundown South Seattle area of Riverton, about two miles north of SeaTac airport.

By winter of 1956, we learned another blessing was on the way. Our third child, Lon, was born on June 9, 1957. We were thrilled, but now our house was jammed full with a small bed for Brenda, Kent's crib, and

Lon's bassinet, plus our own almost wall-to-wall bed. We speeded up our plan to find a good lot and build a suitable home.

Building Our Own Home—as Our Family Expands

I finally found a great building lot for our badly needed larger house. It was on Southwest 186th Street in the Normandy Park area. It offered a sweeping 180-degree view of Puget Sound and the Olympic Mountains. The price was $2,500, about twice what it cost to buy a new Volkswagen Beetle that year. Today that lot would probably sell for nearly half a million dollars.

Barbara and I cleared off the kitchen table and designed a 3,000-square-foot home on two levels, complete with a two-vehicle carport. I designed a deck that went out over the driveway leading to the carport. We both wanted a truly social place for partying and picnicking with family and friends.

Construction began in late September 1957, three months after Lon was born. Thanks to the fact I was on salary with Hal's construction firm, we realized we could probably afford a new home, but the family budget was always tight. To economize, I decided to do much of the construction work myself at night and on weekends. I was also constantly hijacking buddies and friends to help out with such projects as drywall or plumbing or installing windows. Acquaintances of mine who were builders also helped get the house framed in near-record time. We spent all our spare time, often working into the night, on painting, finish carpentry, and other projects to get ready for occupancy.

Meanwhile, Barbara got pregnant again, and we knew we *really* needed that bigger place, since we would have four children. Her due date was sometime in June 1958. With this pregnancy, her tummy became enormous, and just a few weeks before delivery, the doctor told Barbara she was pregnant with twins.

Back then, the only method doctors had to learn if a mom was carrying multiple babies was to put a stethoscope on her tummy and listen closely for multiple heartbeats. Given how eternally competitive the twins were with one another, I sometimes suspect that one brother pushed the other into the background so only *his* heart would be noticed. I can tell you that it took a while before the doctor heard more than one heartbeat.

So on June 23, 1958, our two exclamation marks to the Halvorson family parade, our twins Randal and Rodney, were born. We were excited and happy to have them join our family.

Barbara shares her memories of those days:

> My emotions were all over the place the day the doctor told us we were having twins. I was so thrilled and honored by God to have this double blessing. Then the reality set in—we were going to have five children in four years. Lonnie wasn't even a year old yet! How was I going to care for all these children—and Elling too?
>
> Elling had picked out Rodney for a boy's name, and I had picked out the name Randal, so we settled it and had both! Looking back, these were wonderful happy days. We had a Christian home and a deep faith. It was during these years that we really learned to depend on God's grace and his strength, one day at a time. Our children were very fortunate to have parents and grandparents who knew the Lord.
>
> As a young family, we were very active in a small church. I can remember Elling directing the choir that sang from a small balcony. I sang alto with a baby in each arm. Randy and Rod didn't care much for the nursery, and they let it be known. I don't remember the boys ever adding anything extra to the choir number.

People who saw us as a close family in those days had no idea how close we really were, especially after Barbara's mother, Charlotte, came from Iowa to stay with us. Her assistance in caring for the kids, preparing batches of formula, and keeping the twins on their feeding schedule helped Barbara maintain her sanity. In a letter she wrote to Barbara's sister Kay and Kay's husband, Irv, in 1958, Charlotte used her over-the-top sense of humor to give a sense of the bedlam that was reigning in the Halvorson household:

Tuesday Evening, 9:30 PM

Dearest Kay and Irv,

Everything's quiet on the western bottle-front right now, so will write you a few lines. One never knows just when the bottle will start again though. Barb and Elling are over at the new house, working again, and I'm babysitting. Sometimes I think I don't *sit* hard enough.

Things are quite peaceful tonight for a change. Lonnie screamed himself to sleep a couple times already, Kent hit Brenda over the head with a block of wood and drew blood (good red color, too), and when I got in the room, Brenda was howling at the top of her lungs, and Kent was crawling under the bed as fast as he could go. I imagine Brenda had it coming, don't you suppose?? But of course I couldn't let Kent know he was justified either, so had to slug him a couple times to sort of teach him he'd better use his *rubber* hatchet next time!

The twins are really some honeys tonight. Very unusual. Roddy had his bottle a bit ago and settled right down, and Randy is still sleeping, so don't know how he'll act. Last night the twins were awful! I'd hold one till his brother almost lost his voice from crying, and then I'd take him and let the other one yowl a while. They were *really, really bad*!! If Barb hadn't used my suitcase to move some stuff down to the new house, I'd have been in Southern Texas by the time she and Elling got back. No, there *is* a grain of truth in this whole paragraph, but it's not as bad as I made it seem. You know I've always loved children. Wonder if I will after this?

Our babies look so much alike that we don't dare remove their identification bracelets that they got at the hospital. Sometimes I think I can tell them apart, and then again I'm completely lost. They are the darlingest things!! They sort of like night life but are improving. We've been trying to keep them awake more in the day time so they'll sleep nights, and they are getting better. When you pick them up, they look so angelic, as though they'd never been bad.

Lonnie is awfully sweet when he feels well, but has had a rugged time lately with teething and earache. Is he ever a big load to handle! He walks now but isn't half as bad to get into things as little Tommy was.

Brenda and Kent are regular three- and four-year-olds, I guess. One minute they are so happy and lovable, and the next they are fighting like cat and dog.

Barb is pretty good now. It sure took her a while to perk up this time. Her only trouble now is her "sitter." She's been so lazy, I've had to boot her around to get her to do anything!! Or it could be from all the shots she got at the hospital. Ha!!

Elling is OK. I've heard of proud papas getting big-headed or even swelling the chest, but it affected Elling entirely different. Barb has to sew up the seam in the seat of his pants every day. Ever heard anything like it?

Grandma is the only really decent one around here, and sometimes I wonder if she isn't a little looney!! What do you think?

You know the old saying, "Absence makes the heart grow fonder"? Well, it's true!! Know what I got in the mail one day from mine Papa? A *beautiful* wristwatch. I just lay awake nights and drool over it. Course I can wear it only at night. All day long I'm in the dishwater, diaper water, or somebody's bath!

Well, this nutty letter better come to an end now. Am not even sure I should send it. You know I always get silly when I'm tired.

Love,

Mom

While Barbara's mother was helping us with the children, there were eight of us living in that 1,100 square-foot rental home until we moved into our new place at the end of July 1958. The quality of our completed home and the amazing speed of its construction reflected how many good friends I had in the construction trades then. Looking back, it reminds me of old-time barn-raising efforts on the American frontier that drew volunteers from miles around. There was a shared spirit of cooperation among us and our many friends.

Adventures in the New House

Thanks to our lively children, the one thing our new home never had was peace and quiet. In fact, the sound of quiet put us on full alert.

A few months after we'd moved in, I started a weekend painting project downstairs in the family room. I had just opened a fresh can of purple enamel paint when I remembered needing something urgent from the hardware store. Off I went, taking Barbara with me. As Barbara scooted out the door, she asked Brenda, who was practicing on the piano, to keep track of the kids while we were

The "Halvorson Herd" in the early 1960s.
Back row: Barbara, Kent, Lon, Elling
Front row: Randy, Brenda, Rod

gone. Brenda was used to having to help ride herd on her often-wild brothers.

When we returned from the store, Brenda was still playing the piano. Was it possible that everything had remained okay? At first it appeared so. But heading downstairs, I nearly went into cardiac arrest. Purple paint was everywhere! Our toddler twins had discovered a wonderful new game. Just stick your arm into the paint can, then smear purple stuff anywhere you want to—all over your twin brother, all over the patio floor, across the cabinet, and up the walls!

Of course, everyone who is part of a large family gets accustomed to constant chaos. One time Barbara needed shower curtains for one of the bathrooms. Off she and I went, taking three-year-old Lonnie with us. At some point inside the Sears department store, I realized Lonnie had wandered off. As a free spirit, Lonnie wandered about often, so we didn't panic. I said to Barbara, "You stay here, and I'll locate him."

While calling out Lonnie's name, I walked through the bathroom-fixture area. Soon I spotted him, but I couldn't believe what I saw. Lonnie was seated on one of the display toilets, grunting hard and pooping.

Not sure what to do, I ran over, scooped him up, pulled up his pants in a blur of motion, and took off like a bank robber. Descending two steps at a time down the escalator, I abandoned the store with the stinky perpetrator under my arm.

They never caught us. But I am certain they never forgot us. The next time we went to Sears, I noticed the toilets were neatly displayed on slanting shelves, out of reach of anyone, including our perpetrator.

Other memories of those times include the friends who often came to visit. Kent remembers the fun we had:

> As far as us boys are concerned, those years in the Normandy Park home that Dad and Mom built were some of the best years of our lives, particularly as we saw more of Dad then than we would later on. We had fun, and Dad had fun.

After leaving Salem 10 years before, he still had a core group of friends who always seemed a little crazy to us. Some of those who occasionally visited us were past members of the original Central Lutheran Gospel Team in Salem. We called them our bosom buddies. Those buddies included Dean and Dennis Vetrus, and many more, including Paul Vetrus, the Hoiland Family, and additional friends who would drive up from Salem from time to time. The group expanded as Don and Irma Goertzen, plus Maynard and Nancy Nelson and family, joined in along with Anna Marie and Bob Larson. All of them had attended school together—high school and/or college. Those friends who were close decades ago are still close friends today.

Dad traveled an increasing amount for his new business, which meant Mom had to take an increasingly stronger role. Brenda was her right-hand helper then, riding herd on us four boys. When Dad was home, we seemed to focus on purely family activities. Looking back, I feel that when you're a family of five kids who are forced to do many things together, you ultimately have a tighter bond with your siblings than does a more typical family with one or two kids.

While it was rewarding to bring children into our family, I worried I wasn't helping Barbara enough. She had her hands full. The trouble was, so did I, for we had another high-maintenance "toddler" in our growing family—our new construction business. It was just starting to make a little money and needed my full attention. The situation definitely was becoming stressful for both Barbara and me. And the more dangerous jobs, such as the ones up at Snoqualmie Summit and then at Echo Summit, always bothered her.

She was also very concerned about the dangers I faced from flying to construction work. Brenda picked up on Barbara's fears and wrote a poem about it in school:

My Dad

My father's name is Elling.
What he is would be telling.
He flies a plane, and mother's insane.
She doesn't like him up in the rain.
He is six-foot one and weighs about a ton.
But I still love him 'cause he's lots of fun.

"Fortunately," Barbara says now, "I think the babies and growing kids helped take my mind off the dangers a little about Elling flying alone in the air. I was right in the middle of motherhood at the time, and we didn't have an introvert in the whole group. Life was never dull."

As Barbara's little helper, Brenda had a unique perspective on the situation:

My mother was 19 years old when she married Dad. Having five kids in four years was really stressful. If you can imagine being at home with five kids all day long and my dad being gone so much, often on dangerous jobs, you can appreciate the stress Mom felt. We did have a nanny and some live-in helpers. But we kids would absolutely drive Mom insane—to the point where she would be so upset, she would bawl.

I also realize a major part of the stress was having four boys and one girl. It would have been easier if she'd had a more even mix of boys and girls, since girls tend to help out in the mothering. That's what I did for Mom. I was her number-one babysitter. Mom tells me that when I first entered kindergarten, the teacher told Mom, "All Brenda wants to do is go around and help everybody." So, my brave mother, having all these wild boys and just one girl to help her, had a rough time of it in the early years.

On top of it all, Mom was a perfectionist. Her home had to be perfect all the time. That belief was the result of being raised in a home with tons of rules about what was right and what was wrong. Looking back, I see her life had to be in conflict at so many times. Yet through it all, my mother always stuck up for her kids and made sure that we kids were the most important focus in our parents' lives.

She was and is the center and protector of our family. Family is what makes her heart beat. She has outside friends and some social life, yet she really makes family her prime focus.

I was a fairly stable part of her life because I lived on the straight and narrow at least until I was 30. As a child growing up, I think I was more congenial than my brothers, although occasionally I stepped into fights between Kent and Lon and would take some hits.

I would watch in awe at how Barbara somehow always found a way to have all our kids, twins included, dressed properly for church. I often used to kid her about having 100 toenails and fingernails to clip each week, just before church. And bear in mind, every single one of our kids was a born rebel. Barbara's amazing work included polishing five pairs of kids' white shoes every Sunday morning. She'd been brought up by her parents in Iowa to dress nicely for church, and that reverent tradition stayed with her.

One particular Mother's Day, the kids and I were happy, although a bit weepy, when Barbara won three corsages at church. The first was for being the youngest mother there, the second was for having the most children, and the third was for having all of her children in church with her.

Learning to Take One Day at a Time

As if rearing a brood of five Type-A children wasn't challenging enough, we would soon be given staggering news from our family doctor.

We think it started when, early in her pregnancy with the twins, Barbara had treatment for a small peptic ulcer. Her doctors used a fluoroscope, a state-of-the-art device then, to try to discover the size and location of the ulcer. The procedure required Barbara to drink barium sulfate, which is visible during fluoroscopy, an imaging technique that uses x-rays. The liquid the patient swallows coats the esophagus with a thin layer of barium. This enables the hollow esophagus to be imaged by fluoroscopic x-ray radiation.

As the doctors watched the barium go down Barbara's throat so they could learn where the little ulcer was, she and our two babies were being exposed to radiation. We didn't know the danger at the time, but nearly 20 years earlier, one of the nation's top physicists, Dr. Carl Braestrup, warned that a medical fluoroscope "could be classified as a lethal diagnostic weapon."

Today, medical literature states that because the barium technique uses radiation, *it should be avoided as much as possible for children and pregnant women.*

Our lives were so hectic and our children seemed so healthy, we didn't think about any possible dangers the doctors had exposed Barbara and the babies inside her to until Rod and Randy were five years old. That's when they received the devastating diagnosis of Duchenne muscular dystrophy (DMD). DMD is the most severe form of the wasting disease that worsens one's health with every passing year.

Until the 1980s, not much was known about the cause. Then in 1986, researchers discovered a gene on the X chromosome (a chromosome that just women have) that can carry a DMD-causing mutation. Each son born to a woman with the mutation has a 50 percent chance of inheriting the flawed gene and ending up with DMD. Each of the woman's daughters has a 50 percent chance of inheriting the mutation and being a carrier.

Both Barbara and Brenda have had blood tests to determine if they are carriers, and they are not. In families with no history of DMD who suddenly have sons with the disease, a possible explanation is that a mutation occurred during early pregnancy due to medication or radiation. After we learned these facts, we've always suspected the fluoroscopic test to have had something to do with our sons' gene mutation.

We were told the boys would steadily lose their ability to walk, to eat and drink, and even to turn their heads. And we would probably lose them when they were still young. Barbara explains how the devastating news affected us:

Randy and Rod were always a little slower physically than our other children, but the doctor kept assuring us it was because they were twins. When they were around five years old and we were about to leave the office of the third pediatrician, I asked, "Where do we go from here? Something is wrong!"

The doctor looked at this "problem" mother and said, "Well, I can make an appointment for you at the Child Study Clinic at the University of Washington if it will make you feel better. It's a three-week study, but you'll have a thorough physical and psychological evaluation when they're done."

We will never forget the day we went back to the university for the results. Duchenne muscular dystrophy was the last thing in the world we ever expected. Learning that their life expectancy was only to the late teens threw us into shock.

We drove out to the Washington Park Arboretum and cried like babies. We would have given our youngest sons anything money could buy, but there was no cure available for love or money.

But God was there for us—one day at a time. He made it clear to us that we had five children to love and nurture and that our responsibilities were just as great to each one of them. We didn't tell anyone about the diagnosis for two weeks, and then we shared it first with our pastor and his wife, dear friends with whom we sang in a quartet. They cried and prayed with us over our news.

The next few months were a real spiritual journey for me as I set out on a quest for healing for my sons. We never felt God was punishing us, because that was not the Lord we knew. But we certainly asked the question "Why?" I read one book after another—a book in one hand and the Bible in the other—making sure I was on solid spiritual ground. Then one day it came to me quite suddenly. There was a real peace and a calm as I realized I didn't have to understand everything God was allowing; I just had to accept it. *Okay, Lord, it's in your hands. Help us, lead us, guide us, and may this all turn out for your glory.* And he has been with us every step of the way—one day at a time.

About a year after the boys were diagnosed, a Jerry Lewis telethon was on TV. That night when I was helping Randy get ready for bed, he said, "Mom, can you tell me something? Are there really grown-up people out there studying about my disease?" I told him about the research labs, and he looked up at me with big tears in his eyes as he said, "I didn't know that!"

I have to say that Barbara held up better than I did. Receiving the diagnosis was one of the most devastating events in our entire lives. We'd gone to the Child Study Clinic thinking we had a healthy brood of kids, and suddenly we were told we would lose our youngest boys within five to six years, which was the life expectancy then.

I can hardly describe the shroud of numbness that tightened around me. At the same time, my thoughts seemed to go in a million directions at once, all of them arriving at a dead end. If this had been a construction challenge, I quickly would have come up with a dozen solutions. But now, I was afraid even to look at the twins for fear I'd fall apart. Had I finally met an impassable detour?

One thing I knew for certain was that with the added challenges of Rod and Randy's condition, we needed live-in help to handle all the children. That's how Bonnie came to stay in our Seattle home. Then, when the Grand Canyon construction job took all of my time and I decided to move my family to Arizona, our entire herd moved into a double-wide mobile home in the Grand Canyon area.

Although Bonnie moved with us to Arizona, there wasn't enough room for her in the double-wide, so she got a local job with the Fred Harvey Company. Eventually, she married and moved to the little town of Williams, south of the canyon.

Barbara was still trying to cope with Rod and Randy's diagnosis when I had the nearly fatal helicopter accident in December 1965. That about put her over the edge. Neighbors took care of kids while Barbara sat by my side at the hospital. But when Bonnie heard about the situation, she moved in again for a month to help with the children until I was released to go home. We all deeply appreciated Bonnie's help.

It was an extremely difficult time for all of us—including for Bonnie. Her marriage was rocky, and eventually she became divorced. When we moved back to Seattle after the stop-work order on the Grand Canyon pipeline project so I could recover my health, Bonnie and her little boy, about two or three years old at the time, came with us. They were like members of our own family. In fact, Bonnie's son called me Uncle Dad.

15
THE LEGACY OF FAMILY CHARACTER

Character is everything. In daily life and business, nothing else comes close to character in importance. I've learned that character is just about the only quality that people ultimately value.

Growing up, I not only had a foundation of love and encouragement, but I also learned much about character from our church and through the example that my parents, brothers, and sister showed me.

Too many people assume they should leave their principles and character at the door when they enter the business world. That's far from the truth. In a National Business Ethics Survey a few years ago, nine out of 10 American workers surveyed said they "expect their organizations to do what is right, not just what is profitable."

I am so pleased that my children—Brenda, Kent, Lon, Randy, and Rod—have all practiced this philosophy. Every one of them is an intelligent, Type-A, motivated person with high morals. They are all 100 percent dependable and very honest in their dealings. I've seen situations where they didn't have to be so honest, but they always took the high road. And from my years in the business world, I know integrity is a lasting key to success.

I could tell lots of stories about each of my children. In fact, I think I will.

Brenda

Brenda has been Barbara's little princess from the beginning and has also been daddy's girl all along. We love each other greatly and still have fun together. Because she was the oldest and had four brothers in quick succession, out of necessity she was very helpful around the house. To this day, helping others is one of her qualities.

At age 11, Brenda was a cheerleader at her grade school in Grand Canyon Village. When we had guests for dinner, I would often say, "Brenda, do a cheer for the guests."

After the guests left, she would get stern with me and say, "Daddy don't ever do that to me again." But I repeated my request a number of times before I realized it was best to stop.

When we moved to Seattle, I would ask her to play the piano for our guests. She would give me the same stern comments after the guests were gone.

From the day she was born, Brenda was a pretty girl. While we were living near the Grand Canyon, one of the young men, about 15 years old, came to me and said he would like to work for me on the pipeline. I told him he was too young to work on the pipeline. The next day he returned and said, "I would work for you for nothing, Mr. Halvorson." That's when I knew he really wanted to be Brenda's friend, not mine.

From the time Brenda could read and use the telephone directory, I had her call restaurants and make reservations for me. I also asked her to look up airline schedules, write down the information, tell me what was available, and then make the flight reservations herself. I did this with her in as many different situations as I could. I believe it helped her when she grew up. She is very adept at finding her way around in the world.

She demonstrated strength of character during a period in her life when she was a single mother. To support herself and her children, she took up housecleaning. She did so well, she soon had others working for her.

A few years later, I hired her to be my administrative assistant. She proved to be an excellent assistant and was eager to take on increasing responsibility.

Some years later, she moved to the Grand Canyon with her husband, who was going to work for Grand Canyon Airlines. After she had been there for a short time, I realized she had the capability to be the general manager of Papillon Grand Canyon Helicopters. Because we had worked together for a long time and knew how each other thought, I was confident in the decisions she would make as general manager. So, even though she wasn't a pilot and didn't have a lot of experience around helicopters in aviation, I offered her the position.

Then I warned her that as the young daughter of the business owner, she was going in with some deficits hanging about her neck. She would have to earn her own respect. Undaunted, she had an interest in learning every part of the operation. She was a quick study and swiftly rose to the challenge. Today, as Chief Executive Officer, she has taken that company to its next level. She is also CEO of Grand Canyon Airlines.

Both companies have terminals at the Grand Canyon National Park airport and at Boulder City, Nevada. Additionally, Papillon has a terminal at the McCarran Airport in Las Vegas across the road from the MGM Grand Hotel and Casino.

During the summer, both companies fly approximately 3,000 passengers per day, so instead of keeping watch over four brothers, Brenda has the responsibility for more than 600 employees during the summer season and about half that during the winter.

Brenda is a wonderful businesswoman, respected and honored by her staff. Today she has two wonderful adult children, Geoff Edlund and Jackie Edlund, and seven grandchildren.

Kent

Our second-born child is Elling Kent Halvorson III. A good name, eh? But when we took our son to church, the older Scandinavian ladies exclaimed about what a beautiful child he was and what a great name he had: "Elling, da turd." From that day on we called little Elling by his middle name. Kent was a good boy, with a very good temperament. Growing up, he and Brenda were close.

In 1962, my company was bidding on the construction of a new high school at Eureka, California. We had to be competitive, so we focused hard on our estimates and prices. With our cost estimating done right, I felt we had a good chance to win. But important last-minute work remained to be done, so I jumped into my twin-engine Piper Apache airplane and took seven-year-old Kent as my "associate." We flew to Eureka to attend the bid-opening event held by the Eureka school board.

Our San Mateo office was preparing the final bid documents, so once Kent and I settled into a hotel room, I manned the phones to handle the flurry of calls coming in from San Mateo. When it was time to leave for the meeting, I dressed Kent up in the little suit and necktie Barbara had packed for him, and boy, did he look great! That gave me an idea to help the school board to remember us.

At the meeting that night, I handed Kent our sealed envelope with our bid inside. I said, "Okay now, you go up there, and you be a proud, proud Halvorson. Walk up to those men and women and hand them this envelope. Say, 'Here is my bid.'"

Kent followed my instructions, and the school-board members loved Kent's presentation. Our company turned out to be the low bidder. That was a big win! I tapped my son on the shoulder and said, "You did it! You got us the job. We're the low bidders."

We were going nuts together. It was absolutely time to celebrate, so I took Kent to the best restaurant in town. I said, "You can order anything you want. You can have the biggest steak, you can have lobster, you can have anything."

Kent saw frog legs on the menu and ordered them. I nearly fell off my chair. He'd never had them before. I asked, "Are you sure you want those frog legs?"

He quickly said, "Yes I do." And he ate them all. That was so funny, I couldn't resist asking him how they tasted.

"To tell you the truth, Dad," he said, "they tasted like fishy chicken."

From the time he was a child, Kent always wanted to be a contractor. He's been in business now since 1983, doing strictly commercial construction. Through his business, Halvorson Construction Group, he has completed buildings all over the western US, including churches, schools, hotels, shopping centers, office buildings, high-rise apartments, and IMAX theaters. He has lots of friends in the Seattle area, is on several charitable boards, and has made his mark in the region.

Kent and his wife Susan have two adult children, Christi and Katie. They each have two children as well, making Kent and Susie grandpa and grandma four times over. They love it and are good grandparents.

Lon

Our third-born, Lon, was a little more mischievous during his childhood years than his siblings were. He liked to tease his sister and brothers, especially Kent, and often would get the best of the situation.

He loved our next-door neighbors' collie, named Lady. Lady was the best-fed and most well-treated dog around. Her owners brushed her teeth and cooked special foods for her, such as beef stew and other good dishes. Lonnie liked to go down the hill to the backyard of the neighbor just below us and have a party with Lady. They would both lie on the ground and eat out of the same bowl.

Lon has always been a great community builder. He had friends all over the neighborhood, old and young. One time he had a big bag of nasturtium seeds, and he planted those seeds everywhere—in our yard, Lady's yard, and in every yard along the street. Every house had colorful nasturtiums, thanks to Lonnie. His beautification work was the talk of the community.

Lon was never rebellious and always loved his family. He was a good boy. However, he had his stressful days where we thought he was going to make poor decisions. For instance, when he was in second or third grade, he decided to run away from home. He could already write in cursive, so he wrote out a note in his best fancy penmanship and left it on the kitchen table. The note said:

Dear Mom,
    I am running away from home because you are so mean.
    Love,
    Lon

Barbara saw him go out the door and start to walk down the hill rather briskly. After he walked about 50 yards down the street, he stopped, thought for a while about what he was doing, and then he turned around and walked slowly back home. The threat was over.

This is typical of Lon. After he makes his first decision, whatever it is—good, bad, or indifferent—he thinks it through and always comes back with the right decision. I am very proud of him for his choices.

One day the lady who lived across the street telephoned Barbara. The neighbor was rather disgusted about Lonnie since Lonnie had told his class during show-and-tell time about what he had done for Mother's Day. Lon had told them we'd gone to Hong Kong and had taken a swim. The neighbor explained that she called to tell Barbara about it because she figured that Barbara needed to know the stories Lon was telling in school.

Barbara retorted that what Lon had said was exactly what we had done. We'd gone to the Hong Kong Café and then we went swimming at the Washington Athletic Club. That was the last time we heard any complaints from the woman about Lon.

A Rainier Heli International helicopter scoops seawater at Big Sur, California, to fight a wildfire.

Today Lon leads a number of companies. He is the chief executive officer of Rainier Heli International, Inc., which focuses primarily on forest-fire-fighting and heavy-lift construction work. It also leases aircraft in the United States and around the world in such places as Central America, South America, Australia, and Papua New Guinea.

He is also executive vice president of Halvorson Aviation Group, which includes Papillon

Helicopters, Grand Canyon Airlines, and Monarch Enterprises Inc. With these companies he deals primarily with bank financing and the helicopter manufacturers with regard to new equipment and the settling of any issues. Lon is the managing member of about 13 LLCs that own equipment, property, and other entities.

Prior to taking the helm at Rainier Heli International, Lon managed construction projects for our construction company, so he got a lot of experience in working with difficult logistics at remote construction sites, many of which required aircraft utilization for their successful completion. In addition to aviation, Lon is involved in several commercial real estate developments.

Randal and Rodney

The boys learned to pray at a very young age, and there were times Barbara and I knew God must be grinning. It is amazing what can come out of the mouths of babes. One memory that stands out is when the two were having a heated argument over whether the birds outside were blue jays or stellar jays. Barbara never said a word but just stood there in amazement at how angry the boys could be. Blood vessels were even popping out on their necks.

Then Rod stopped, folded his hands, and looking up as he prayed, "Dear God, are these blue jays or stellar jays?" Unfolding his hands, he looked Randy in the eye and announced, "He said stellar jays, and he knows!" Randy stared at Rod for a minute and then just walked away. It was all over. He knew he couldn't argue with an apparently divine pronouncement.

Remember when I was in a Phoenix tack store looking for 18,000 hog rings to make Gabion baskets for streambed stabilization? At the time, my family was traveling with me. The twins were part of a medical study that required collecting and freezing their urine every day and then sending it to the laboratory packed in dry ice. Talk about a travel challenge! Another requirement of the study was that Rod and Randy had to receive a couple of shots daily.

After learning that the tack store didn't have as many hog rings as I needed, I was on my way out the door when I spied an enormous hypodermic syringe, about a foot long, for use with horses. The needle itself was about eight inches long and the diameter of a small straw. I decided to buy it and chuckled to myself at the fatherly joke I was about to play on Rod and Randy.

When I returned to the car, I announced to my youngest sons, "I have good news and bad news."

"What's the good news?" the boys chorused.

"The good news is you'll have to get only one shot per week from now on."

They thought that was great indeed. "So, what's the bad news?"

"The bad news is you'll get that weekly shot with this." I pulled the huge syringe from the bag.

At first they just stared at me with their big, round blue eyes. Finally, one of them said in a shaky voice, "You wouldn't! . . . Would you, Dad?"

A Hot Life Lesson

When we lived at Grand Canyon Village, our double-wide trailer was located in the Coconino National Forest, just outside of the National Park boundary. One afternoon, the boys were playing in the woods. The minute I got home from work, I could hear people shouting, "Forest fire! There's a forest fire!"

We happened to live directly across the street from the district forest ranger's office, so I immediately called the office and reported the fire. Just then, our two older sons and a neighbor boy came running back to the housing area. Guilt was written all over their faces. I immediately asked my sons to come into the bedroom because I wanted to talk about the fire. With their heads hung low, looking like guilty convicts, they slowly revealed what had happened.

"We were burning red ants with matches," the boys confessed. "They would pop, and we were having a lot of fun doing it, when all of a sudden, a fire started in the sawdust the ants had made, and it started to spread. We did our best to put it out. All three of us peed on the fire, but we couldn't get it put out, so we ran home as fast as we could."

I thanked them for telling the truth and told them it would be necessary for them to go across the street and tell the district ranger what had happened. "As you know," I said, "someone has to pay for the forest service putting out the fire. Maybe there's a way you could pay for that."

I asked them to call the district ranger and make an appointment for the three of them to meet with him. The ranger cordially set a time for the next afternoon.

I can still see Kent and Lonnie walking toward the highway, hand in hand. The problem was that the father of the neighbor boy who'd also been involved would not let his son confess anything to the chief ranger, so only two of the three banditos kept the appointment.

In a very nice way, the forest ranger thanked them for coming to confess what they had done. He explained they would have to pay for the firefighters and fire engines, and he would make arrangements for them to do that. Since they weren't old enough to work alone, they could go with one of his rangers for several days and pick up tin cans and rubbish along the side of the highway. So, that's what they did.

The result was that our sons confessed their wrongdoing and paid their debt, while the other boy was not allowed to confess or have the opportunity to clear his guilt. Unfortunately, that man did not turn out to be a contributing member of society and has even spent time in jail.

16
NEW SCHOOLS, NEW SURPRISES

During the two years my family lived in Grand Canyon Village, I believe one of the advantages our children had in attending the local elementary school was learning to live with and understand people of different cultures, including Native Americans. It was also at the Grand Canyon where they nearly lost their father—twice. We all grew closer after that and learned how to function during difficult times.

Around September 1967, when we moved to a new home in Redmond, a Seattle suburb east of Lake Washington, we enrolled the children at Bellevue Christian School. This turned out well for Brenda, who was 14 and in ninth grade.

It was also a good experience for Kent. He made many lasting friendships at that school, some of which have lasted to this day. He became a real popular guy and was class president and captain of the varsity basketball team. He was even the pet of some of the teachers. As a result, he was able to get away with a lot.

Lon, on the other hand, found it difficult to compete with his older brother. Barbara and I realized the resentment that was building up in Lon, so we transferred him to Redmond Junior High, which worked out well.

Regrettably, after the twins spent their first four months or so of third grade at Bellevue Christian, it didn't seem to be going well for them, so we reluctantly took them out and decided to keep them at home the rest of the school year. That fall we enrolled them in third grade at Redmond Elementary School.

Barbara has many memories of those fast and crazy years. One day when the children returned home from grade school, Rod was sitting in his wheelchair, sputtering over and over, "Dumb kid, dumb kid!" When Barbara asked what happened, Rod said, "A kid came up to me and kicked me as hard as he could right on my leg. That dummy thought I couldn't feel anything!"

As disabled students, when the twins were ready to enter junior high, they came to the attention of Ed Houck, administrator for the Lake Washington School District. Barbara and I soon realized what an excellent administrator he was, as well as a constant champion for our twins.

When Ed met with junior high teachers and told them that Randy and Rod were enrolling, the teachers feared not being able to handle their disabilities and wanted our youngest sons to attend special education classes instead. But we knew our boys would never agree to that plan. Their minds were keen. It would have been the worst kind of putdown for them to have the same instruction as those who struggled with mental disabilities.

When we presented our case to Ed Houck, he arranged for us to meet with the teachers, warning us again about their negative attitudes. He opened the meeting by stating, "Here are Elling and Barbara Halvorson, Randy and Rod's parents. Ask them all the questions you want about having the boys with us in junior high. They are prepared to answer your questions."

Immediately, one teacher asked us, "Do you know how *mean* junior-high-school kids

Randy and Rod never let physical challenges slow them down.

are? Do you realize what could happen to your twins?" One by one, the teachers' questions painted the most dismal picture imaginable. Realizing that most of the teachers had very little awareness of the actual capabilities of our two sons, we did our best to make it clear that each twin was completely able to cope with whatever situation developed. Nevertheless, the mood in the room was very unfriendly.

After the last objecting teacher had been heard from, Ed Houck stood and said, "Okay, you teachers have gotten all that off your chest, and these parents have just about died. Now, from this moment forward, we're *all* going to figure out how to make this work."

We loved Ed Houck's persistence and courage. He proved to be a genuine help to us with his get-it-done attitude. I'm happy to report that few, if any, of the dire warnings from the teachers ever took place. In fact, Randy and Rod became popular almost immediately and made a ton of new friends, which included the teachers. Everyone took good care of the boys at school, and many are still best friends today.

While Rod and Randy couldn't play sports, they could still write and compose reports. Soon, coaches took a liking to them and had them help out by keeping statistics on the players and teams. From 1968 forward, our guys were not just observers on the sidelines, but they were also an active part of the school's sports activities.

Runaway Chair

Back then, reliable electric wheelchairs were rare, so Randy and Rod used regular wheelchairs. They could move about themselves to a small degree, and they always seemed to have friends who pushed them to where they needed to go. During their teen years, they didn't need resident nursing around the clock, so we were able to handle their care at home.

They still managed to find ways to get into trouble, however. Our hilltop home had a steep driveway that descended about the length of a city block. One day not long after we moved in, Randy headed down the driveway in his wheelchair. It was evident he underestimated how steep the hill was, because in a few seconds, he was traveling at full speed. Lonnie and Brenda ran after him to try to help, but the wheelchair was out of control and flew into a field.

Fortunately, the landing was soft, but when Brenda reached Randy, she saw that his hands were both horribly raw from trying to stop the wheels, and he'd filed off all his toenails when he'd dragged his sock-covered feet against the asphalt, trying to slow down his wheelchair.

With episodes like that, we learned never to underestimate our youngest sons. They, in turn, learned never to underestimate the steepness of a hill.

Rod and Randy have always been very social people. When they were juniors in high school, a man and his wife who lived just a few blocks away and also attended our church would take them in their van on camping and fishing outings, as well as to many other activities. Our guys just loved the trips.

Sports Fanatic Times Two

As parents of children with disabilities know, each school district is obligated to provide transportation for disabled students. After we moved to our home above Lake Sammamish in 1966, the school district sent a taxi to take the twins to their grade school each morning and bring them home again after their classes. Rod and Randy got to be good friends with their regular cab driver.

While they needed the extra assist with physical mobility, nothing could hamper their interest in sports. Almost before they could talk, Randy and Rod absolutely lived and breathed basketball. When they got a little older, they could tell you in a flash the statistics of any player in the NBA—their shooting stats, the schools they came from—they knew it all. They were human encyclopedias on NBA players and teams. One of the members of their personal Hall of Fame was Lenny Wilkins, the famous star of the Seattle Supersonics basketball team.

One day after school, just like usual, the twins were waiting for their taxi to take them home. As the familiar cab pulled up, Rod and Randy realized that someone was riding in the taxi's backseat. Who could it be? They were barely able to see the man. As the cabbie helped the boys into their seats, they were astounded to recognize the stranger as Lenny Wilkins. They let out yelps of delight.

Lenny came home with them and sat in our kitchen. Barbara put out milk and cookies, but being a disciplined athlete, Lenny didn't eat any cookies. He talked basketball with our sons instead. Then he headed into our backyard and casually shot some baskets. The news of Lenny Wilkins being at our home sizzled through the neighborhood, and in mere seconds it seemed, kids showed up from all over.

Not only were Rod and Randy huge fans of Lenny Wilkins, but over time, Lenny also became a longtime fan of the boys. Many other major athletes have also come to know about two of the sharpest, most well-informed fans around. Our youngest sons have many friends in professional sports to this day, including Edgar Martinez of the Seattle Mariners, former NFL defensive lineman Manu Tuiasosopo, and University of Washington Huskies football coach Don James, who passed away in 2013.

Barbara talks about the twins' success in sports:

> Randy and Rod started coaching basketball and softball teams when they were in seventh grade—men's teams, girl's team, and men and women's teams. Three teachers at Rose Hill Junior High were mainly responsible for getting them inspired to do this: Mr. Bowser, Mr. Hung, and Mr. Mescash. Randy and Rod would go to PE class, and before they knew it, they were keeping statistics and blowing the whistles.
>
> On their last day of junior high, they rolled into the house, and I looked into their laps, and I had to quickly go into the other room to cry tears of happiness—I couldn't let them see me out of control.
>
> There they sat, each with an athletic letter. They had been named lettermen for their work in assisting two coaches throughout the school year, and I learned they had also

received a standing ovation from the student body! They were rather humble about it, but their mother was overwhelmed.

Those two coaches became longtime friends of our family, often visiting at home and going out with Rod and Randy.

In their years since high school, our guys developed real skill at coaching basketball and softball. In fact, their coaching work won them more than 100 major trophies.

Barbara and I vividly remember when Congress passed the Americans with Disabilities Act of 1990 (ADA), a wide-ranging civil rights law that prohibits discrimination based on disability. One result was that government facilities and private companies were required by law to provide better for the needs of the disabled. This meant building sidewalks and providing curb cuts, along with ensuring access to bathrooms, elevators, and more. That badly needed legislation produced significant improvements in the lives of all people with disabilities.

An Anniversary Surprise

Dealing with many challenges over the years as our family of seven zipped along through life at high speed, Barbara and I were surprised when our 25th wedding anniversary approached in 1978. Each of us wanted to do something special to celebrate the occasion. And for a few days at least, we wanted to be alone, just the two of us.

Our anniversary fell very close to the beginning of summer when the days are long and the temperatures mild in the Pacific Northwest. We booked a four-day weekend at the popular Harrison Hot Springs resort north of us in British Columbia.

After checking into the hotel and finding our way around the resort, we went to the spa where we'd made reservations for massages and the use of a private room with a small pool. After enjoying the relaxing massages, we went into the beautifully decorated room we'd reserved, illuminated only by candlelight, and closed and locked the door behind us. Barbara and I enjoyed a most beautiful romantic time together. We then had British-style afternoon tea, took a nice walk about the town of Harrison, and, upon our return to the resort, we relaxed and sunbathed.

We had late dinner reservations at the Copper Room, the resort's upscale restaurant known for fine food and a great live band that played five nights a week. We looked forward to the evening with great anticipation.

In those days, people really dressed up for special events such as anniversaries. Barbara looked like a vision of beauty to me in her beautiful long, white dress, highlighted by the corsage I had presented to her. The fabric of my suit featured a very faint blue-and-white plaid, and with it, I wore a white shirt, an elegant blue necktie, a light-blue belt, and light-blue shoes with white socks. I was dressed to kill.

Our dinner reservation was for 8:00 o'clock on the gorgeously calm, comfortably warm evening. Our table was located next to a wall with an open panel-fold door that fronted one of the swimming pools.

Toward the end of our sumptuous dinner—seafood for Barbara and rack of lamb for me—we heard an announcement from the podium: "Elling and Barbara Halvorson are celebrating with us on this evening of their twenty-fifth wedding anniversary." The band played a number for us and invited us to dance. We weren't the greatest dancers in the world, but we were oblivious to anything except the love that raced between our hearts.

After dinner, around 11:00 PM, we decided to stroll along a vine-covered arbor that encircled the grounds. The setting was pure romance, and with each step we took along the dimly lit wooden walkway, I was feeling more amorous.

As we neared the first turn in the walkway, we realized that the arbor lights were out in that area, and we could no longer see what lay ahead in the pitch blackness. I whispered, "Stay here and let me take a few steps to see what's ahead."

Not many steps later, the walkway vanished from under my feet, and I suddenly went airborne, landing with a belly flop in the lagoon slough. I found myself surrounded by tadpoles, frogs, water skimmers, and the like. Fortunately, the only thing that got hurt was my pride. But Barbara, hearing the splash and unable to see anything, was shocked with fright. I yelled to her that I was okay.

After finding her way to the edge, she extended her hand in the darkness to help me crawl over the slough's muddy bank to the sidewalk. We made our way to a lighted area and saw that my gorgeous blue-and-white anniversary outfit, now soaking wet, was covered in mud, grass, and bugs.

We both laughed almost hysterically and wondered how I would return to our hotel room without being seen by other guests. Then we remembered my Hillcrest Academy "ledge walk" and put together a tactical plan. Barbara returned through the lobby and up to the fourth floor where she opened the door to our room. Then she went to the end of the hall and opened the fire-escape door.

When I saw the door open, I jumped up, grabbed the escape ladder, and pulled it down. Leaving a dirty and dripping trail as I climbed, I hustled up the ladder some 40 feet and squished in my wet shoes, *ker-slush, ker-slush*, down the hall to our room before anyone could see me.

Despite muck, insects, and ruined outfits, however, our 25-year romance enjoyed a bright flame that anniversary celebration of 1978, and we ended the night beautifully sleeping arm in arm.

17
LEARNING FROM THE PROFESSORS

In spite of the fact that muscular dystrophy produces a steady loss of many physical abilities, Rod and Randy were able to graduate from Redmond High School in 1978 and then take classes at Bellevue Community College.

The following year, however, they were confronted with a new crisis in late spring. Just when Randy and Rod were turning 21 years old, Barbara and I realized they were losing the ability to breathe on their own. We purchased a "bird respirator," similar to the medical ventilators I'd used when recovering from my helicopter crash. The device worked well enough when held up to the patient's mouth, but that required a caregiver. Barbara and I, as well as our hired assistants, did that as often as our sons needed breathing assistance.

I discussed the situation with a friend, Dr. Frank Sennewald. We came to the conclusion that it would be beneficial for each boy to have a permanent trach (pronounced *trake*). A trach is a hole (stoma) made through the throat into the windpipe (trachea) to form a direct airway so the patient can get air into the lungs. They are most often used in emergency situations. For a permanent trach, the edges of the stoma are stitched all the way around so the hole can heal cleanly and be permanent. While someone is still breathing on his or her own, the decision to make a trach permanent is a very difficult one. Unfortunately, most people have to be in an emergency situation before they are mentally prepared to make this decision.

All too soon, we had just such an emergency on our hands. A few weeks after getting the medical ventilator set up in our home, we woke one morning to see Rodney in enormous discomfort as he struggled to breathe. Feeling gut-wrenching helplessness, we dialed 911. Paramedics responded immediately, calling ahead to Overlake Hospital's emergency room. Their presence of mind helped save Rod's life.

But that morning in the ER, Rod was diagnosed with pneumonia. Barbara and I remember every second, every detail of that terrifying emergency. We were about to lose a son! Medical personnel moved like lightning, clearing Rod's airways and inserting breathing tubes through his nose and down into his lungs.

We stood paralyzed by fear in the midst of the frenzy of needles, injections, pumps, air blasts, and shouts for medicines. We had never been as frightened for our son as we were in those moments. Our mouths were so dry, we couldn't talk. But we could *pray*. And a miracle took place before our eyes.

As a doctor slipped off his gloves and wiped his brow, the entire staff seemed to sigh. They'd won the first fight; they'd stabilized Rod. They wheeled his bed out of the ER and into the intensive care unit where he remained on a medical ventilator.

Although Rod was stabilized, physicians diagnosed his condition as double pneumonia and warned us that our son still might not survive. Just as we were adjusting to the grave situation, Randy was attacked by the same condition. Again we made frantic calls to 911, did the trip to Overlake's emergency room, and watched as doctors inserted breathing tubes down his nose and into his lungs. Soon Randy was also diagnosed with double pneumonia and attached to a medical ventilator.

Our sons' condition was so serious, doctors warned us they might be in the intensive care facility for months. And sure enough, our sons' healing progress was agonizingly slow. As a result, Barbara and I spent most of our time at the hospital. Even when we weren't there, we continued to pray for their recovery, as did hundreds of others who knew them. Then very slowly, our sons began to overcome the severe pneumonia that had knocked them down.

As soon as Randy and Rod were stabilized to a small degree, I asked Dr. Frank to come to the hospital and do the permanent trachs on both of them. It was a heart-wrenching thing to do, but I knew it would be beneficial in the long run if they could survive the initial blow. After the stomas were permanent, the hospital installed a trach fixture in each opening and removed the tubes from their noses. That helped their comfort levels a great deal during the healing process.

However, we were privately advised that even if our guys survived, they'd likely never be able to speak again due to the design of the cuffed trach devices. The design included a little inflated balloon that maintained pressure on the walls of the windpipe, requiring all inhalation and exhalation to take place through the trach tube. Doctors figured they would never be able to use anything but a cuffed trach for the rest of their lives, and because the cuff was located below the voice box (larynx), it prevented air from passing through the voice box and allowing speech. We all soon learned to read our sons' lips.

Rod and Randy remained in intensive care around two months. One day, as Barbara entered the hospital elevator to go up to their room, she ran into Lenny Wilkins. She asked him what he was doing there, and he said he was on his way to the airport and had just been up to see Randy and Rod before he left town. What an inspiration that generous man has been to our sons! Manu Tuiasosopo also paid them a visit during their lengthy stay.

Barbara and I secretly smiled about how much Rod and Randy changed the ICU's heavy, stoic atmosphere to one that was far more upbeat. Always into sports, they arranged to have their friends regularly slip betting-club choices under the door. They never lost touch with their favorite pastime—evaluating and comparing almost every team in every league. They were visited by a number of other local sports celebrities too.

During their long hospitalization, they developed deep friendships and attachments with doctors, nurses, and pulmonary specialists. When they were finally about to be discharged, they asked Barbara and me to help them thank the medical professionals in ICU by buying them a top-of-the-line coffeemaker. Reading their lips, we saw our sons say, "They have to go to the cafeteria to get their coffee. We think they'd love having their own coffeemaker here." Rod and Randy also asked us to arrange for a small plaque reading, "Thanks for all the TLC – Randy and Rod," to be attached to the gift. They planned to give their surprise on the day they went home.

It turned out that the ICU staff had secretly planned a surprise farewell party themselves in a room just outside ICU. It seemed as if virtually *everyone* on the staff came to say good-bye and enjoy the delicious cake. I counted some 25 people. It was an emotional event. Then, when we presented the staff with the coffeemaker from Randy and Rod, many in the group broke into tears. Our sons asked us also to say that when they got stronger, they'd be inviting everyone to their home for a party. Three months later, about 35 people came for a great spaghetti feed.

Such a tribute to the guys! What more does a parent want? Many of those friendships have lasted decades.

Mechanical Helpers

When Randy and Rod were quite young, they were still able to get around with help from family and friends. Schoolmates carried them on their backs or pulled them in a wagon from class to class and helped them get into their seats. But when they were nine years old, the boys needed wheelchairs. Later, their first electric ones had four small wheels about six inches in diameter. Each boy operated his wheelchair with a joystick.

As Randy and Rod grew, their wheelchairs became heavier and more complicated, not only because of their physical growth but also because of additional life-support machines that needed to be added. Eventually, each wheelchair weighed around 750 pounds and carried several batteries, a water heater, a complex respirator, and a suction machine.

Those huge motorized chairs are essential for our sons, enabling them to move around in our home entirely on their own. They can pull up to their computers and adjust our various television sets and sound systems. Our elevator can carry them from the main floor down to the basement and also up to the third level.

But while the motorized wheelchairs were valuable inside the home, they were so heavy and unwieldy that they became a huge problem outside the house. My sons' health needs were also more difficult to address away from home. That's because Randy and Rod were basically kept alive by wires, fuses, batteries, motors, and electrical connections. Since hoses can leak or come off and electrical connections can be broken, our sons' lifelines were at risk of being interrupted at any time. If a caregiver driving the vehicle got distracted and didn't remain constantly aware of the guys' needs, the result could be serious, indeed.

I searched the truck market in hopes of finding a vehicle already equipped to meet my sons' mobility and health needs, but I found nothing suitable. At that point, the years of experience I'd had in custom-building entire machines—such as the equipment we created to fit the narrow trail deep inside the Grand Canyon—came to the rescue.

I launched into the custom truck-building business. I visualized what my sons needed, then I drew up a shopping list. The first item was a powerful, industrial-caliber truck with dual tires to lessen the risk in the event of a flat tire. I didn't want their attendant to have to get out of the van to change a tire and leave Randy and Rod alone inside.

Another requirement was that the motorized chairs could be placed side by side toward the front of the vehicle. That way, the driver could stop the vehicle, quickly leave his seat, and maneuver between the motorized chairs to tend to each young man as needed.

After research, I purchased a new, one-ton Chevrolet chassis with an "open back" cab. Then it was delivered to a company in Portland that builds refrigerator boxes on truck chassis. This was an ideal application for our needs because the refrigerator truck's foam insulation helps keep the vehicle cooler in the summer and warmer in the winter. Then I brought the custom-made truck to Seattle and outfitted it with windows, a hydraulic wheelchair-lift in the back, plus a DC inverter to provide 120-volt AC power for electric blankets and suction machines, as well as respirators on long trips. I also installed an unusually large battery, much like those used in golf carts, to even out the electrical load.

Next I had lighting installed, along with carpeting and other finishing touches. On the outside, it looked more like a delivery truck, but it was comfortable on the inside and served us well for many years. The addition of a standard-size van as backup came to Rod and Randy's rescue several times and also allowed them to go separate ways if they wanted to.

After using our custom-equipped van for quite a while, we ordered a new one. Then we gave the first one to a family in Olympia, Washington, who had three sons with muscular dystrophy and needed a wheelchair van. The mother called to thank me, tell me how thrilled they were to receive it, and describe how the van was benefiting their lives. Eventually, I went to Olympia to meet them all. When I saw those children, ranging in age from kindergarten or early grade school into the teens, I saw many of the stages of life we had lived through with Randy and Rod. The reminder of our past tugged at my heartstrings and deeply affected my emotions.

Making Hard Decisions

When Randy and Rod were coming into their teenage years, they explained to Barbara and me their desire to be treated like any other teenagers, including having the freedom to go places and do things, to have friends, and to participate in events. Also, they wanted to have the freedom to come and go in their custom van and not always have to have a hired driver, which was our practice. Instead, they wanted it to be okay to have one of their friends be the driver.

That was an incredibly difficult, emotionally stressful decision for us. Barbara and I went around and around with one another. What if the boys ended up too far away from hospital care in an emergency? What if a friend offered them drugs that might make everyone else feel high but could be lethal to our sons?

However, in the end, despite our pain and fears, Barbara and I were in complete agreement on one truth: each of our sons had the right to live as normal a life as was humanly possible. And they deserved our support. So we said yes to their request.

A short time later, Rod and Randy and some friends were headed in their new van to a baseball practice at Marymoor Park. One of their high school buddies was driving. They arrived at the park, and one by one everybody exited the van. We'd equipped the vehicle with a small fold-up ramp on the passenger side. First, Rod in his electric-powered wheelchair went down the ramp and around to the front of the van to join some buddies. Then Randy went down the ramp in his powered wheelchair, but he drove around to the back of the van. Not aware that Randy was behind the van, his school buddy put the van in reverse and backed over Randy in his wheelchair. The young kid knew he'd hit something, and in a panic, he reacted by putting the car in forward gear and driving over Randy a second time. Randy was horribly injured.

We lived in fear and constant prayer for many days. But Randy survived, though his condition was permanently weakened. Barbara and I were nearly consumed by the situation. In approving the expanded freedom that had led to the accident, we almost lost our son. Sorrowful and speechless, we wept and hung on to each other. For weeks afterward, I often saw quiet tears running down Barbara's cheeks as she was fixing meals in the kitchen or walking alone in our home. Her pain for our son was very visible.

Many parents have to make hard decisions that affect their children's lives, and if you're in that situation, I hope our story of Randy will be a help to you. Over time, Barbara and I felt we had made the right decision, even though it ended in terrible pain. Our boys were growing up. Despite their muscular dystrophy, each had a right to try to have as normal a life as he possibly could. Out of love, we had an obligation to help them do that. One of them got horribly injured, but pain is a part of life. At times in parenting, one simply has to take chances, come what may. You can't obsess about your own needs. You have to try to walk in your children's shoes too.

Moving Forward

Life is rarely dull at the Halvorson house. Close calls with our youngest sons continue. In the summer of 2004, at a little office party we were hosting at our home, someone ran out onto the patio and yelled, "Randy's having trouble! There's something wrong with Randy!"

We rushed in and saw that his eyes had rolled back into his head. The ventilator seemed to be working, so he was still breathing, but his heart was stopping. I pounded him on the chest. While I was trying to figure out if something was wrong with his breathing machine, I kept saying "Call 911!"

Lon, however, ignored the machinery and focused directly on Randy. In fact, I credit Lon with saving his brother's life. He screamed again and again into his brother's face. "Randy, look at me! Look at me! Randy, don't leave us! Randy, open your eyes! Look at me!" Lon also pounded on his chest.

Randy would almost come to, but then his eyes would roll up into his head again. That happened about half a dozen times. I was sure we were going to lose him.

When medics arrived, they took his vital signs and injected a medication into his arm, but they didn't know exactly what else to do. They needed to get him to a hospital, "But how," they asked, "are we going to get him in the ambulance?"

I said, "He'll go in the special van we have for them. You see, you can't just lay him down. Trying to put him on a gurney will traumatize him." Randy's tendons and joints were not protected by muscles the way most people's are. Lifting him correctly required a very delicate maneuver. He had already been hurt many times before. I knew that trying to transport him to the hospital in the ambulance would have been time consuming, as well as very painful for him and likely would have intensified his already perilous condition.[10]

One of the medics said, "We're not about to go screaming through town in a private van!"

"We won't scream through town," I assured them. "We'll drive responsibly, but he's got to be in our special van. We'll get him there much quicker than you can."

Finally, the paramedic in charge said, "Okay, let's do it."

---

[10] That risk never went away. When injury occurred to either one, the road to recovery proved to be long and painful.

191

With the aid car in front of us flashing its emergency lights and a fire engine behind us with all of its lights flashing too, we drove the custom van down State Route 520 toward the hospital.

It happened that Kent was returning home from Seattle on the same freeway when he saw emergency vehicles speeding toward him and recognized our families' special van between the aid cars. It scared him nearly to death. Whenever any of our family sees emergency vehicles heading somewhere, we always worry it could be Randy or Rod. That's just something we live with.

Our fast-moving caravan took the 520 off-ramp to I-405, and at the next exit we drove to Overlake Hospital's ER location nearby. Meanwhile, heading east on 520, Kent took the first off-ramp he reached, sped across an overpass in a big U-turn, and zoomed back onto the freeway going west. He reached the hospital just moments after we arrived.

Doctors soon wired Randy with an external pacemaker. "In the morning, we'll take him into surgery and install a permanent device," they said. Using their diagnostic equipment, they learned that his heart had been stopping completely. Before Randy's planned surgery the next morning, Rod, along with his attendant, went to see his brother. As they started to visit, Randy flatlined. At the code blue signal, people raced in from all over the hospital. Several of them already knew Randy from his previous ICU stay.

Since Randy had earlier been pre-wired for an external pacemaker, the medical staff turned on the pacemaker right then to restart his heart. His doctor made immediate preparations to surgically implant an internal pacemaker. We were all limp with relief that Randy survived the emergency.

A number of months later, Rod's heart began failing too, but instead of stopping, his heart raced at well over 230 beats per minute, too fast even to allow us to take his pulse.

With a paramedic escort, we rushed Rod to the hospital, just as we had done with Randy. The doctor tried different approaches with Rod's medicines. Soon, Rod stabilized, so we were able to bring him home, but just a couple of days later, we had to call 911 again. This time, physicians installed a pacemaker/defibrillator in his chest.

Not long after Rod's heart emergency, doctors replaced Randy's pacemaker with a pacemaker/defibrillator too. As you can guess by now, we learned that if one developed a condition, we could expect the other to develop it also, almost without fail.

Keys to Longevity

After our guys had their tracheostomies, they weren't sure how active they'd continue to be. "You really don't know what's going to happen until after it happens," Randy told *New Mobility* magazine for an April 1996 feature. "We didn't know if we'd ever talk again or be able to go out of the house again—you just don't know."

"We've got a lot in common, but sometimes we get sick of each other," Rod confessed when the interviewer asked if having a twin makes living with ventilators easier. "It's a lot more expensive with two of us," he added. "You know how you see on TV shows? When one twin's hurting, then the other one is? I think that's a bunch of hogwash. Because when he breaks a leg, I don't feel it. But we can watch over each other. If we're out with friends and there aren't any attendants around, the other guy can tell them how to fix a respirator."

As far as we know, Randy and Rod have been the oldest living Duchenne muscular dystrophy survivors in the world. I believe several factors contribute to their longevity.

First is their optimistic attitude toward life.

Second is their strong faith in God, a faith that supports them as it supports Barbara and me.

Third, we've been able financially to provide these two men good, round-the-clock health care in our home, each and every day of the year. In fact, three daily shifts are filled by a permanent staff of seven people.

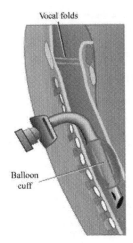

Vocal folds

Balloon
cuff

*Traditional trach
devices like these
didn't work well. I
knew the design
could be improved.*

A fourth factor in their longevity is how, in desperation, I discovered a way to make a reliable seal for their tracheal fitting. As you may recall, a trach is a hole made through the throat and into the windpipe (trachea) to form a direct airway so the patient can get air into the lungs. This graphic illustrates how the trach device fits into the patient's neck in a completed tracheostomy.

The cuffed tracheostomy tube, prescribed for our sons when they left the hospital, worked poorly. I felt it was a continuous threat to my sons' health. In fact, I maintain that Rod wouldn't have lived so long and Randy would not be alive today if we hadn't invented a tracheal fitting device that was significantly better than what was then available.

The unreliable, "off-the-shelf" tracheal fitting leaked and slipped around, leading to risk of infection. And when the balloon cuff was blocking their airways, rendering their vocal cords unusable, Rod and Randy could not speak at all, just as doctors had told us. In fact, they'd said that the loss of speech would be permanent. I simply couldn't accept that prediction.

I began thinking through different solutions, and then, over time, I tested a variety of approaches to find a way to make a superior tracheal fitting that my sons could trust. I had a lot to learn and produced far more failures than successes. I started the process by working with the doctor friend who did each son's original tracheostomy.

My doctor friend agreed that the medical system's tracheal fitting at the time was old-fashioned and that something better simply *had* to be invented. He and I began working to develop a fitting that could be sealed to the neck in some fashion, but our efforts never really resulted in a good solution.

My doctor friend gave up, but thanks to the attitude of perseverance I learned as a boy, I continued to chew on the problem the way dogs chew on bones. Then one day, I happened to see a man at the airport who had an artificial larynx. That sparked an idea. I bought the fittings for an artificial larynx and discovered that the piece going from the artificial larynx to the trach would work well in my application.

My challenge was that where a respirator's fitting attaches to the stoma in the neck, air pressure is high. That's because the respirator must force air into the lungs and then let the air out again. However, an artificial larynx doesn't need nearly as much air pressure in order to allow the user to vocalize, so the fitting had to be modified in order to be used with a respirator.

To meet the challenge, I adapted the soft plastic fitting by placing non-allergenic pressure-sensitive double-sided tape on the inside. But tests revealed that the seal wouldn't last longer than a few hours.

My next attempt was to add a second strip of pressure-sensitive tape to the outside of the ring. That increased the diameter of the fitting on the neck. That version worked better than anything before it. But it began leaking six or seven hours later. Changing the fittings three times a day was a huge inconvenience. Worse, the twins told me their necks started getting a little irritated from it. Randy even told his mother, "Get that mad scientist away from me!"

Obviously, I needed to find an even better way to attach the fittings. I pondered how to get something to stick to the skin without allowing leakage and without leaving a tape residue or causing harm and discomfort. Then a long-ago memory surfaced of when I played football in college. We wrapped our legs with athletic tape to protect against ankle injuries. But first we brushed a liquid called Tuf-Skin on our skin. The liquid left a tacky surface that helped the tape adhere to the skin.

Research revealed that Tuf-Skin was tincture of benzoin, long-known in medicine as a safe, natural substance to increase surface tackiness.

With this discovery, I was ready to take a big gamble and use my sons as test patients. I put the tincture of benzoin on their skin around the tracheal opening where the unsuccessful, leaky trach had been. Wow! It stuck for 24 hours and did not leak.

What a satisfying moment—for my sons, and for the mad scientist they shared a house with. In fact, my sons have worn those leak-proof plugs for four decades—ever since they were 21 years old.

A few years ago, I accompanied Randy and Rod to the engineering department of the University of Washington to look at some new medical appliances. The doctors who saw Randy and Rod were extremely surprised because they hadn't seen or heard from them in years. In fact, they couldn't believe our youngest sons were still alive.

When doctors learned that Randy and Rod were about 50 years old, they closely examined my tracheal fittings. They even brought out cameras and took pictures. Although they were very interested in the design, I don't know if they've done anything with it. I've never seen or heard of anyone who has adapted my design to their trach fitting. As far as I know, Rod and Randy have been the only people in the world to use it.

I have offered to give others the small engineering drawings I made, but so far, no one has taken me up on the offer, which I think is rather sad. That doesn't preclude someone from designing something similar, of course, but I think the possibility is rather doubtful. Nevertheless, having the drawings and specifications allows me to go to a machine shop with the plans and an 18-inch-long Teflon rod and say, "Make me six of these."

The mad-scientist fittings are like Volkswagens in that they work well and last for years. I also think they're a little like Corvettes in the design department. With the fitting I designed, the wearer can hide the trach with a shirt collar and necktie. Can't do that with the old-fashioned kind!

Celebrating Life

When a 76-piece brass band from Sweden was touring the US in 2003 and indicated an interest in taking a Grand Canyon flight tour, I gave them deeply discounted tickets.

A short while later, on June 18, Barbara and I celebrated our fiftieth wedding anniversary. Since the date was close to Randy and Rod's birthday on June 23, we included their birthdays in the event and invited around 150 people to celebrate with us.

On the day of the party, I received a call from Dave Anderson, the Swedish band's US tour director. "Elling," he said, "the band wants to do something special to thank you for your generosity." The only thing I could think of was to invite them to play for our party at the country club that day. The band arrived in two Greyhound buses and set up under the clubhouse's porte-cochère.

I chatted in Swedish with some of the band members and then announced to everyone that I'd flown the band in from Sweden for the event. Our guests knew me too well to take that remark seriously. Chairs had been set in front for Barbara and me, and we enjoyed the concert very much.

Toward the end of the festivities, Rod and Randy's birthday cake was brought out, and the guys were asked if they'd like to say anything to the crowd. Rod made a teasingly derogatory remark about his older-by-15-minutes brother.

Randy retorted, "Remember, Rod. You're the only one in this family who wasn't planned."

Everyone roared so hard with laughter, they almost fell off their chairs.

Learning to Dance

I am grateful that God has helped our family and extended network of friends and professionals to keep our youngest sons with us for so long. Let me share with you a short essay that Jack Bentler, a friend of Lon's, wrote about Rod and Randy's influence on others in spite of their apparent limitations.

The Professors

Always be open to learning something new from someone, as you never know when a great teachable moment has arrived at your feet.

That's been my experience when it comes to Rod and Randy. I had been friends with their brother Lon for some time but had only heard of the twins.

My first encounter with them was at a concert at the Chateau Ste. Michelle Winery. Rod rolled up in his wheelchair, a rolling mass of technology, with his assistant. I will never forget the empathy in my heart.

Throughout the night, I observed a man who was living life on his terms, soaking up the experience like anyone else at the concert would. How could someone so limited be so, well . . . so *unlimited?* Heck, if I so much as have a head cold, I want to stay home, but this guy is using his tongue controller to make his wheelchair dance in rhythm to the music!

Now I felt pathetic, soon to be followed by inspired. That's the effect that those who rise above adversity gift to us all. The Latin word for inspiration is *inspirare*, "breath from God."

Here is how the evening wrapped up. It began to drizzle. Some people left the concert. Lon and I wanted Rod to get right up to the stage and experience the concert front row, so I took the role of lead blocker. People parted like the Red Sea. It was a precious moment of kindness, and we got Rod literally one foot from front-center stage. The lead guitarist played for Rod as though he was the only person in the crowd. Dave Mason sang from his soul, Rod danced in his chair, and there was not a dry eye within 50 feet—and not because of the rain. So much for my empathy. Something told me Rod didn't need it or want it.

Fast forward to the next concert season, and in rolls Randy to a Turtles concert. Not to be outdone, Randy dances all night, and again we crash the mosh pit to front-center stage and hit the repeat button of Rod's night.

Is a theme going on here? I think so. These two men are the greatest teachers you will ever know, hence the nickname

Professors. I think anyone who knows Rod and Randy would agree with this definition, although it seems funny to try to define two men who refuse to be defined.

The moral of the story is this: dance and teach. Regardless of what life throws at you, dance to the music of your life, and teach others how to find their music.

Jack is right. Randy and Rod have always been amazing individuals—bright, good humored, courageous, and always full of optimism. In fact once, when they were running low on patches for their tracheal fittings, they ordered more—5,000 of them! How's that for optimism?

Barbara and I are deeply, deeply proud of how these two courageous men, along with our entire family, always made the best of life's extremely challenging detours.

PART IV: FROM GROUND TO SKY

✦ ✦ ✦ ✦ ✦

18
UNIQUE PROPERTIES AND PAYMENTS

In 1962, Seattle hosted the Century 21 Exposition, a hugely successful world's fair. Open from April 21 to October 21 that year, the event drew nearly 10 million people and actually made a profit, which world fairs in that era didn't always do. What's more, it left Seattle with fine gifts, including the Space Needle, financed entirely by private investors, as well as the Alweg monorail transit system. Even Elvis Presley caught the excitement with his movie filmed on location, *It Happened at the World's Fair,* released the following year.

For my fledgling construction company, the world's fair looked like bonus business, since a crash effort was being made to get all the fair pavilions built and opened on time. But almost every exhibitor delayed much too long. My company built several projects: the Government of Thailand pavilion, the Christian Witness in Century 21 pavilion, the Government of the Philippines pavilion, and some commercial exhibits. My team also built a number of facilities in the Food Circus, including a shop for Fisher Flour Mill's famous fair scones.

But the project that proved to be the most challenging was the Philippine pavilion. It got off to a rocky start because their government officials procrastinated until almost too late. As a result, our crews were working around the clock, even pouring concrete all through the night.

We were also hampered when a ship that was supposed to bring us hand-carved mahogany timbers for an exotic stairway, along with other special materials from the Philippines, didn't arrive in time. We ended up improvising with materials we could obtain locally. Fortunately, their architect from the Philippines worked with us day after day. Our gang really sweated the job, cramming three to four months of normal construction time into about six weeks. Everyone—all our crews and subs—worked tirelessly to meet the opening day deadline.

Construction went so fast, we finished the job even before they paid the billing for our initial work. When our final billing was added, the Philippine government owed us some $250,000, the equivalent to what would be about $2.5 million today. That was a lot of money to me. I had done lots of previous work with government contracts and typically was promptly paid. So I never imagined getting shortchanged by a sovereign nation.

When week after week went by without payment, I inquired into the matter. All I got was a flurry of excuses. They alleged that the outgoing president, Carlos Garcia, had drained their nation's national treasury. A new president, Diosdado Macapagal, had taken office in January 1962, shortly before we began construction, and now, they claimed, their nation had no money. None. I realized I had foolishly accepted a sovereign government's contract without suspecting they would not have funds set aside to pay for their nation's pavilion at a world-class event. I made several telephone calls to Manila to speak with the people I had been dealing with.

By this time, the Seattle World's Fair had its glamorous official opening. The pavilion I built for the Philippine government had not only opened on time, but it also was receiving high praise from the public and in the press. Finally, during one of my many overseas phone calls to Manila, I was told that coming to Seattle to meet with me were several Philippine government executives, including their Director of Economic Affairs, the equivalent of our US Secretary of the Treasury.

I said "Okay." But as the telephone call ended, I realized that in this situation, I could not allow myself to become Mr. Nice Guy. I was a young contractor, not part of the establishment. I had no way to be certain anyone on the Century 21 Executive Committee would take my side.

Working around the clock, we managed to complete the Philippine Pavilion on time. Trying to get paid on time was another matter.

So, I arranged a meeting with the Executive Committee and the contingent of Philippine government officials. Then quietly, without discussing the matter with anyone, I filed a formal Notice of Intent to Lien against the Century 21 fairgrounds, and then I provided the Philippine Consulate in Seattle with a copy of my Intent to Lien.

The filing of Intent to Lien immediately captured the attention of the Executive Committee, which included many of Seattle's elite, well-known citizens. No doubt I probably lost the good will of some of the directors. Nevertheless, I decided that if our discussion at the meeting and the Intent to Lien filing did not bring a satisfactory resolution to the problem, I would also picket the entrances to the exposition itself.

A day or two later, the Philippine government officials arrived on time for our meeting. We sat around a long table at the fair's headquarters. After formal introductions took place, I opened the session by telling the Philippine officials that if I did not receive immediate payment for the work my company had completed for them, I would perfect (activate) my lien against the fairgrounds, plus immediately initiate legal proceedings against the Philippine Consulate in Seattle. Further, I told them I would picket the fair itself to embarrass all parties into action, if necessary.

After a period of silence, the Philippine government officials assured me they wanted to pay. But when they fell silent again, I finally asked them, "When and how are you going to pay?"

There were additional moments of silence. Finally, one of the officials said, "Well, we could ship you a boatload of bananas." That brought chuckles from around the table.

"I can't use a boatload of bananas," I explained. "I don't know how to sell bananas. And even if I knew how, they'd rot on me before I could get my money out of them." I looked at the officials one by one and said firmly, "I have bills I must pay. I have subcontractors to pay. I need money. I need cash."

Another long silence in the boardroom. Then a different Philippine official said, "We could send you a boatload of coconuts. They'd be more durable."

Smiles from the fair's executive committee went around the room again. Repeating my point, I said, "I have bills to pay. I need money. I need cash."

The room fell silent again. This pause was longer than the others. Then one of the Philippine officials raised his hand energetically as his face lit up. "Mr. Halvorson," he said, "we can give you an island and three wives!"

I was stunned, and the Seattle representatives cracked up. But once the laughter faded, we all realized the official wasn't kidding. He was serious. He went on to explain that the Philippine nation had 7,107 islands clustered into the island groupings of Luzon, Visayas, and Mindanao. About 3,000 were uninhabited, so they really could give me one in payment. What he left unsaid was the fact that in those days, women in the Philippines were considered almost a commodity.

Defeated by the laughter in the room, the Philippine Director of Economic Affairs told us his group would fly back to the Philippines to see what else they could do. So I had my meeting, but I still did not have the money that was due me.

I spoke clearly to the Executive Committee in that crucial moment. I explained that even though I did not want to harm the fair, I absolutely was prepared to exercise my right to lien on the last day before my filing expired. I also told them, "If I don't get paid within a certain number of days, I'm going to start picketing the main entrances as well as the Philippine pavilion."

Of course, the committee didn't want a picket line at the fair, and the Philippine government didn't want one either, as it would have created negative press in the United States and throughout Asia.

Having made my point, I walked out of the meeting but without real assurance of payment, though I did have a couple of weeks before I would have to perfect my materialman's lien.[11]

A few hours after that meeting, I went to the National Bank of Commerce and met with my banker, Carter Shannon. As I walked into his office, Carter looked at me over the top of his glasses, grinning from ear to ear. He'd already heard about the island-and-three-wives offer. It must have zipped around the business community within minutes. By the time I sat down, he was roaring with laughter.

On my drive home after meeting with the committee and then with Carter, I considered different ways to tell Barbara of the Philippine government's offer. "Imagine, Barbara!" I said when I got home, "they're offering a whole island and three wives to go with it."

Barbara waited about a nanosecond and then said flippantly, "Uh, huh, well three wives is what you'd have."

On the last day of the time frame for the Notice of Intent to Lien I'd filed, I went to the King County Auditor's office to perfect the lien. Meanwhile, as I waited for the clerk to retrieve my paperwork from where it had been filed, the Seattle office of the Philippine Consul General called my business office. My secretary told him where I was. He immediately called the County Auditor's office and asked to speak with me.

By this time I had come to know the guy on the other end of the phone quite well. He'd lived in the US a long time. When I got on the line, he said, "Elling, I've got the check, and the money is in a Seattle bank. Please don't perfect that lien."

Now I wasn't sure what to do. Should I trust the man, or should I continue to perfect the lien? For a while, I stood just outside the wall of

---

[11] Essentially the same as a mechanic's lien, a materialman's lien gives a security interest in property to someone who supplies materials used during work performed on that property.

the auditor's office so I could sort out my options. If I relied on the official's claim that he had the money, I would at least have a check in my hands. And if for some reason the check bounced, I would have a "material default" to pursue legally. But taking the Philippine government to court would be a long and costly proceeding.

Still, I knew the Philippine consul well. I felt he would be honest with me. So, taking a chance on his integrity, I left the auditor's office, went to the consulate, and picked up the check. I took the check immediately to the bank it was drawn on and got a certified check. In the meantime, I couldn't restrain myself from asking the Philippine consul where the money came from to make the payment.

"It came from pari-mutuel betting on cock fights in Manila," he said.

I suppose after the island-and-three-wives offer, I shouldn't have been surprised at anything, but I'll admit that the source of payment was a bit of a shock to me. Still, in the end, I came to respect the Philippine people. Theirs was a new and growing nation, and ultimately they honored their word to me.

When the world's fair closed in late October, exhibitors were required to tear down most of the pavilions and exhibitions. When my company built the Christian Witness pavilion, we already knew it had to come down as quickly as it had gone up, so I originally designed it using removable panels.

My client had no use for the building after the fair, so we dismantled the structure into panel sections and stored them at a lot I'd purchased in Seattle's South Park industrial area. Later, we reassembled the sections at that location and used the building as our office for years.

Reassembled, the Christian Witness pavilion became our office in Seattle's South Park area.

Building for More Room, More Accessibility

After the catastrophic Grand Canyon flood in 1965 and the subsequent stop-work order issued by the federal government, I returned to Seattle to work from my office there. So, in the spring of 1966, with my left leg still in a full cast, I moved my family out of the cramped, double-wide mobile home near the Grand Canyon and brought them with me to Washington State.

Barbara and I were still adjusting to the new reality of our twins having muscular dystrophy. We recognized they needed to be closer to first-class medical facilities in order to receive expert help. The future of Rod and Randy, as well as of our entire family, was uncertain.

So, with the help of a good architect, Barbara and I worked diligently on designing a larger home that would give our boys easier mobility and allow us to provide the many different types of medical care they would increasingly need. I've already talked about crises with Randy and Rod's health that took place at this home, but now I'll tell you how we came to build such a house.

Of course, we were in prayer about the right location. Then I came across a remarkable piece of view property. It was five acres (which later grew to 20 acres through subsequent purchases) located at the north end of Lake Sammamish. The hilltop setting was near Marymoor Park in Redmond, Washington, a city once known as a suburb of Seattle but now better known as a suburb of Microsoft. To the east we could see sweeping, panoramic views of Redmond valley and towering, snow-covered peaks of the Cascade mountain range beyond.

Aware of my strained financial situation, my sweet mother, Beda, gave us $10,000 toward our new home. With that gift, we were able to pay cash for one full acre, which we mortgaged, and then we got a contract for the balance of the land purchase price. We also had the proceeds of the sale of our Normandy Park home. And while our new home with its splendid views was under construction, we were able to rent the house—the one we'd just sold in Normandy Park—from the new owners and continue living in it until our new house was ready.

Within just one month of hiring the architect, we had a building permit. And since I owned a backhoe and a bulldozer, I was able to excavate the crawl space myself. I also counted on friends in the building trades to lend a hand, and many did.

Since Barb and I were still quite young, we thought nothing of doing as much construction as possible ourselves. So on most days and most evenings, we worked on the house and did all of our own painting. I contracted out the framing to get it done quickly.

Our new home went up significantly faster than expected. One evening, the two of us stood outside the new home and each had a cocktail to celebrate the fact we could move in within a few days. We were proud of our achievement. We'd built a U-shaped California rambler, all on one floor, with 5,000 square feet of space, plus a carport and garage. Our family rumbled into the new house early in 1967.

As I look back, I am always amazed. We purchased this unique piece of land, got our permits, nailed down a mortgage, and completed construction in just six months. That's a miraculous achievement in house building. Best of all, *everyone* in our Halvorson herd loved the new Marymoor/Lake Sammamish "Home on the Hill." Maybe the most-pleased members of the family were Rod and Randy. Thanks to the efforts we'd made to remove barriers and increase their ease of mobility, it was much easier for them to get around.

Not too long after we settled in, I noticed that on our property, some 200 feet behind the house, was an artesian spring about three feet wide at the broadest point. Clear mountain water bubbled up through fine, white sand and flowed downhill in a little creek.

The spring's beauty inspired me to create some water features. I inserted a little intake structure to allow the piping of spring water down to the front of our house. Then I excavated a small pond and lined it with concrete, featuring a great-looking exposed-pebble aggregate. At first I stocked the pond with koi, but predators got them, so we replaced the koi with trout. In that pure spring water, the trout thrived on a diet of Purina trout chow. Those six-inch fingerlings grew to become six-to-eight-pound trout. When they saw us approach at feeding time, the water became alive as the trout rushed toward us in anticipation. We had to be careful not to get bitten by the hungry, leaping fish. Even putting a fingertip in the water was an invitation to be snapped at.

We caught trout with fishing poles, nets, even our hands. Whenever the fish population became abundant, we'd invite neighborhood kids over or hold a church picnic on our property and tell the young ones to bring fishing poles. After everyone had a blast catching the large trout, we would restock the pond with more fingerlings.

I created a meandering stream that flowed out of the pond and back to the creek. Then I installed a pump in the pond to use for watering our lawns and flowerbeds. The finishing touch was to build a bridge about 25 or 30 feet long that went from the parking area, gracefully arched over the picturesque pond, and continued to our home's front entrance.

We didn't restrict water to the yard, however. An especially wonderful feature of this home was an indoor swimming pool, 32 feet long by 16 feet wide, facing sliding doors to the outside. It became a year-round Mecca for children, including the neighborhood kids. Those kids also enjoyed the spacious yard, with its great basketball court. Many times those basketball games would go on well into the night. When we had picnics or group meetings, very often on cool nights we'd all end up around the blazing fire pit, harmonizing together in song.

Remember the shipment of hand-carved mahogany timbers and other exotic materials from the Philippines that didn't arrive in time to be used in the Philippine pavilion at the Seattle World's Fair? When it finally did show up, the fair was already underway and we'd improvised with local materials. The Philippine government no longer had use for the imported wood, so they gave it to me.

The unique wood proved to be simply dazzling in our new home. The mahogany panels were 14 inches across and boasted little hand-carved scoops that added more visual interest. I used some of it to panel one wall of the entryway. Between each of the mahogany panels, I left four-inch strips. Into each of those openings I inserted a thinner board with foam padding covered by gold-colored velvet. The dark mahogany boards accented by velvet strips consistently drew compliments from our guests.

So, while I turned down the Philippine government's offer of an island and three wives, I was happy to benefit from their gift of surplus mahogany. We loved our home and added a new feature to it at least once every year.

How to Treat a Good Friend

Living just a few miles from our new home were Ralph and Gerry Lindquist, some of our very best friends. When it came to practical jokes, Ralph and I always tried to outdo each other.

One Christmas, I decided to give the Lindquists a nice present. Carefully, and with love in my heart, I lifted the bag from our trash compactor. It was well-formed from its compaction and as heavy as could be.

I folded over the top of the bag evenly, covered the firm package with gorgeous wrapping paper, and placed a big, beautiful bow on top. Then I lugged the gift to the Lindquists' doorstep. As I rang the doorbell, I was almost giddy with anticipation. I definitely was going to get the best of Ralph this time.

When Ralph saw the package, he said, "Aw, you shouldn't have done this, Elling. It's so nice of you. We're embarrassed we don't have a gift for you too." While Ralph and Gerry put the heavy package under their tree, they went on and on about how beautiful the wrapping was and how they couldn't imagine what would be inside.

The next evening Ralph and Gerry were sitting in their living-room easy chairs when Ralph turned to Gerry and asked, "When's the last time you cleaned the refrigerator?"

"Why, I did it only three days ago," she replied.

The next evening the odor was even stronger. Together they checked the refrigerator and all the kitchen cupboards, and then they went through every closet in the entire house. After thoroughly checking the basement and still unable to find the source of the stench, they were totally perplexed. Then one of them happened to walk by the Christmas tree and said, "Ah! I think it might be Elling's gift to us. Maybe he gave us cheese or fish or something else that might spoil. We'd better open it."

Moments later, they knew what the problem was. "Oh, that darned Elling," said Ralph. "He did it to us again. I'll fix him. He'll pay for this."

By now it was quite late, so, rewrapping the package the best they could, they put it out on the front porch. Ralph planned to dispose of it properly in the morning. However, while they slept that night, neighborhood dogs strewed the garbage all over the lawn.

The entire time Ralph was stooping over to pick up the mess, he muttered, "I'll get Elling back for this. I'll get Elling back for this."

I loved Ralph. He was one of the sweetest, kindest people I've ever known. Unfortunately, he passed away before we could finish having fun together.

19
EXPANDING OUR HORIZONS

In 1973 I entered into an agreement with Seattle developer Paul Schuler to do a project together at Sun Valley, Idaho, located on the north side of Bald Mountain, directly across from the Greyhawk chairlift station. Shortly after we completed the project, Paul was riding an off-road dirt bike in the area when he fell, hit his head against a tree trunk, and died. I was shocked to hear the news but knew Paul liked to participate in some risky sports.

A man named George Osborne was Schuler's manager. George and I got along very well and seemed to share the same creative sense about construction work. Eventually, I offered George a job with Elling Halvorson Inc. as my right-hand administrator.

North to Alaska

High-logistics jobs were somewhat limited in the Lower 48, so, after several years, George and I decided to do some work in Alaska, where all jobs required greater logistics and planning, at least to some degree.

All of our projects in the Arctic required us to ship our supplies and equipment to the site on barges during the few weeks of summer ice-break-up. Everything we needed for each job was in numbered containers stacked eight stories high on container barges. Once the barges arrived and were beached, we would unload the containers in reverse order they'd been packed in. That way, when the materials were removed, every bolt, every beam, every little thing we needed for the project would be available in the order we needed them. We had to work quickly before the seawater started to freeze again.

We always continued our construction work throughout the winter. High logistics were required for doing that type of work in the Arctic where winter was so bitterly cold that engines had to be kept running 24 hours a day or they wouldn't start again.

Some of our biggest jobs involved military housing and schools. Alaska was on a mission to put a real high school in every village, so we got building contracts for quite a number of them. Our first was in Unalakleet, on the Bering Sea, a little southeast of Nome.

My company earned a reputation for handling high-risk projects well.

Unalakleet

Unalakleet was populated with an unusually high percentage of well-educated students. Prior to the village's school system being run by the state, the elementary and high school had been operated by the Evangelical Covenant Church of America. The Covenant schools' high-spirited student body was proficient in sports and scholastic education, as well as understanding the tenets of Christianity. It was a good group of teachers and students.

When we built our first project there, we used all of the creative techniques and ideas we had used on other remote jobs. We batched our own concrete, produced our own sand and gravel for the concrete, and shipped all other materials to the site by oceangoing barges out of Seattle. Once the barges were beached at Unalakleet, we would unload our equipment.

Brenda, who was 22 years old at the time, managed our camp for employees. It was her first time handling that responsibility, and that camp was the best-managed one we ever had.

On one of my business trips to the site, I brought Barbara along to visit with our daughter and experience Alaska for the first time. When Brenda invited Barbara to go berry picking with her, Barbara was amazed to see Brenda strap on a .357 Magnum pistol. The wilderness area had many bears and other wild animals, so everyone had to be prepared.

Close to Unalakleet was the White Alice Communications System, built by the US Air Force in the late 1950s to provide reliable communications in isolated and often rugged locales. The early warning defense system had been advanced for its time, but by the end of the 1970s, most of it was deactivated due to the advent of satellite communications.

One of the unusual features of our project there was the requirement to relocate a full-sized gymnasium from a mountaintop at the White Alice project to the site of a new village school several miles away. The only pathway between the two sites was a steep dirt road.

We had shipped all our necessary supplies—timbers, beams, wheel dollies, jacks, etc., on a barge. So we carefully jacked the gymnasium off its foundation and placed timbers and beams underneath the structure, which we reinforced for shear loads that would be imposed on it during its trip down the mountainside.

After widening and making improvements to the primary dirt road going up to the White Alice site, we placed a large crawler-tractor in front of the gym and another one behind it and carefully navigated down the mountainside. We handled that building like it was a load of eggs. Once at the new school site, we gently set it on the new foundation we'd prepared. We were all relieved that the project was a huge success.

Prudhoe Bay

When we looked for jobs from then on, we focused almost all of our attention on the Alaskan bush and Aleutian Islands. At Deadhorse, above the Arctic Circle, we built the Prudhoe Bay Hotel at the end of Alaska's Dalton Highway and on the edge of Prudhoe Bay Oil Field. We also built a primary power turbine facility to provide the electricity for the Prudhoe Bay Oil Field. Power was provided by huge turbine generators. Gas was simply piped directly from a nearby well. We also built the solid-waste disposal facility, the freshwater facility, and a number of other projects there.

Kuparuk

At the Kuparuk Oil Field, we constructed maintenance and storage buildings for schools, and we did other projects. We also relocated a radome (radar facility) in a similar manner to the way we'd moved the gymnasium off the mountain top at Unalakleet.

Adak

We removed all of the World War II ordnance—including fuel tanks, piping, buildings, and bunkers—at Adak, which was located at the end of the Aleutian Islands. Adak originally had a sizeable population in the 1800s until many people left to follow the fur-trade business to Russia. The small contingent of people who remained behind struggled through difficult times, including famine.

During World War II, the village became a strategic location for the US military. It was our country's closest military base to Russia and Japan. Later, during the Cold War, Adak served as a significant surveillance center for submarines. At one point, the US military had more than 6,000 people based at Adak. Today, however, the population has dwindled to slightly more than 300 people, leaving large numbers of vacant homes, apartments, and dormitories. Due to its naval-aviation past, Adak has an unusually sophisticated airport for its location. Although there is no control tower, it does have instrument-landing capabilities and two paved runways, each 200 feet wide by close to 7,700 feet long.

Sand Point

Sand Point, one of the primary fishing villages in the middle of the Aleutian chain, is located about 1,000 miles from Anchorage. When we bid a school-building project there, the village boasted a fleet of fishing boats and several canneries. There were about 950 permanent residents, and in the summer many hundreds of people would swell the ranks to work in the fish-packing plants.

The village was serviced by propeller-driven aircraft that held approximately 20 passengers, in addition to cargo. When booking a flight, passengers didn't know how many seats would be available due to the amount of space the cargo required.

As the successful bidder on the project, we believed we had a good job in a good community. We had located sources of aggregate that could be screened for concrete aggregate. The fact that the project called for a lot of concrete may have given our bid a fundamental advantage. Teachers were conducting classes in very substandard conditions, so everyone was eager to get the new school.

We hurriedly planned the project. To find a responsible job superintendent, we interviewed several applicants and selected a man who came with good recommendations.

Next we secured equipment and materials to load on a huge barge, and we contracted with a marine towing company to undertake the hauling to Sand Point. Once the barge was securely beached at its destination, all the cargo was moved to the job site.

Our relationship with the community grew into an unusually good one. At first we weren't sure why we were being given such a warm welcome. Then we started hearing rumors that our job superintendent was selling our aggregate and bags of portland cement on the side. Since we had sent the appropriate amount of supplies to the job site and were now coming up short of powdered cement, we suspected the rumors to be true. But how could we prove it? By that point, construction of the school was well underway.

We sent testing equipment with one of our good employees, field estimator Mike Richie, so he could determine the strength of the concrete in the building's foundation.

To perform the test, he took a hardened steel probe that had a blunt conical tip, and he fired it into the concrete with a special gun that used a powder-filled cartridge. Then he was supposed to measure the depth of penetration and compare it to information provided by the manufacturer.

The problem was, it took Mike quite a while even to find the probe. It had gone clear through the foundation, proving beyond a shadow of a doubt that our job superintendent had cheated on the amount of cement used while batching the concrete. The entire foundation would have to be replaced.

We faced a serious detour in trying to make a profit on that job.

I asked the job superintendent to come to Seattle so we could discuss the situation. I said I would pick him up at the airport, but I actually had no intention of bringing him to the office. When he stepped off the airplane, I looked him in the eye, said, "You're fired!" and then turned around and left. I figured he could find his own way home. I was so upset I was reluctant to say anything else for fear I would regret it later.

To fix the problem, we had to ship in new supplies of cement. Then we had to jack the building up high enough to crush the old foundation, haul out the chunks, and build entirely new forms, footings and foundation walls. That work cost us about one million dollars.

Yes, we fixed the problem, but the job's earning potential had been destroyed. Because of one man's greed, all the hard work our people had spent organizing, planning, bidding, and supporting the project resulted in zero profits.

We finished the school, and the town's residents were happy with their new concrete driveways, retaining walls, patios, etc. I guess it was good that someone could win.

From Ground to Sky

During the Grand Canyon project, after construction crews had been delivered to their job sites each morning, our pilots often flew inspectors, surveyors, insurers, engineers, lawyers, photographers and park service staff to different places along the pipeline's route. Everyone was overwhelmed when they saw the canyon's beauty from a helicopter's perspective. To some it was even a spiritual experience.

Most people back then had never seen a helicopter up close, let alone had the opportunity to fly in one. A helicopter flight is in itself a unique thrill. But when you add the Grand Canyon's astonishing vistas, you can understand how people came away with an experience they would never forget.

As guests thanked us for their flights, many of them would say, "That was the best adventure of my life." After hearing that month after month, I became convinced of the potential for a profitable business based on flying tourists into the canyon.

So, with a mix of caution and enthusiasm—after we completed the rebuild of the Grand Canyon pipeline—I started a new business, Grand Canyon Helicopters. We had an initial staff of four people. But even that small number couldn't fit in our first "building," an eight-foot camping trailer. Company meetings were held in the great outdoors.

Soon enough though, we had two pilots, two mechanics and two ticket sellers while I worked on growing the seedling we'd just planted. Our big advantage was the experience we'd gained

For many years, a double-wide mobile home was our terminal at Grand Canyon Helicopters.

flying as many as 60 construction workers a day into the Grand Canyon and learning how to operate a helicopter fleet.

Then, in 1968, I and Pat Sullivan, the attorney who had helped me prevail against the federal government after the catastrophic flood, each purchased a 50-percent interest in Grand Canyon Airlines.

From the beginning, I focused all my energies on building a professional flightseeing business. I use the word *professional* because most helicopter flight services I had visited or heard of at that time were pretty small outfits. That's why I stressed the importance of radiating professionalism and competence. My goal was to set a higher standard in how we looked and in how we treated our guests. I insisted that we keep our helicopters *spotless*. We made sure our pilots and hosts were dressed well. We insisted on the highest level of professionalism throughout our guests' flightseeing experiences.

Nevertheless, for the first few years, business was slow and I had to use my construction company to underwrite the helicopter operation. In our startup years in the late sixties and early seventies, it was difficult persuading people to take a flightseeing ride when they'd never been near a helicopter. After all, helicopters were still new to most of the public. People often asked me, "How can a machine fly when it doesn't have wings?" I would explain that the propeller blades *are* wings.[12]

During our initial years, almost everyone I met in business—from bankers to lawyers to airline people to my own accountant—told me to sell out or bail out. They had never seen a flightseeing business make a good profit. But every day, my crew and I experienced something most of my business contacts did not; we saw how thrilled people were with the Grand Canyon flights. I always told the naysayers, "No, there's real value there. It just hasn't hit yet."

Fortunately, just a few years after we opened our doors, our flightseeing business got a huge boost from a surprising source—the hit 1970 movie *M*A*S*H*. In that film about the Korean conflict era, helicopters brought the wounded to a Mobile Army Surgical Hospital. The movie and the subsequent weekly television series that began in 1972 created great publicity for us. The TV show was consistently number one in the ratings every week for 11 straight years, making helicopters familiar to millions of viewers.

But, even with that terrific promotion, it took a long time to steadily build our Grand Canyon Helicopters business into a profitable, according to my calculations, we provided helicopter flights to about 300,000 people before the business got enough word-of-mouth buzz going to turn the corner. I always knew that if we could cross a critical mass of past customers who were ecstatic about the product, we would become

---

[12] See Appendix A for a detailed explanation of how helicopters fly.

successful. Sure enough, once our enterprise took off, we increased business about 10 percent a year for many years.

To this day, our passengers are so enthusiastic about their canyon flights that they continue to recommend us to others. Those heartfelt person-to-person endorsements have always driven the core of our success, since there is no recommendation stronger than that of a friend or family member. It is more important than any advertising one could buy.

Over and over, we'd welcome visiting aviation people who heard about our success and professionalism in both maintenance and operations. We had taken flightseeing out of the mom-and-pop level, slowly building not only a Grand Canyon service, but really, a new flightseeing industry, which has since grown to worldwide reach. Many helicopter touring companies are now providing a wide range of services, from winging over glaciers to scooting over African tropical forests. Nevertheless, to the best of my knowledge, I'd say we are still the largest in the world in terms of numbers of flights per year.

Whenever the big commercial operators have gotten together with me, they tell stories about each other. They've confessed that they used to look at us and laugh while thinking, *The Halvorsons aren't going to go very far with a flightseeing business.* But our business model has proved itself.

A key factor in our business success today is the Internet. In fact, the Internet generates a remarkable amount of our business. Also, in an ongoing effort to introduce our service to travel agents all over Europe, Japan, and the United States, we've sponsored booths for many years at the International Pow Wow, a global event for travel agency professionals. As a result, nearly half of our customers are from other countries. We welcome at least a half million international visitors annually. They bring our nation valuable international currency, and our international guests also take home a very positive feeling about America's great sights.

Although there are many wonderful ways to experience the Grand Canyon, most take several days of time investment, and even then one cannot see the canyon as a whole unless one flies over it. I believe that's why aircraft touring has grown to become the number one way to enjoy the canyon's size, breadth, and beauty.

Borrowing Trouble

To complement our flightseeing business at the canyon, I felt that building a nice hotel would also be a good investment. Around 1969, I became interested in key acreage near the South Rim that was owned by a member of the Robert Thurston family. Robert's family members had been among the earliest settlers at the Grand Canyon. The property was located at Tusayan, a conclave of a few families, plus a gas station that had a small coffee shop and bar.

This parcel, approximately 160 acres, was the only property on US Highway 64 within 20 miles from the canyon's South Rim that wasn't owned by the federal government. I was convinced it would be an excellent location for a hotel. So, after acquiring the land, I called Pat Sullivan and asked him to be my partner in the venture. [13]

During that economic era, the early part of the seventies, it was very hard to borrow money. For more than a year, Pat and I looked into various possible sources. Seafirst Bank (now Bank of America) referred us to an offshore bank with whom they had done satisfactory transactions. Seafirst assured us it was a good bank. We arranged to meet with the offshore bank's representatives at their office on the second floor of the First National Bank building in Fort Lauderdale, Florida.

We scraped together all the money we could find for the required deposit and had a certified check drawn on the Old National Bank in Spokane, where my brother Hal was on the board and Pat and I both knew the president.

When we got to the offshore bank's office in Fort Lauderdale with our sizeable deposit, we were met by David Mayfield, the broker and our

[13] For more information about our developments in the town of Tusayan, see Appendix C, "Witnessing the Birth of a Village."

contact with the lender bank. We also met an escrow agent who had been brought in to handle the transaction.

But then we were told that the bank had filled its quota on loans. However, they had a commitment from a similar quality offshore bank that we could get the loan from. This bothered us, but after deliberation and questioning the broker and escrow agent, we finally decided that maybe it would be okay. So we gave our money to the escrow agent. He said they would like to meet for cocktails at Mr. Mayfield's home and then go to dinner at a particular nightclub. We agreed to meet them that evening. When we arrived at Mr. Mayfield's home, we discovered it was the penthouse suite at the top of one of the biggest hotels in Fort Lauderdale. He was known by everyone in the hotel—which, incidentally, was owned by the Teamsters.

That evening a Sicilian guy, who had flown in from Los Angeles to meet us, joined us for dinner. Then, while we were eating, two women slipped in with us too. Pat and I wondered who they were and where they had come from. After a couple of toasts concerning our business-loan deal, the women started getting rather cozy with us. At that point, Pat got up to go to the restroom. He gave me a nod, so I got up and joined him. Once we were away from the table, we agreed that situation did not look good, and we pledged to take care of each other that night.

During the course of the evening as everyone was having a lot of drinks, the Sicilian guy put his arm around me. He said, "I'm going to know you and your family just really well, Elling. We're going to do a lot of things together."

Pat and I became increasingly uneasy about the whole thing. It just didn't feel right. Meanwhile, the women got very drunk, and one of them finally left, deciding we weren't very good prospects. After everyone else had gone, the other woman didn't have a way home and Pat and I were alone with her. We volunteered to take her to her home and ended up having to help her into her house.

As we left, Pat and I said to each other, "This is really bad. Something terribly wrong is going on." We'd already agreed to meet the men for breakfast in the morning, so Pat and I talked over the situation and came up with a plan. The plan was that I would show up for breakfast, and Pat would take the rental car and check out the escrow company at the address we'd been given.

When Pat returned, his face was white. As soon as he could get a private moment with me, he said in a low voice, "Elling, the escrow company is nothing more than a room with something like thirty telephones in it."

We had put up all the money we could muster, and now it looked like we'd gotten ourselves involved in a mafia-type operation. We figured that while we were on their territory, we couldn't do much, so we decided to return home—Spokane for Pat and Seattle for me.

The first leg of our flight home went from Fort Lauderdale to Tampa Bay. During that flight, Pat was reading the *Wall Street Journal* and came across a feature article about the people we had been working with. An accompanying photo nearly gave him a heart attack. It was a picture of David Mayfield. The man was wanted in connection with fraud and other charges.

When our plane landed in Tampa Bay, I stayed on the airplane and Pat went into the terminal to call officials at the office of Florida's Attorney General. They knew exactly who we were talking about and were very familiar with the covert operations we described. They explained that the mafia-type of operation was too large for Florida to deal with. But when Pat told them the mafia guys had used the United States Postal Service to communicate with us—sending material to us and receiving drawings and financial statements and other documents back from us through the mail—the Attorney General's office told Pat to call the post office. It sounded like a mail fraud case.

When Pat came back on the airplane, he again looked like an albino. He was deeply disappointed. "Elling," he said, "if I had been your attorney on this trip instead of your partner, I never would have let you turn that check over to the escrow agent. I would have insisted that we delay payment until we had time to check out the source of their commitment, along with that of the escrow company. I got so caught up in the spirit of doing this thing that I abandoned my legal conservatism for a moment. But in that moment, the damage was done. I got caught up in the transaction."

So, here we were, involved in some sort of mafia thing. My first evening at home, I gathered my family together and explained what had gone on. My kids were still quite young, probably about 10 to 15 years old. I said, "If any stranger comes near you, if anyone wants to talk to you, don't talk to them. Just run away. I don't know exactly what's going on, but we've been in contact with some bad people." I warned them never to get in a car with anyone they didn't know.

Pat, being an attorney, carried the ball concerning our legal matters. First he called the US Postal Service, who involved the FBI. Then he went to Old National Bank in Spokane, where the banker knew both of us and we both knew the president, and he was able to get Old National to stop payment on our certified check. Stopping payment on a certified check can happen only when fraud is involved.

After the bank agreed not to honor its own certified check—an unusual move that would put any bank under Federal scrutiny—we waited. We wouldn't know what bank our check had been taken to for deposit until the check arrived at the Old National Bank. But now we had a partner bank in Florida who was on our side and had our same interests.

A private investigating firm hired by the Florida bank tracked down the culprits. The mafia guys were brought to trial, and at least one or two of them went to jail for using the US postal service in some of their dealings. We got all our money back, and the Florida bank ended up getting money back too. We were grateful for the successful outcome.

Adventures in Paradise

By the mid 1980s, with a steady, profitable flightseeing business, we began looking for a way to extend our flying season, since few visitors come to the Grand Canyon during the winter. We decided that Hawaii might hold the key to our solution.

We learned that the Hawaiian Islands have innumerable hidden places of beauty, many of them impossible to experience without wings. This South Pacific paradise, with its volcanoes, jungles, and vast, untouched shorelines, has literally hundreds of sights that people would remember for a lifetime if they just had a chance to experience them.

Kauai

On the island of Kauai, we found a helicopter touring firm that needed an infusion of capital and fresh ideas to upgrade its facilities at Princeville.

I especially liked the name of this going concern, Papillon, the French word for butterfly. A butterfly is light. It flits around here and there like a helicopter is able to do. The word itself is endowed with intrigue and is one that people remember. Our established touring company was named Grand Canyon Helicopters, but after the Hawaiian purchase, we changed our trade name to operate as Papillon Hawaiian Helicopters in Hawaii and Papillon Grand Canyon Helicopters at the Grand Canyon.

Our first project was a major remodel of the terminal facility, which included adding a theater. We utilized some of the finest photographers in the nation to capture Hawaii's magic, and then video professional Gerry Gawne produced a fantastic multimedia show that we presented to our guests. The complimentary show gave visitors a preview and helped them interpret the visions of beauty they would see on their flight. As a result, our new Kauai Flight Center was very successful. We also brought new life to the business by providing brightly colored aircraft and buses.

Maui

Soon after we had the Kauai heliport operating successfully, we opted to develop a flightseeing location on the island of Maui. Kapalua was considered one of the most beautiful regions of the island. The company we acquired there was negotiating for a heliport on Pineapple Hill, overlooking Kapalua Golf Course, an incredibly attractive development. We succeeded in signing a five-year contract for the heliport. We developed a terminal building and invested in roads, curbs, gutters, and utilities.

Maui's heliport

The location, the professionalism of our operation, and the flightseeing trip itself developed into a financial home run for us. Guests told us they loved our location and found it easy to get to. Upon being airborne, they were astonished at the hidden miles of primitive Maui they'd never see from a resort or beach. As a result, we benefited from excellent word-of-mouth endorsements.

The Big Island

Our second acquisition (but the third island we operated from) was Hawaii Helicopters, a company operating four aircraft on the island of Hawaii. This was a nice opportunity for us to begin operations in the Big Island since there was already a book of trade that came with the acquisition. We succeeded in getting a location for a heliport on an abandoned airport at the intersection of State Highway 19 (Queen

Our terminal on the Island of Hawaii

Kaahumanu Highway) and the road to Waikoloa. I created a little tropical oasis heliport there. Everyone on the way to the mega resorts north of the airport had to drive past our heliport. We had good visibility from that road, business built up quite quickly, and it proved to be a very successful location for us.

Oahu

Many tourists don't realize that the island of Oahu is alive with rare and memorable jungles, bays, and tropical mountains. The island's bustling city of Honolulu and vast naval facilities give some people the impression that Oahu lacks the magic of the other islands. Not true. It has unique paradise locations of its own.

Oahu's beauty prompted us to purchase a long-established helicopter flightseeing firm based in Honolulu. The small but successful company owned rights to a heliport on Waikiki Beach itself, next to Hilton Hawaiian Village Hotel. The fact that the firm had operated from its beach site for years gave us a false sense of security about the location's future viability.

Copying our successful ideas at the revamped Kauai facility, we opened a center with a state-of-the-art flight-preview theater. But not long after our acquisition was complete, we had to give up the prime Waikiki location. The key factor was helicopter noise. Without that site, we came to learn that an Oahu flightseeing business was marginal, so we gave up operations on that island.

Blowing in the Wind

During the first week of September 1992, tourists on the island of Kauai were having a great time in the sun—golfing, swimming, surfing, boating, fishing, hiking, and more. No one had any reason to be concerned about a storm that had formed three days earlier, 1,700 miles southwest of Cabo San Lucas, Mexico.

The storm moved quickly across the Pacific Ocean until it grew to be a tropical depression on September 8. The next day it intensified into a hurricane. At that point, it was 450 miles southeast of Hilo, Hawaii. The National Weather Service acknowledged the hurricane but, according to their calculations and traditions, predicted it would miss the Hawaiian Islands and continue west.

However, El Niño was strong that year, and that weather phenomenon sometimes caused unusual things to happen. On September 10, the hurricane turned north and headed toward the island of Kauai. The National Weather Service issued a warning to the island only 24 hours before the storm struck.

As soon as we received the warning on the afternoon of September 10, we instructed our pilots to fly their aircraft to the islands of Oahu or Maui. We gave them permission to take along their families, at their own discretion.

As they were loading their families and personal belongings into the helicopters, the Princeville fire department came to the heliport because of a desperate situation. They said 72 hikers were at various points on the 11-mile-long Kalalau Trail, which is located along the cliffs of the famous Na Pali Coast. The hikers had to be rescued from imminent danger, and our helicopters were the only way they could be saved. But could we possibly find them all?

The pilots and the crew immediately unloaded the helicopters and dispatched them to the coastline. After several hours of searching, our crew found every one of the hikers, several of whom couldn't understand why they had to leave their backpacks behind and get into the aircraft. Some even became upset. But our pilots convinced them to abandon their belongings and get aboard.

By then the wind was gusting, and it was too late to evacuate the aircraft to another island. Menacing skies to the south were changing from dark gray to black as the fierce hurricane closed in on the shoreline.

Well in advance of the storm's arrival, authorities had realized that a Category 4 hurricane was headed in that direction, but they waited until 24 hours before landfall to issue a warning. That didn't give people enough time to obtain food and supplies, board up windows, or prepare for inevitable power outages.

Kent and I didn't wait around for an official warning. As soon as we learned the storm, named Hurricane Iniki, had turned toward Kauai, we went to a Seattle-area Home Depot and bought all the generators and Visqueen they had in stock. We immediately sent it via air cargo to Kauai.

Meanwhile, telephone lines hummed regularly between Maui (where Brenda was), Seattle (where I was), and Kauai, as we tried to determine the best course of action. We decided to have our crew move as many of our aircraft as possible inside the hanger. However, one helicopter was left over, so they took off its blades and tied it down to the taxiway.

Iniki landed the next morning. Waves grew larger each hour as winds registered up to 145 miles per hour with gusts to 175 miles per hour. All the phone lines went dead. Some 30,000 people had made it to shelters, but some of our employees were not among them. They huddled inside their homes, trembling and praying—or some went to be with friends so they could ride out the storm together. When exterior walls collapsed, many retreated to interior bathrooms they deemed to be safer, climbing into bathtubs and pulling mattresses on top of themselves as the houses' roofs blew off.

Wind, rain, and surf pounded the beach for hours like a fury from hell. The tide level rose four and a half to six feet above normal, with waves up to 35 feet high. The debris line was 800 feet from the shoreline, and everything in that area was totally destroyed, including 63 buildings. Across the entire island, some 5,000 homes were severely damaged, and 1,421 were totally destroyed.

Slammed by the powerful storm, the helicopter that had to be left outside our Kauai hanger spun around its tie-down until it broke loose and blew all around the airport—never tipping over, remarkably—as the wind changed direction many times. The employees reported that at first, the wind blew in primarily from the south. Then an eerie aura filled the dark atmosphere and everything became completely calm. As the eye of the storm passed over the island, the wind resumed its intensity, this time coming from the north.

The helicopter we had to leave outside ended up being damaged but was repairable. The rest of the helicopters, however, didn't fare so well. They were all destroyed when the hangar collapsed on top of them.

Amazingly, only seven people were killed in the storm, and about 100 were injured.

FEMA (Federal Emergency Management Agency) immediately shut down all air transportation to Kauai. Meanwhile, after Iniki had passed, many of the hikers we'd picked up were stranded at the heliport. Hungry and thirsty, they broke the glass on the heliport vending machines to get food and drink.

The next morning when Kent and I arrived in Oahu from Seattle, we got special permission from the FAA to fly a helicopter to our airport facilities at Princeville. When we arrived, the airport was perfectly empty of all debris. Everything had been blown clear. So, we requested FEMA to open the airport, explaining that we had a good, clean runway. However, they would not cooperate with us and kept the airport closed.

Many of the hikers we'd rescued did not have their medicines with them, and we had no food or drink to serve them. They were desperate to get food, shelter, and their medications. Fortunately, one of our employees was a ham radio operator, and he got in contact with some aviators on the Big Island (Hawaii) who had good twin-engine aircraft. They were willing to come to Kauai and take people to where they could get the proper help. Some hours later, based on the assurances of our people that the Princeville airport was in good condition, the aircraft owners flew in and landed without seeking permission from the FAA or FEMA. In doing so, they risked being disciplined.

Before the passengers got onboard, our manager took up a collection to pay for fuel and other costs. However, while helpful, it certainly didn't cover all the expenses the airplane owners incurred.

The hurricane's effects were felt for a long time on the island. Every leaf on every bush and tree had been stripped off. More than 25 percent of the telephone poles were down, most of them lying across roads. Buildings were destroyed, sheds swept away, and the windows of every hotel had been blown out. Some of the hotels took two years to open again; one remained shuttered permanently. It took repair personnel about a month and a half to restore electricity to about 60 percent of the homes, and up to four months for the rest of the homes to have power again. It was an extremely trying time for the residents of Kauai.

The generators we'd sent to Kauai before the storm, along with Visqueen to put over damaged roofs, eased the suffering of a lot of people during those difficult months.

A few weeks after the hikers' evacuation, the FAA charged Papillon Helicopters with a violation. They said we had illegally collected fares from people to fly on airplanes that weren't certified to fly passengers for hire. We explained the emergency situation, but it took about three months of persuasion before we were absolved of the violation.

After the disaster, we reflected how our decision to respond to the needs of those stranded hikers involved changing our plans to get all of our own aircraft off the island. I don't know how many would have died had we not rescued them. Changing our original plans cost us seven helicopters and a challenge from the FAA. To the best of my knowledge, the only formal thanks we ever received was a two-inch-long column in the local newspaper reporting that we had rescued the hikers.

However, a large photograph of our hangar collapsed on top of our helicopters made the front page of *USA Today*.

Would we respond the same way again? Of course!

Leaving Paradise

Eventually, we owned and operated 25 aircraft in our Hawaiian fleet, making us the largest flightseeing operation in the state. Nevertheless, trying to operate two growing flightseeing companies simultaneously—one in the Grand Canyon, another on various Hawaiian islands—turned into a real logistics problem for us. At the same time, I was also dealing with construction jobs in Alaska. So, when an excellent opportunity came along to sell our Hawaiian company, including all 25 of our aircraft, I agreed to the offer.

The operator who bought us had realized a fair amount of cash from a recent initial public stock offering. We took payment mostly in cash, along with some stock. However, in less than one year after the purchase, the parent company in Atlanta, Georgia, became insolvent and went through Chapter 7 liquidation. It had cross-collateralized all of the equipment from its Atlanta operation, together with the equipment from Hawaii, and it created an unbearable burden for the Hawaii operation. The operation continued for another year before it collapsed under the financial burden.

To this day I still believe Hawaii is a wonderful location. But at the time, we did the right thing by focusing our energies on the Grand Canyon. It had "grand growth" in front of it.

Our Grand Canyon terminal as it looked just before the new millennium.

20

ADVENTURES WITH SOVIETS, SILENCERS, STADIUMS, AND THE SEVEN SEAS

In 1991, I accepted an invitation from the Russian government to visit their Mil Design Bureau to meet the designers and discuss international helicopter operations, including a possible joint venture. This was a great opportunity, since I was very interested in their Mil Mi-26, the most powerful helicopter ever to have gone into production. It would lift up to 20 metric tons (44,093 pounds) and carry that load a distance of 150 miles. It was huge, with equally massive engines, more than 11,000 shp (shaft horsepower) each.

Disembarking from a Scandinavian Airlines plane, I entered Moscow's somewhat dark airport terminal. All the signs were in Russian, and I was totally confused. I got into what I thought was the correct line. I soon realized, however, that no English-speaking people were anywhere around me. I began to feel intimidated. Was it possible I'd gotten into the wrong line due to my zero ability to read Russian signs? Were the people standing in line with me all Russian citizens? Ahead of me I saw immigration and customs officers tearing everything apart in travelers' suitcases. My intimidation meter kicked up another notch.

But just then, a friendly smiling Russian in front of me in line asked in broken English, "What color passport you have?" I showed him my US passport.

He said, "Good passport," held up his Russian one, and added, "Not good passport." Then he asked why I was in that line. I told him. My new Russian friend kindly explained I was standing in the wrong line. By now, all the people in the line I should have been in had already been processed and were gone. The officials who had processed them had left too.

My friend asked those ahead of us if I could go to the front of the line, explaining, "He's been here a long time." Once I was at the front, he assured me, "You'll go through easily." And I did.

The customs man, who spoke English, was about to sign my paper when he asked, "Can I borrow your pen?"

I thought it strange he didn't seem to have his own pen, but I replied, "Sure," and handed him a gold-filled Cross pen from an $80 pen/pencil set. The customs officer finished his note and placed my pen on the table. I picked it up and put it back in my pocket. Little did I guess the trouble that pen would be to me later.

Once out of customs, I spotted the person that the Mil Design Bureau had sent to pick me up, and from that point on, I enjoyed red-carpet treatment. That first night, my hosts took me to the legendary Moscow Circus, a performance alive with incredible acrobats and artists. I felt sure I was the only American in the place. The next day they assigned a female guide to accompany me on my sightseeing during my free time. She took me everywhere. In fact, she stuck so close, I began to suspect that her real employer was the KGB!

The next day, after my initial meeting at Russia's Mil Design Bureau, I again had opportunity to explore amazing Moscow. I could not help but notice how Communism had utterly failed to work. While Moscow had some beautiful areas, many buildings were visibly falling apart. The roads were especially bad. I saw no flowers at all, grassy areas were never mowed, and the parks, marred by litter, were unkempt.

At every turn in my tour, I noticed many cultural differences, as exhibited by the Russian women. The young ones were gorgeous. The older ones, having had a lifetime of poor nutrition, looked as if they'd been sentenced years before to hard labor. In truth, as far as I could see, the older women were doing all the hard work.

In sharp contrast to the poorly built and ill-maintained buildings, Russia's modern, nicely finished military equipment was first-rate. I also noticed that the computers and testing equipment at Mil Design Bureau's test facilities were at least a generation behind what Bell Helicopter and Sikorsky were then using in the US.

That night, my hosts took me to an almost-hidden casino. We had to go through several doors to get in. Casinos were totally new in Russian life and, I understand, were not approved at that time.

My final tour through the Mil Design Bureau was fascinating. My hosts hoped to persuade me to help them introduce their Mil Mi-26 helicopter to the West. That machine was easy for me to endorse. As the largest helicopter in the world, it was truly remarkable.

During my week-long stay, a group of Design Bureau engineers invited me to lunch. They started the meal by putting a bottle of vodka on the table. I realized they likely wouldn't go back to work until that bottle was empty. I had no affection for vodka, but I was trying to be a friendly guest. However, after just a couple of shots over lunch, I asked to be taken back to my hotel. How they could go back to work was beyond me!

Shortly before my trip, hard-line members of the Communist Party, who opposed Soviet president Mikhail Gorbachev's reform program, had attempted a coup on August 18, 1991. Gorbachev was held in Crimea while Russian president Boris Yeltsin raced to Russia's equivalent of the White House in Moscow to defy the coup. Yeltsin had climbed to the top of a tank turret where he made a memorable speech. Military troops surrounded the area, but they backed down in the face of mass popular demonstrations. Although the coup collapsed in only two days and Gorbachev returned to office, the event is widely regarded as the beginning of the end for the Soviet Union. Before the month was over, the Communist Party of the Soviet Union had effectively disintegrated, and within four months, the Soviet Union itself would be no more.

I was thrilled at the opportunity to have a firsthand look at this huge Union in the throes of breaking up. The disintegration of the Soviet Union had actually begun in the Baltic region in 1987, followed by nationalist movements in the southern region and Central Asian republics. Everywhere I looked, I saw signs of how the power of the central government had been considerably weakened by these movements. But the closest the anti-Communist revolution came to me was when my gracious host took me to the airport for my flight home, and on the way, we passed by the building where Yeltsin had climbed up on a tank and made his speech.

At the airport, I told my host that he could leave and I could just wait there until they opened up the immigration kiosk. But he said emphatically, "No, I *can't* leave you." That made me a bit nervous. And, in fact, he didn't leave until after I walked through the gate to Immigration. The memory of that scene is still vivid in my mind, since the kiosk was guarded by two soldiers, each holding a submachine gun.

I was directed to the enclosed kiosk, where I handed the agent my passport. After thumbing through my passport, the agent looked up and asked, "Can I borrow your pen?"

I thought, *How strange, none of these guys ever have pens.* But aloud I said, "Sure," and handed over my Cross pen. He accepted the pen and did paperwork under the kiosk counter where I could not see his hands. Minutes later, the agent finished checking me in and handed back my passport—*without* my pen. Instantly, I recognized what game the immigration officers were trying to play, and it made me so angry, I decided to confront him, though I wasn't sure it was smart to do so.

I said loudly, "Would you give me my pen?"

He replied, "I don't have your pen."

That made me even angrier. In an even louder voice, I said, "Yes, *you do* have my pen, and I am not leaving here until I get it back."

The agent played with me for a little bit but ultimately returned my pen. At that moment, I realized the risk I had just taken. Could this guy have become irritated enough to stop me from getting on my flight?

My heartbeat sped up, and I got increasingly nervous. I was waiting by the gate all alone. No other passengers were around. I began imagining newspaper stories back home, such as "Disorderly Seattle Man Arrested for Pen Fracas at Moscow Airport, Sentenced to a Year in Siberia." All over a dumb pen!

Finally, another passenger showed up, and eventually the gate opened for the two of us to board the Scandinavian Airlines flight leaving Moscow. I was so pleased to get out of there, I could have kissed the stewardesses or even the floor of that jet!

That August, Mikhail Gorbachev came home from Crimea, and Elling Halvorson came home from Russia. Both were grateful to have avoided any harm.

Whispers of Success

Anyone who works around helicopters for very long recognizes that the noise created is a distraction to many people. In fact, it was the complaints of just one local resident that forced us to shut down our key helicopter site near Waikiki Beach.

I understood the noise complaints. For years I had felt that noise was the helicopter's Achilles heel. Working for decades in the Grand Canyon, a pristine area that is super-sensitive to unnatural sounds, caused me to be very conscious about the noise issue. It is also a major concern not only for the National Park Service but also for environmental groups and most cities worldwide.

In an effort to improve our industry, I took on the sound issue as a personal cause. When I was a keynote speaker at a Bell Helicopter marketing seminar in Dallas in the mid 1980s, I talked about designing a quiet helicopter. I addressed what could and should be done, how important such a development was to the industry, and how we needed to recognize that noise was a hazard to our industry's success.

At the end of my speech, engineers came up to me and said, "Elling, what you're talking about is a pipe dream. It can't be done. It would cost too much, and you'd have to sacrifice too much in performance." Sales people, however, patted me on the back, shook my hand, and said, "Elling, you're exactly on target. What we need is quiet technology."

At many of the international helicopter industry events attended by virtually everyone in the field, I was always trying to convince the manufacturers of the many benefits of quiet helicopters, but I couldn't get any of them interested in the idea.

Since my speeches from the podium failed to interest anyone, I wondered if face-to-face contact might let me get the quiet-technology messages across. In 1989 I went on a world-circling journey to sit down with executives at virtually all the helicopter manufacturers in the United States and Europe. At those appointments, I tried my best to convince each manufacturer to adopt quiet helicopter technologies.

Since I had served twice as chairman of the Helicopter Association International, I knew that these aviation businessmen and scientists were not ignorant or stubborn people. As helicopter designers and builders, they first had to respond to their customers, both military and civilian, who typically wanted new machines with more lifting power or with greater flight range or with lower operating costs. Although all of those goals could be achieved with quiet technology, no one wanted to try. So, as before, I struck out.

Making Quiet Technology a Personal Mission

After getting what amounted to 100 percent industry rejection, my Viking stubbornness kicked into gear. I told myself, "I know I can find ways to reduce much of the helicopter noise. I'll build a quiet helicopter myself if it comes to that."

My early training in principles such as "No job is too big; it's just that the tools are too small" made the engineering challenges of developing noise-reduction technologies irresistible to me. So, I decided I would personally build the world's first helicopter with quiet technology. That vow of "I'll show them" cost me $5 million per word, since it took some $15 million out of my pocket and a dozen years of frustration to achieve my goal.

In 1990, I started on my mission by searching for an older production helicopter that already had a fairly soft noise footprint. I soon zeroed in on the famed Sikorsky H-19 Chickasaw, also known by its Sikorsky model number, S-55. The Sikorsky was a popular proven machine in its time, used by the United States Army, Air Force, Navy, Coast Guard, and Marines, as well as by private industry operations.

I then sat down with my friend and fellow industry executive, Fred Clark, who owned Orlando Helicopter Airways. Fred had built up a fleet of the S-55 Sikorsky models, and, after the S-55 went out of production, he'd wisely purchased most of the available S-55 surplus parts and materials. Fred and I agreed to partner in my quest for quiet flying.

We decided to utilize the hot new Lycoming LTS-101 engine that had a combining gearbox. We also planned some radical changes to the airframe itself. But just as we were set to begin, some early failures of the new engine caused Lycoming's factory output to be canceled. That meant we had no engine to work with on our project.

Our first step failed before it even began. Fred gave up on my program. But I couldn't give up. After all, someone had to show the industry that quiet-technology machines could be designed and manufactured with no loss in performance.

To be able to go forward, I negotiated the purchase of Fred Clark's entire fleet of S-55 Sikorsky helicopters. Of course, I knew that at least a year of difficult engineering was needed before we would be ready to build. I began looking for the best engineers I could find for this unprecedented project. I got lucky right out of the chute by being able to hire Ralph Alex, the very engineer who originally designed the S-55 Sikorsky helicopter itself!

I was pumped. Hiring Ralph was a coup! We began our work by recognizing that I could reduce the helicopter's noise footprint by adding two more blades and reducing the rotor RPM. That would accomplish several things:

1. It would reduce the tip speed of the rotor, which approaches the speed of sound in many helicopters.
2. The helicopter could fly with less pitch in the blades, thus producing less disturbed air behind the advancing blade, which would in turn reduce slap from the following blade.

3. With the addition of two main rotor blades, and by installing a larger, more powerful engine, we could improve the aircraft's performance instead of sacrificing any. In fact, the modification would also improve useful load, high-altitude performance, and air-speed performance.

However, the engine we had to work with was not adequate for five blades. So, instead of using the engine that came with the Sikorsky S-55—with just 600 horsepower—we installed a much more powerful engine, the Honeywell TPE331-10, rated at 1,000 horsepower.

Tackling the Acoustics

More engine power meant more noise, of course, and that Honeywell engine was an absolute screamer. But I had a plan. I brought in an outstanding acoustic engineer, John L. Alberti of J R Engineering. We measured the sound frequencies of both the intake and the exhaust of the turbine engine. Then John and I built a silencer intake plenum on the front of the engine using passive noise cancellation built on the knowledge that *high-frequency sound cannot bend*. We also built a special exhaust muffler for the low frequencies.[14]

I'm pleased to say that our efforts met with success. Today you can actually stand next to a modified helicopter while it's running and have a normal conversation with someone.

We did one other thing that one of the planet's largest aircraft builders, Airbus (formerly Eurocopter), has done now in their EC130. We certified it under two rotor speeds—one for takeoff and maneuvering, and one for cruising. We included a silent mode where we slowed the system down.

As for the speed capability, the helicopter could lift its full gross load to 14,000 feet—and still does to this day. Being an S-55, it was originally certified to 100 knots, and the pilot had to reduce air speed by about 3

[14] See Appendix B: "Developing Whisper Jet Technology" for more detail on how we accomplished our audacious goal.

percent for every 1,000 feet of altitude. We didn't change the 100 knots, but we are now approved to fly the 100-knot speed at all altitudes. It will fly a lot faster than that because it always has a rotor blade in the critical quadrant of the rotor plane. The aircraft is now capable of increasing speed to around 120 knots.

Soon after we certified the modified aircraft, NASA agreed to test our new quiet technology over the course of an entire day, making dozens and dozens of runs in every configuration. They determined it was the quietest helicopter ever built. I felt vindicated. *That designation made our helicopter the only one in the world with quiet technology.*

The distinction prompted me to come up with a trademarked name for our bird: the Whisper Jet. In 1993, I founded Whisper Jet Inc.

After that NASA report, I displayed the World's Quietest Helicopter at the Helicopter Association International's HELI-EXPO, the world's largest helicopter trade show and exposition. At that time, the annual event typically drew 15,000 people from around the world. I had the helicopter on display for about four conventions in a row. The aircraft looked marvelous, and I wanted people to be able to see it up close. Many came up to our display, asked questions, saw the NASA report, and applauded what we were achieving.

One engineer from a major helicopter manufacturer told me, "I'm ashamed, Elling, that you had to do this when we, as a major manufacturer, should have been the leader in this."

Hovering to Get Attention

At one HELI-EXPO in Las Vegas, I hovered a Whisper Jet over the entrance to the exhibit hall for almost an hour at 500 feet. Most of the convention attendees below never noticed since there was no loud sound to catch their attention. Ultimately, though, some people looked up and were amazed to see the hovering helicopter. They began pointing upward, capturing everyone's attention. The industry people were astounded. They could see our Whisper Jet hovering in flight, but they could barely hear the lower level of sound that people coming in and out of the convention center didn't even notice.

I repeated this popular stunt with our new Whisper Jet in various places around the country, gradually building both awareness and understanding about how practical and affordable quiet helicopters could be.

One of the most personally satisfying phone calls of my life came from Eurocopter. They had become convinced of the need to incorporate into their future some helicopters with the same technology used in the Whisper Jet. What's more, they asked if I would join a group of other fleet operators to review and make suggestions on their proposed designs for a to-tally new, quieter machine.

I enthusiastically supported their plan. After years of being a one-man band, I now had top people in our industry who also believed that quiet technology helicopters were practical and affordable. I assured them I'd participate. I also congratulated them on their perspicacity.

Soon, Eurocopter brought together a number of helicopter fleet operators in the scenic-tour business. At their factory in Toulouse, France, they took us step by step through the initial designs for their quiet-technology craft. The group of operators—none of them shy—also gave Euro-copter's staff input on everything about the proposed helicopter, including the lift, the passenger's viewing ability, and more.

The result of our collaboration with Eurocopter resulted in the successful introduction of a new design called the *Eurocopter 130*. It's a derivative of the AS350 B3 series helicopter and was substantially quieter than any other helicopter in the marketplace.

I had challenged manufacturers to begin providing quieter helicopters, to add space in the cabin area for passenger comfort, and to reduce internal noise. Those three things are very important to an operator. I'm glad to see that Eurocopter/Airbus has taken some steps in the right direction, and there are a number of things they could do to continue improvement.

A Whisper Jet glides quietly over downtown Las Vegas.

I was pleased that my stubborn approach to developing quiet technology on my own led ultimately to the production of new, quieter machines. All the effort and finances I invested are changing the entire field of helicopter flight. It may even have influenced one of the most successful sneak attacks the USA ever conducted. Noiseless stealth helicopters were used in the raid on Osama Bin Laden's hideout in Pakistan. Yet, I know from hands-on experience that still more acoustic improvements and advances can be made. I guarantee it!

Detoured by a Delinquent Dirigible

Not all my ventures have turned out as well as the Whisper Jet, of course. Earlier in my quest to conquer the issue of helicopter noise, I researched airship capabilities, even traveling to an East Coast manufacturing plant to spend the day examining and flying a blimp myself.

A few years later, I was approached by Grant Murray, who was president of Scenic Airlines at one point before Papillon bought it. Murray was looking for investors for his new blimp company, Airship USA. All he had at the time was a concept, so I declined.

Murray kept going forward. When he called me again, he'd connected with Igor Pasternak, a Russian immigrant who had an idea for a digitally controlled dual ballonet airship. Eventually, with 20 employees and a shoestring budget, Pasternak's Worldwide Aeros Corporation out of Chatsworth, California, would develop a 143-foot, five-seat ship, called the Aeros 40B. Most blimps used cables to maneuver; Pasternak's ship featured a pneumatic system that could be operated with a joystick, cutting pilot fatigue.

When he contacted Murray, it was to sell him on the idea of using blimps for scenic tours over the Grand Canyon. But the advertising potential is what really caught Murray's attention. Banners attached to the blimp's exterior turned the airship into a flying billboard. After sundown, interior lighting transformed the craft into a glowing message in the night sky. Intrigued, Murray looked for advertisers and investors.

Since there was now a firm price for the airship, along with complete drawings and other specifications, I considered the proposal more seriously. The design was certainly unique. Strips of Velcro held together sections that, in an emergency, could be pulled apart with ropes to allow gas to escape, giving the pilot a measure of manual control.

Grant Murray anticipated maximizing the advertising potential by getting mentioned on sports telecasts when cameras were mounted to the blimp. "You can't not look at a blimp," he assured me. "People love them when they see them because they're so graceful. They just float there."

Murray already had potential advertisers lined up, so I told Kent, Lon, and Brenda about the investment opportunity. The longer we thought about it, the more excited we became. Our blimp would be seen by thousands—maybe millions!—at huge events and on TV.

By this time, Pasternak's creation had passed all its test flights, received FAA certification, and looked great, so we decided to go into the blimp business. We procured a bank loan to make it happen.

AWOL Airship

Our first advertising contract was to fly over the Sun Bowl football game in Phoenix on December 29, 2000, where Wisconsin and UCLA squared off in front of 49,093 fans. It was the seventh largest crowd in Sun Bowl history.

Unfortunately, no one there saw our blimp. A necessary repair had been delayed, making the airship unavailable, and we were forced to default on the contract. That should have been our first clue. But we were committed.

Our second contract was with the brand-new XFL football league, a joint venture between Vince McMahon's World Wrestling Federation (now the WWE) and NBC. The XFL promised exciting games because its league would have fewer rules than other major leagues and would also encourage rougher play. Their telecasts would feature extensive usage of aerial skycams, and players would wear microphones to provide additional perspectives.

Everything went according to schedule at the AFC playoff game in Oakland on Saturday, January 6, 2001, between the Oakland Raiders and Miami Dolphins. We were pumped. Vast numbers of people saw our blimp, emblazoned on the side with the name "XFL," along with "Spaulding," the XFL's first official licensee. We could hardly wait until the following Tuesday's AFC championship game, also in Oakland.

As scheduled, our blimp flew over the crowd again at the Oakland Coliseum stadium. But then, things started to go wrong. Black clouds headed in our direction, and the FAA warned that a tremendous storm was approaching. The blimp's pilot and copilot turned the ship around and flew back toward the airport, where a crew awaited with a truck and tether lines.

But before the blimp could complete the short, two-mile journey, it was hit full force by the storm. Water entered the control panel, rendering the ship's rudder and elevators useless.

Somehow, the blimp managed to touch down on the airfield, but in the hard landing, it damaged a couple of airplanes, along with the propellers on its own engines. Before the ground crew had a chance to tether the craft, it started to lift off again.

Emergency time! The pilot reached out one window of the gondola, his copilot reached out the other, and they started yanking on the ropes to release enough gas to land again.

Nothing happened. The blimp continued to rise. The pilot gave the order to crawl out the windows and use their full body weight as they dangled from the ropes. Still nothing. When they were about 13 feet in the air, the pilot yelled, "Jump!" Both men let go and dropped to the ground.

Everyone stood by helplessly as the errant albatross took off on its own, heading toward the coliseum and continuing north, at one point reaching an altitude of 1,600 feet. Eventually, enough gas escaped through a hole in the bottom to allow the craft to slowly descend. But where would it land? No one knew. For 20 minutes, wind pushed the pilotless airship on a zigzag path along the shoreline and over the bay.

Our blimp advertising venture snagged publicity we weren't looking for.

Of course, by now we no longer wanted the blimp to capture anyone's attention. We wanted memory of it to fade into oblivion. But that was not to be.

The airport control tower had called 911, and news of the disaster sizzled over radio frequencies. As fire engines, law enforcement, and our crew scrambled like Keystone Cops after the flying fugitive, disk jockeys gave the blimp more airtime than we ever imagined possible.

First responders raced from one anticipated landing point to another as the wayward airship led them on a merry chase all the way to the Central Basin marina, some five miles north of the airport. Eventually, the blimp's gondola caught on the mast of a moored sailboat. The deflating envelope sagged over the boat, the Oyster Reef restaurant next to it, and a nearby power line.

When first responders arrived, adrenalin pumping hard, they attacked the hapless escapee with axes to ensure it stayed on the ground. Fortunately, the pilots, sailboat, and restaurant suffered only minor injuries. The blimp, however, needed $2.5 million in repairs.

The XFL didn't do so well, either. NBC and the WWF both lost $35 million on their $100 million investment in the league's inaugural season. Vince McMahon conceded that the league was a "colossal failure." Many reports recapping the XFL's history included photos of our promotional blimp draped across the restaurant's roof. Reporters said that in retrospect, the debacle had been a bad omen for the league.

I'd be tempted to call it a bad omen for us Halvorson investors too, except that this particular detour taught us a valuable lesson. We realized we'd invested in the blimp for all the wrong reasons. Never again would we let our egos get involved in a business decision.

Something about having to repay the bank $1.5 million for a destroyed dirigible helps you remember lessons like that.

Halvorson's Navy

You wouldn't know it from most of my life's adventures, but the truth is, I'm crazy about boats and boating. Back in the sixties, I built a speedboat at home that was powered by a 35-horsepower Mercury outboard motor. We had many great family times boating, fishing, and water skiing on the saltwater of Puget Sound. Kent remembers one of those times like it was yesterday:

> That speedboat ran like crazy. For us kids it was the most exciting machine in the universe. It flew! There was lots of waterskiing. And great trips. We'd start out from Redondo Beach Marina on a fishing expedition with Dad and his buddies. The day began by all of us getting up super-early. Next we'd get a big thermos full of hot cocoa, enough for five kids.
>
> With everyone on board, we'd head out toward Vashon Island. The boat was not only fast, but it also had high sides

on it, making it especially good on the Puget Sound where you can often run into choppy water.

Then, after Dad and his buddies consulted the fishing oracles about the best spot, we'd drop anchor there, pull out some cocoa, add a few marshmallows, and enjoy. We kids were in paradise, especially since Dad would often get us onto a beach at Vashon Island. I felt we were Tom Sawyer and his clan out there. We always collected driftwood and shells and never tired of skipping rocks over the water. Those were great family times.

We enjoyed those outings so much that some years later I purchased our first factory-made boat. It was a Cruise-A-Home houseboat, and it had much more power and speed than a typical houseboat. In many ways it was a perfect choice for touring the ports, villages, and dozens of islands that Puget Sound offers.

But one day something took place on board that, by a strange coincidence, Barbara heard about while it was still in progress, upsetting her greatly. She'd happened to tune in to a local radio station for her listening pleasure. At that moment, an "eye in the sky" reporter over Puget Sound was reporting on a houseboat fire. Barbara's instinct told her immediately that the houseboat was our family's newest vessel, no doubt skippered by a Norwegian/Swede she knew well.

She was right. It was our boat. When the alarm went off in the engine room, everyone scampered like crazy to put on lifejackets and get the dinghy overboard. Our foremost effort was to get our guests into the dinghy. Kent and I stayed behind, grabbed fire extinguishers, and did our best to put out the blaze. As I look back, I don't think we used good judgment in staying on board. We would probably have been better off to have climbed into the dinghy and left the boat to drift. However, it turned out all right. Several other boats approached us, and from their bows, handed us extra fire extinguishers. We were successful in putting out the flames, and then we drifted until a marine rescue boat arrived and towed us into port.

The fire provided me with one of the rarest excuses a husband could get in an entire lifetime. Keeping a straight face, I could say to my loving wife, "We've learned a lesson, Hon. For our own safety, we need to get a newer, bigger, longer, wider, faster, safer boat than the one we had before. After all, we need to make sure the kids stay safe, don't we?"

The 57-foot Bayliner yacht we purchased next proved to be perfect for cruising the waters of the In-side Passage each summer with friends and family, including Dean and Phyllis Vettrus. This coastal route—from northwestern Washington State, along western British Columbia, and on up to south-eastern Alaska—is the most popular cruise-ship path on the planet.

One of our friends, Cathy Boshaw, tells about some teasing I had to endure during those cruises:

> My husband and I have been longtime friends of Elling and Barbara, and we also had a modest yacht, so our families sometimes sailed together. Barbara's sister, Kay, and brother-in-law, Irv, often sailed on the Halvorsons' yacht with Barbara and Elling.
>
> Eventually, our voyages resulted in Elling losing his given name because we renamed him Captain Let's. He earned that nickname by always suggesting things for us to do—"Let's do this, Cathy" and "Let's do that, Doug!" Typically, Elling spoke these suggestions over a bowl of cereal in the morning, and everybody would say, "Oh Lord, what is it today?"
>
> But to Elling, nothing was too big a deal, and he always replied that his idea was going to be fun. It didn't matter what anybody else thought. He just dragged us along with his enthusiasm. Even when we'd rather lie in bed and read a smutty book, it didn't matter. Thanks to Captain Let's, none of us would be doing that.

One of his "let's do it" items involved traversing over a melting glacier. But fortunately for me, I threw my back out and thanks to my husband, Captain Pharmaceutical, I was comatose a lot!

The glacier incident took place in 2005, the year we were all at Glacier Bay National Park near Juneau, Alaska. In fact, that yacht cruise turned out to be one of our last in our Bayliner.

My love of boating is why, when I attended a 1972 charity auction in

We really enjoyed our "newer, bigger, longer, wider, faster, safer" Bayliner yacht after the houseboat caught fire.

Seattle, I jumped with gusto on one particular auction item. It was a day cruise on a nuclear-powered aircraft carrier. I bid with such determination, everyone else was scared off. In fact, the amount I bid scared even me. Still, it was worth every penny.

Barbara and I decided to invite Kay and Irv to go with us on the day cruise. On the way home that Saturday, about 11:30 PM my time, I called them on my cellphone. Irv sleepily answered at his home in Minneapolis, where it was 1:30 AM. I said, "Can you two be at Pier 19 in Oakland, California, at 7:30 next Friday morning?"

Irv replied, "Absolutely. We will be there, no problem. By the way, *why* do you want us there?"

I said, "We'll board the USS *Abraham Lincoln* and ride the carrier out into the Pacific Ocean. It's an experience you won't regret!"

Barbara and I met Kay and Irv at an Oakland hotel on Thursday evening, and the next morning we were treated to one of the most remarkable adventures of our lives. The USS *Abraham Lincoln* is the fifth

Nimitz-class aircraft carrier in the United States Navy. Its four propeller shafts, driven by two pressurized water reactors, allow the ship to roar through the water at more than 30 knots per hour. The ship is capable of operating for 20 to 25 years without refueling. But one of the most amazing things to me was the ship's crew: 3,200 seamen and 2,500 airmen, for a total of 5,700 crew members.

As we headed out to sea on our 13-hour cruise, we went under the Oakland Bay Bridge and then the Golden Gate Bridge, enjoying the beautiful sights. About an hour later, the show began. Airplanes were continuously taking off and landing during the afternoon, displaying all forms of flight—propeller-driven aircraft, jet aircraft, helicopters. We witnessed emergency demonstrations of all sorts.

On our tour, the entire ship was open to us everywhere except the atomic-reactor area. We enjoyed meals and snacks with the skipper and our tour guide Cmdr. Stevens. That day on the USS *Abraham Lincoln* enhanced our admiration for our US Navy, Marines, and all US military services. We were proud to be Americans.

Bigger and Better Boats

After cruising for 25 years and owning three different boats—a 40-foot yacht, 45-foot yacht, and a 57-foot yacht—we finally came to the realization that we needed to get a still-larger boat. I was finding it a little more difficult to get around in the engine room and make repairs. Maintenance and cleanliness of a boat's interior and exterior are always necessary, as well as repairs to the water system, the generator system, the toilet system, the engine, the batteries, etc.

We decided the minimum we needed was an 85-foot boat to have adequate quarters for two crew members. However, Barbara and I came to an impasse concerning the type of crew we needed. Barbara wanted a cook and a hairdresser. I wanted a deckhand and masseuse. Since we couldn't agree, we decided to sell the boat and be landlubbers once again.

In the early nineties I was attending another charity auction where one of the items up for bid was the opportunity to spend a day on a nuclear-powered submarine. Again I stepped up with a strong-enough bid to allow me, along with five others, to spend a day aboard the most powerful submarine and weapons system in the world's oceans. Getting security clearances and background checks took a long time, but eventually the day arrived for our adventure.

This Ohio-class nuclear submarine was one of a fleet of six nuclear-powered subs that roamed the Pacific Ocean. It had 24 missile tubes and employed the Trident missile with independently targeted multiple warheads. The skipper told us that this submarine alone had more firepower than all of the explosions used in battle since the origination of gunpowder.

The sub also featured four torpedo tubes equipped with a number of Mark 48 torpedoes. While we were aboard, the crew did a simulation exercise of firing torpedoes. It was quite interesting. The torpedoes were fired with compressed air, and such a surge of compressed air left the submarine's hull that a wave of frigid air filled the torpedo room. We also experienced crash dives, used the periscope, and climbed the conning tower. Most of the day was spent underwater. Since this was not long after the end of the Cold War, we did a simulated attack on Russia.

One of the most rewarding experiences during this submarine cruise was to be with the crew. There were 140 enlisted men and 15 officers on the ship. These men were underwater continuously for two and a half months as the ship roamed the Pacific Ocean. During each trip, no one was fully aware where they were located. Even the president of the United States could not be informed as to their whereabouts. At any time in the Pacific Ocean, five of these submarines are roaming the seas, surreptitiously waiting for the emergency that everyone dreads. There is likewise a fleet of six nuclear-powered subs roaming the Atlantic Ocean. After being at sea for 77 days, each submarine spends 35 days in port for maintenance and refurbishing. Every 15 years the submarines are refueled and overhauled.

From surviving Russia to quieting helicopters to dodging blimps to taking many sea excursions, my life has continued to be blessed with exciting adventures. But I also believe in sharing with others the abundance that I've been privileged to receive.

PART V: GIVING BACK

✦ ✦ ✦ ✦ ✦

21
THE PRINCIPLE OF COMPENSATION

As I've said before, my entire life has been guided by the principle that there is a solution to virtually any problem. My parents and siblings continually modeled for me that the secret was simply to keep working until I found the answer.

Armed with that belief, I was able to detour around every obstacle . . . until the end of 1965 when I lay in the hospital, barely hanging onto life after the devastating helicopter crash. I struggled to understand what was happening to me. Everything seemed to be going sour.

I mentally reviewed the downhill slide that had begun the year before when my youngest sons were diagnosed with a terminal disease and not expected to live past their teens. I thought about our construction jobs that were losing money because I had been spending all my time on the Grand Canyon project. In my mind's eye, I could see all the uninsured equipment that had been destroyed in the catastrophic flood. Now unpaid bills stared me in the face, and I was physically broken. I simply couldn't understand how God could have let all of these reverses happen to me. Perplexed, I went to the Lord in prayer.

Later, I would learn that prayer was going up for me all over the United States. A few of my former classmates at Hillcrest Academy had found out about my accident, and they contacted other classmates, who contacted still more people. Prayer meetings were being held in Seattle, in Minnesota, and in many other places across the nation.

Soon I started receiving get-well cards from people telling me of their prayers and best wishes. So much mail poured in, it filled a large shopping bag and made me wonder if the crash had been on national news. It was humbling—and encouraging.

As I heard about prayer group after prayer group interceding for my recovery, my spirits rose. Not just two or three groups, but as the weeks stretched on, it seemed there were hundreds of such groups. And I could feel their prayers. When I recuperated enough to be able to sit up and read, I opened the pile of mail. The outpouring of concern and affection buoyed my spirits.

One envelope was from a woman I'd known when I was young. I'd even had a bit of a crush on her at one point, although we'd never dated. She wrote me a nice letter and included a card that meant so much to me, that today, many decades later, it is still framed on a wall in my home. The card contained this poem:

Compensation

Who never wept knows laughter but a jest;
Who never failed, no victory has sought;
Who never suffered, never lived his best;
Who never doubted, never really thought;
Who never feared, real courage has not shown;
Who never faltered, lacks a real intent;
Whose soul was never troubled has not known
The sweetness and the peace of real content.

— E. M. Brainard[15]

A decade after I received the card, I again met the schoolmate who'd mailed it to me. I thanked her for that thoughtful kindness as I explained how deeply the poem had touched me. It contained many truths about life and the struggles I was going through. It reminded me of the good that can come out of adversity. It was also a reminder that if you don't

---

[15] E. M. Brainard, "Compensation," in *Poems That Touch the Heart*, ed. A. L. Alexander (New York: Doubleday, 1956), 292.

show initiative and strive to master challenges, you are not really living. If you don't push yourself—don't stretch yourself, don't take risks—you *shrink.*

Each line of the poem contained a powerful insight that I meditated on during my recovery.

Who never wept knows laughter but a jest. You have to weep before you can truly understand laughter.

Who never failed, no victory has sought. I had certainly failed—a number of times.

Who never suffered, never lived his best. Until you've really suffered, you just can't appreciate good life.

Who never doubted, never really thought. I was in a time of doubting and wondering. "What have I done, God? What are you doing? Why are you letting this happen? Everything in my life has turned to sour apples."

Who never feared, real courage has not shown. I was wrapped in the heaviest blanket of fear anyone could know. I feared I would die or be paralyzed or handicapped in some way. My children needed a father and good financial support. I feared the unreasonable pressures my wife would have to bear trying to raise five children, two of whom had significant challenges. Our completed Grand Canyon project was now damaged and in disarray, cluttered by tangles of aluminum pipe across a worksite that no longer existed, all caused by an act of God. I feared what would happen next.

Who never faltered, lacks a real intent. Reading this helped me realize that the pursuit of achieving certain goals naturally comes with risks. And the bigger the goals, the greater the risks. Again and again, I had undertaken many significant projects. The fact that I was faltering now was, in effect, proof that I had real intent in life. That realization brought me a measure of comfort.

Whose soul was never troubled, has not known / The sweetness and the peace of real content. Yes, my soul was troubled—almost indescribably so. But at the same time, I had faith, and I realized that I had to rely on my faith if I were to come to enjoy the sweet peace of real contentment.

Pondering these things reminded me there was a purpose behind what I was going through. God had a reason for keeping me alive. And that the number-one reason was my family—Barbara and our five young children.

My troubles weren't over immediately. I still had no income and was on State medical aid at that point. But it was about one month later when Marshall Miller, the Lloyd's of London adjuster, handed me that check for $100,000 so I could deal with the federal government out of a position of strength.

Some might believe all this was coincidence.

I believe it was the miracle of divine compensation.

Why would I be granted such favor? I believe part of the reason was because God knew I had the desire to bless others financially, once I was in the position to do so. In fact, I strongly believe that if a person is blessed with financial resources, he or she has a responsibility to give back to the community. Once I recovered my physical health and emotional strength, I gave back in an abundance of ways.[16]

One venture I devoted an entire year of my life to involved a fascinating exchange between the US and China.

Son of Heaven: Imperial Arts of China

In the mid-1980s, when I was serving as chairman of the Seattle Resource Center for the Handicapped, the center's president and executive director, Rich Walsh, approached me with an idea. He suggested that an exhibition of Chinese treasures could possibly produce revenue for our nonprofit association.

The idea captured my interest. I'd gained experience with exhibitions when my company designed and built a number of exhibition pavilions for the Seattle's World's Fair nearly 25 years earlier. And of course I was in favor of generating revenue for the center.

Arrangements were made for us to go to a hotel in Vancouver, British Columbia, Canada, and have dinner with Mr. Deng Pufang, founder of

---

[16] See Appendix E for a more complete list of charitable giving and service.

the China Welfare Fund for the Disabled. A couple of years later, he would initiate and become chairman of the China Disabled Persons Federation. His interest in assisting people with disabilities was a personal one. During the Cultural Revolution, Red Guards had thrown him out of a three-story window, leaving him a paraplegic.

Also included at the meeting was Mr. Zhang Deqin, Director of China's State Administrative Bureau of Museums and Archaeological Data, and Dr. Robert Thorp, the Chief American Curator and Associate Professor of Art History at Washington University in St. Louis. As an expert on Chinese culture and history, Dr. Thorp became an important part of our endeavor.

We went through all the formalities of meeting each other and socializing at dinner. Rich Walsh was sitting next to me, and recognizing that we were talking with a Communist (Deng Pufang), Rich asked me to put my ear to his mouth. When I did, he said, "Elling, ask him if he wears red underwear." I chuckled but didn't ask the question.

The more I learned about the story of China's emperors and their feudal predecessors and how they ruled China from the seventh century BC until the last emperor in 1911, the more my enthusiasm for this project gained momentum.

A trip to China was arranged in early 1985 so that the newly formed Son of Heaven National Committee could meet with representatives of China's Ministry of Culture and discuss a possible exhibition tour. United Airlines provided complimentary air transportation, and it turned out to be an amazing trip.

We were taken to Tiananmen Square and the Forbidden City and shown all of the back rooms and treasured tombs in the very inner sanctum. At the end of our tour, we were invited to partake in a feast hosted by Deng Pufang himself in the Great Hall of the People, the venue for China's parliament. Also in attendance were representatives of the Chinese Overseas Archaeological Exhibition Corporation (COAEC). Because China was willing to send its national art treasures on tour for the first time in the nation's history, we agreed to work together to create an extraordinary exhibition in North America.

Our commitment was based on mutual respect, friendship, and professional enthusiasm for the potential good that would be generated by such a project. Because our goal was to reveal a true glimpse into the life of each "Son of Heaven" ruler—how he reigned, lived, worshiped, and prepared for his afterlife—we agreed to call the project Son of Heaven: Imperial Arts of China.

Harvey West was the executive director of the exhibition, I served as chairman, and Robert Thorp was the anchorman of the whole thing. He was fabulous. Over the next couple of years, I worked tirelessly to help make the event happen. I gave money to support the nonprofit organization, Son of Heaven, Inc., and I also worked with Rich in persuading many others to contribute.

For three and a half years, representatives from both countries worked with the curators of 21 Chinese museums and institutions from eight provinces and Beijing to contribute more than 200 art treasures, covering a period of 26 centuries, to represent China's imperial institution.

I was thrilled to see the exhibition capture so many hearts and minds. From July 28, 1988, to January 1989, some 600,000 Pacific Northwest residents patiently stood in long lines to see the once-in-a-lifetime event and catch a rare glimpse of national historic treasures.

To enhance each visitor's understanding and enjoyment, a multi-media slide show produced by Gerry Gawne offered a sweeping overview of China through the centuries.

After the Seattle exhibit, the art treasures traveled to Columbus, Ohio, for a nine-month exhibition that enjoyed an even greater attendance. Our next venue was to be Denver, Colorado, and we had already booked venues in Orlando, Wichita, Chicago, Washington DC, and a city in Canada. We were sailing along so well that proceeds benefitted the Resource Center for the Handicapped, the Vesper Society charity, and we were even able to send half a million dollars to China for their Ministry of Culture. That built long-lasting friendships. In fact, I still get Christmas cards from some of our friends in China.

Then on June 4, 1989, about three months before the show was finished in Columbus, the Tiananmen Square Massacre took place. The resulting media focus on China actually boosted our exhibition attendance.

But the mayor of Denver and the governor of Colorado decided to cancel the exhibit for political reasons. The cultural-exchange benefits didn't matter to them, or that people were still interested in the exhibit. That cancellation put us into untenable situation, even though we had been making money.

You see, each venue cost us a couple million dollars for the necessary construction, insurance, procuring special truck trailers to haul the treasures, and the arrangement of other critical details. We then had to be at each location long enough to generate sufficient revenue to pay for those expenses.

The venue we'd set up after Denver was in Orlando, Florida. That city desperately wanted the exhibit, but we'd booked the convention center for the time we expected to be done in Denver. It wasn't available that many months earlier after Denver canceled.

The chairman of the Orlando exhibit was a member of the Dupont family, which owned a lot of property in town. They worked hard to figure out a place to put the exhibition but were unable to do so. We were stuck.

Although we'd paid off about $4 million of the $6 million in bank loans we owed, and our next venue would have cleaned up our debt, Denver's cancellation killed us. I had to call on the notes and bank guarantees we had from various individuals and companies in Seattle. The timing could not have been worse for us.

China's uncertain political climate resulted in our being required to return the objects to that country before we had completed the cultural exchange in which we'd invested so much of our lives.

Even though I didn't attain the level of success I'd hoped for with the Son of Heaven cultural exchange, 20 years later I would take great satisfaction in a lasting tribute our family and church was able to make in a different venture.

The Randy and Rod Halvorson ReCreation Center

In 2004, Randy and Rod were doing some coaching at Washington Cathedral in Redmond and dreaming of a space designed specifically so others with special needs could benefit from athletic activities. Then they learned that the 20-year-old church wanted a larger space to meet, along with classrooms and offices. They also desired to provide a recreational facility for community use. Those two dreams resulted in a recreation center as part of the church's master plan.

Our family wanted to honor Randy and Rod in such a way that their legacy would carry on after they were gone, and we wanted that legacy to be something that would help other people, particularly youth. So as a family—including Rod and Randy's siblings—we gave a major lead gift toward the new facility that would inspire the church and others to give.

My son Kent was the general contractor. Work began on the $20-million, 40,000-square-foot, multi-use building in early 2006. Designed to blend in with the agrarian feel of the surrounding valley, it was built into the side of a hill. That decreased its heat load from the sun, better controlled lighting, and avoided requiring stairs for the entries. Other green features included energy-efficient lighting, motion-sensing and light-sensing systems, and recycled and locally manufactured materials.

At the grand opening on March 8, 2009, visitors marveled at the swimming pool, gymnasium, theatre, library, baby nursery, music room, meeting rooms, counseling offices, administrative offices, and other spaces.

Every possible convenience had been provided for those who rely on support for their mobility. Ramps throughout the two-story building allowed wheelchairs to move freely. The zero-degree-entry pool, named "Healing Waters," allowed unassisted access for people who use walkers or wheelchairs. It was especially well-suited for senior adults and those undergoing post-surgery therapy.

The entire recreation center was open to the public, since part of the church's mission was to provide services to its community. Those services included free open-gym night every Monday, open swims, toddler swims, water exercise classes, after-school tutoring, counseling, Holy Yoga, basketball, football, volleyball, indoor soccer, and roller skating. Some type of activity was going on each day of the week.

It was named the Randy and Rod Halvorson ReCreation Center because its purpose was to help those dealing with the isolation of disability to re-create their lives. The center did that by helping them develop lifelong friendships and find opportunities to have an impact on their communities as they shared their gifts and talents with others.

I am grateful for this contribution to the community that our family has been able to make for the benefit of others.

The Elling and Barbara Halvorson Cancer Center

In addition to our involvement with the ReCreation Center, Barbara and I have also been longtime supporters of the EvergreenHealth Foundation in Kirkland, Washington. We strongly believe in EvergreenHealth's motto: "Working together to enrich the health and well-being of every life we touch."

A few years ago, we were privileged to fund the nondenominational chapel on its community campus to provide a soothing, welcoming place for patients and family members. In the back of the chapel—which is open around the clock—a blank book is available for guests to write down prayer requests. These requests are prayed over daily by the hospital chaplains.

Later, when the foundation's leadership was looking for someone to make a major gift to launch fundraising for a new comprehensive cancer center, they came to us and proposed naming the center after Barbara and me. We felt very honored. We had hoped to be able to do something truly valuable for the community, and, like one in three Americans, our family had been touched by cancer, so we wanted to be involved.

We were also humbled by what Al DeYoung, Chairman of the EvergreenHealth Board of Commissioners told reporters. "Doing great things for their community is what we have come to know from the Halvorsons," he said. "It's all an extension of their deep faith and committed family values. This gift will help bring hope to the thousands of people who will come to the center suffering from the full range of cancers."

At the grand opening of the Elling and Barbara Halvorson Cancer Center, held on March 30, 2013, our hearts were full of thanksgiving to God for allowing us to be able to make a difference, in our own quiet way, in the lives of so many people.

Adopting an African Village

For 12 years, my attorney friend Pat Sullivan was chairman of the board of the humanitarian nonprofit, Hope 4 Kids International. He is passionate about bringing relief to areas of severe poverty and disease around the world, and naturally he got me involved in the endeavor too. That's why Barbara and I adopted a village in Uganda.

We began by purchasing a one-and-a-half-acre plot of ground in a rural area plagued by extreme poverty. The subsistence-farming families in that region had no access to basic healthcare, quality education, or even safe drinking water.

The first thing we did was to drill a well 150 feet deep. Previously, the women had to walk six miles in each direction every day for their water, and the water they did have access to was polluted. The new well was an instant hit with people for miles around. They understand that they are responsible for maintaining the sturdy hand pump, and it is in use around the clock by villagers who've brought their five-gallon containers to fill for their families' daily needs.

When the well was dedicated, Hope 4 Kids representatives turned the pump over to the local pastor and the village chief, clearly explaining that it was to be used by everyone. In that largely Muslim area, everyone knows they get their water from Christians, who are sharing it freely.

A latrine is also built a good distance away from the well to provide adequate hygiene.

In that country, where HIV/AIDS is on the rise again, orphans and widows have a particularly difficult time. Pastors step up to care for them, even though it means that they will experience poverty themselves in their calling. The pastor at Nabusera had been holding worship services under a tree, so the next step was to build a church and also a small cement home for him and his family, in addition to providing a small monthly stipend as he ministers to those around him who have physical, spiritual, emotional, and financial needs.

The Hope 4 Kids team also constructed a two-room medical/dental center in the village. When a medical/dental team comes in from the area hospital or from another country, the news of the event is announced, and people arrive from great distances. We hire a nurse and stock the medical clinic with the initial offering of medicine. By charging about a dollar per treatment, we can continually restock the shelves with medicine.

In the local language, Nabusera means *porridge*, a basic staple in the Ugandan diet. I am grateful we've been able to provide nourishment in multiple ways to the people in that region. As my friend Pat points out, empowering faith-based communities with life-saving components begins their journey towards self-sufficiency.

The Blessing of Family

Anyone with grandchildren knows how much of your heart is reserved for the children of your children. Barbara and I will tell you that grandkids make our hearts beat. Our grandson Geoff Edlund and granddaughter Jackie Edlund—both adults now—talk about what it was like to be a Halvorson grandkid:

> Grandpa and Grandma have had a big influence on us, and our concern to not disappoint them has helped steer us in the right direction. They taught us how to love a spouse and gave us the optimism to believe that not only can a good marriage happen, but it's actually possible to be married for decades.
>
> They've been well-off our entire lives, but if you met them, you'd have no idea of that. They're not showy. They've worked hard for what they have. And it's never been about what they possess; it's always been about what they can give with their hearts to help people.
>
> Every Christmas each of us grandkids would receive from them $100 to spend on ourselves, plus an equal amount to shop for the homeless and families in need. Grandpa and Grandma would scoop us up and let us buy something for ourselves. Then it was time to buy groceries for people in need. So, you can imagine the scene, all of us kids tearing through the supermarket. The only rule Grandpa had was, we couldn't buy perishables.
>
> Then Grandpa would drive us to a place like Union Gospel Mission, and we kids would stagger up the stairs with bags and bags of food. Once we went to a home where the person was in a wheelchair, so we put all the groceries away for them. Eventually, we realized that Grandpa's purpose was to get us thinking about others.
>
> He also taught us that family is everything. Our wider family circles—with Great-Uncle Hal's family in Spokane and Grandpa's here—have cultivated a bond that makes our second cousins feel like our first cousins. Grandpa has kept the relationships going with our Norwegian relatives too.

Everyone in the family knows how much he and Grandma love and care about us all.

Our granddaughter Christi Ackerson has similar memories:

Grandpa and Grandma Halvorson were not your typical grandparents. Of course, they were always excited to see you, ask about your favorite things, give you cookies, and sneak you some soda pop every once in a while, but it was rare to see their home not full of people that I didn't know. We'd meet strangers who soon became family to us all, because that is how my grandparents work. I don't know if anyone comes into contact with Elling and Barbara who doesn't feel instantly welcomed and loved.

One of the greatest lessons I have learned from them is to always be grateful for what you are given and to share your blessings with others. They embody Acts 20:35, "I have shown you in every way, by laboring like this, that you must support the weak. And remember the words of the Lord Jesus, that He said, 'It is more blessed to give than to receive.'"[17] The generosity I have witnessed over the years is unbelievable!

As their grandchild, Christmas was always the most special. Grandpa would take all of us grandkids out to the same restaurant every year. A train would bring us our food; we loved it!

Christi recounted memories similar to Geoff and Jackie's about shopping for needy families. Sometimes they would also buy clothing items, and then, when making the deliveries, would sing Christmas carols to the families. She added,

---

[17] Scripture taken from the New King James Version® of the Bible. Copyright © 1982 by Thomas Nelson. Used by permission. All rights reserved.

Those were some of the best moments I have experienced. The feeling you get when you help someone in need was beautiful, and I think Grandpa wanted each of us to understand that.

Even though my grandparents had a lot of money, they never judged those who didn't and never made anyone feel inferior for having less. So many different times I have been told how kind and generous my family is, which is a testament to our grandparents. I know my dad, Kent, has taken those lessons to heart and has also made it a mission to instill the gift of giving in my sister and me.

One of the things that my grandpa always made sure we understood is that to be able to give, you need to work hard. He built his companies from the ground up, starting with nothing but a strong will and amazing work ethic. My grandpa is in his eighties and still hasn't slowed down, still putting in the time and effort that it takes to be where he is today.

As a little girl, I loved to go over to their house, sneak into my grandpa's office, climb up on his lap, and listen to him while he was on a conference call. I always admired how he could cuddle with me but at the same time be fully engaged in his conversation. That is my grandpa in a nutshell—a man who took the job of a leader seriously but always had time to snuggle with his grandkids, even if it was at the same time!

The example my grandparents has set is priceless, and their qualities are too numerous to name. I know that their legacy will last for many generations to come.

As you have seen, family is an important part of my life story. In addition to traditional family members, our home has also been honored to have Rod and Randy's nurses and caregivers—people who've assisted us night and day. We consider them to be part of our extended family and are grateful for the tremendous blessing they've been to all of us.

It's More Blessed to Give

Our granddaughter quoted the words of Jesus, "It is more blessed to give than to receive." Barbara and I continually find that to be true.

Recently, I asked my administrative assistant to print out a list of our charitable giving over the past couple of years. Seeing it in black and white was astonishing. Each name I read brought to mind stories of the great work these recipients are doing—from medical causes, to education, to the arts, to spiritual endeavors, to agencies helping the disadvantaged and those with disabilities. I was almost overwhelmed with gratitude at what is being accomplished.

In addition to our personal giving, we've also set up the Halvorson Charities Fund that grants monies to similar endeavors, including youth camps and vibrant Christian outreaches in Seattle's inner city.

I do not say any of this to brag about my own accomplishments. Not in the least! I've experienced many failures and times of discouragement. At any of those low points, I could have given up and faded from sight. But thankfully, with God's help and the support of my family, I was able to convert those detours into brand-new byways that helped me forge ahead to greater successes.

You can do the same. Oh, your success might not necessarily be measured in terms of wealth, but your ability to give to others and then be blessed in return can be applied to every area of your life: relationships, physical condition, even a healthy self-image.

Being generous with others is a key element in rerouting detours so they lead to your own bright destiny. Try it. You won't be disappointed.

22
THE EIGHTH MIRACLE

Experiencing seven miracles after nearly being killed in the Grand Canyon helicopter crash convinced me that my life and usefulness had been spared for a reason. My narrow escape in a small plane—when compass readings led me in the wrong direction over the Pacific Ocean—reinforced that conviction. I've dealt with other crises as they've arisen, but I haven't let them detour me for long.

Until 2014.

About four decades previously, I'd been told I had a slight heart murmur due to a problem with my aortic valve, but I wasn't concerned. I never bothered to study what it might mean in my older years. Instead, I focused on my blessings—not the least of which was the enjoyment I received from my work. In fact, even after entering my eighties, retirement held little appeal. People would ask me, "Are you thinking about retiring?" and I would reply, "What for?" I simply couldn't see any reason to slow down.

However, my cardiologist, Dr. John Holmes, had been telling me for some time that I would need aortic-valve surgery. We had been through so many medical emergencies with Randy and Rod, I wasn't fearful about having the risky procedure. The big challenge was how major surgery and a year-long recovery would interrupt my schedule.

Whenever I would suggest that I needed to delay surgery to get some work done, my family members would take turns reminding me that I needed to take care of myself first. Everyone always teases me about my Viking stubbornness. The same obstinacy that allowed my long-ago ancestors to carry on after being shot by an arrow is what spurred me to downplay my doctors' advice that I get my heart repaired sooner than later.

But the heart murmur eventually began to put the brakes on my fast-paced life. By the time I turned 82, my aortic valve opening had reduced to 10 millimeters in diameter. So, before my condition weakened me much more, I decided to take the gamble that the procedure would possibly give me another good 10 to 15 years out of life. After all, I still had more to do on this planet.

On my next trip to the cardiologist, Brenda tagged along to make sure the doctor knew the seriousness of my condition. That's when we learned my heart rate was only 35 beats per minute. I was immediately taken off the atrial fibrillation medication that had been purposefully slowing my heart rate, and the doctor began taking away one additional drug at a time to see what else was affecting me. They also measured the pump-rate blood flow through the heart valve.

Surgery to repair the aortic valve with a bit of cow (bovine) tissue was set for the beginning of September 2014. The surgeon told me that while I was under the knife, he also planned to remove a flap in the left ventricle that was slowing blood flow, and perform two small bypasses, as well. Then he instructed me to stop taking the blood thinner Coumadin a week before surgery.

A couple of days prior to the scheduled procedure, ultrasound results revealed I had an 80- to 90-percent blockage—an occlusion—in the left carotid artery. That would put me at extreme risk during valve-replacement surgery, so the blockage had to be dealt with first.

Carotid-artery surgery was scheduled for Friday, August 29. I let the vascular surgeon know how long I'd already been off of Coumadin and asked what I should do. They prescribed the blood-thinner Lovenox (enoxaparin sodium) as a bridge between the two surgeries because it was supposed to have a short lifespan.

August 29 fell on Labor Day weekend. My entire family gathered in Seattle for my surgery, so I called everyone to my home that morning. I led in prayer, thanking God for my beautiful family and all that he had given me. I asked the Lord to take care of me through the surgery so I could continue to fulfill my purpose in life. I added that if this was my time to go, I was ready. Everything was in the hands of the Lord. Tears were flowing, even from my great-grandchildren, as we all felt embraced in the spirit of love.

Since I was a likely candidate for a stroke, doctors wanted to do local anesthesia, rather than general. That way, they could keep me talking and monitor my condition. However, local anesthesia for this operation wasn't common, so several anesthesiologists were on hand to observe and learn.

My anesthesiologist began injecting the drug with needles above and behind my ear, as well as other nerve centers around the neck. It was a very unusual sensation. Then a whistling squeeze-toy was placed in my hand. During the surgery, I was regularly asked to squeeze the toy so they could monitor my alertness.

Surgery appeared to be successful. Immediately afterward they showed me a small bottle with the plug of calcium crystals that had been removed from my carotid artery. The material looked like little rods about an eighth of an inch long.

The next day, as the doctor in another part of the hospital was writing my discharge papers, a nurse in my room gave me a shot of the blood-thinner Lovenox. I went home, and that evening I enjoyed a great dinner with family. As I got ready for bed at about 8:30 PM, I reviewed the discharge papers. I was supposed to give myself another shot of Lovenox at bedtime, so I followed that instruction.

Creating Excitement in the ER

The next morning, Sunday, the incision in my neck was a bit swollen, but I wasn't alarmed. I went downstairs for breakfast. My grandson Geoffrey Edlund took one look at me and said, "Grandpa, you have a problem. A bump on your neck is the size of a baseball. You need to go to the hospital right away."

I wasn't convinced. After all, my neck didn't hurt—and I hadn't even had my breakfast yet. So we spent a few minutes discussing the logic of his suggestion. Except for Mark Rex, Brenda's husband, all the adults in my family were already committed to meetings or appointments. So Mark said, "I'd be glad to take you. Just show me the way."

Now that I look back, I can see I wasn't thinking clearly. As he saw the rapidly ballooning lump on my neck, Mark began to drive in what I thought was an aggressive manner. Calmly, I said, "Slow down. We're not in a hurry. We've got plenty of time. No need to get a ticket."

Then I noticed the windshield splattered with bugs from a trip we'd taken to Eastern Washington the previous week. Seeing a carwash ahead, I said to Mark, "Let's run through that carwash to get rid of these bugs."

He looked at me and said firmly, "Elling, we're not stopping at the carwash. We're on our way to the hospital!"

When we arrived at the emergency-room entrance, Mark helped me out of the car. I walked into the hospital under my own power and was whisked to a room right away. A doctor came in, took one look at me, and the hustle began. He called a surgeon to come check me out. Meanwhile, an anesthesiologist entered the room.

A few minutes later, the surgeon—whom it turned out I knew—arrived, looked at my neck, asked me a few questions, and then said, "I'll meet you in surgery." He hurried off to change into surgical scrubs.

Meanwhile, the anesthesiologist was urgently talking on the phone with someone in the surgery center. I heard him say, "I don't give a shit what is going on there. We're on the way up *now!*"

Then, just like you might see in a movie drama, five people were running down the hall alongside my gurney yelling, "Nobody get in that elevator! Nobody get in that elevator!" They rolled me in and zoomed up one flight to the surgery center where they slapped a mask over my nose and mouth and said, "Start breathing deep and easy." In just a few breaths, I was out.

When I awoke in intensive care, I learned that the anesthesiologist had been frantic at the real possibility that my windpipe might collapse, making it impossible to insert a tube, leaving me unable to breathe. He told me later, "By the time the surgeon arrived in the operating room, the hematoma on your neck was the size of a cantaloupe. If it had burst, there's no way we could have saved you."

It turned out I had been bleeding between every suture in the carotid artery repair, and I lost a lot of blood during surgery, requiring transfusions. The doctor put in one or two additional stitches on the artery before sewing up my neck. Everyone hoped my blood would start to clot soon.

The following Friday, I was discharged from the hospital, prescribed my regular dosage of Coumadin, and sent home. However, as we would soon learn, my metabolism and weight had changed so much, that dosage made my blood far too thin.

A Series of Unfortunate Events

Two weeks later, I knew something was wrong in my body, so, on Thursday, September 18, I stopped taking Coumadin. The next evening, still not feeling well, I went to bed early.

In her mobility scooter in another room, Barbara reached to do something, lost her center of gravity, and fell. The scooter rolled on top of her. I heard her calling me, so I got out of bed and found her lying under the conveyance. My first instinct was to start to lift her. Then I remembered I wasn't supposed to do anything strenuous because of the risk of bleeding again, so I called my neighbor. He came over and was able to lift her about three-quarters of the way up. But then he lost his balance. Reacting automatically, I stepped in to help, but I fell, hitting my head and tailbone.

A short while later, Rod and Randy returned from an outing and were greatly alarmed to see flashing lights from a fire engine and aid car parked in front of the house. Inside they saw paramedics bending over two people lying on the floor. When they realized those people were Barbara and me, it scared them nearly to death. What had happened? A mass murder?

Medics rushed me to EvergreenHealth Hospital in Kirkland, where I was x-rayed and had a brain scan to make sure I was all right. After putting a compression pack on my neck that would hold up to 20 cubic centimeters of blood, doctors sent me home.

When I awoke at 5:00 the following morning, I became dimly aware of something sticky on my body. The saturated compression pack on my neck had overflowed. My pajamas, pillows, and the bed were soaked with blood.

That event landed me in the hospital again as doctors did what they could to stop the bleeding. I developed pneumonia there, which caused me to cough incessantly. Intubation during the second surgery had irritated my throat, and swelling due to the two surgeries pressured my windpipe. The result was a paralyzed vocal cord that remained stuck to the side of my larynx. For three days I struggled to breathe, all the while continuing to bleed profusely.

Then thrush set in. I had to fight to hang on. Everything in my body was affected—appetite, internal organs, brain . . . everything. I lost weight quickly. Even after my breathing eased, I still looked like Muhammad Ali after a good fight.

The Blessing of Praying Friends

News spread quickly about my struggles. Word came back from many places that I was being prayed for by numerous people and prayer groups, coast to coast. Knowing this gave me strength and confidence as I lay in the hospital.

Over the next six months, I grew stronger and was able to return to daily life and work, although with greatly reduced strength and a weak voice. For most people the latter might not be such a big thing, but all my life I have loved to sing. To lose my singing ability was a traumatic setback for me. I was filled with memories of traveling in a quartet and how Barbara and I had sung duets together. It was a pretty frustrating loss, with no guarantee that my voice would ever return.

Messages continued to come from all over, assuring me of the love, prayers, and best wishes of many friends and colleagues. One week before my aortic surgery, I received a note from Jr Ortal, a Papillon mechanic in Nevada. He first met me in Hawaii when we had operations there. His words encouraged me greatly:

Hello Elling –

I want to take this moment to reflect the precious years way back in 1984. I was just a young man, full of uncertainties for my future. I did not have a clue, but God put you in my life to fulfill my dreams. I lack the words to describe how I would like to thank you.

You are the one that molded me, encouraged me, and contributed in a big way to who I am today. I could not have reached my dreams without you. You are a godsend to me, especially in my career, as well as professional and personal growth. You had faith in me and built up my strong confidence to perform my assigned tasks and responsibilities. You made me reach my heart's desire to excel and reach my potential in my chosen profession and career. I would like to take this opportunity to express my sincere gratitude for all that you have done in my life—spiritually, in career growth, and as inspiration to my success.

I pray to our *awesome* God to continue to bless you with excellent health, long life, joy, happiness, and especially wisdom so you can continue to be a blessing to others. God has blessed and will bless you more and more in the years to come to finish the mission God has for you. I believe God has special blessings in store for you, and the best are yet to come. God has promised us, by his *stripes* we are healed, and nothing is impossible with *God*. We just need to trust in him always. Thank you very much and may *God* shower more of his blessing upon you and your family!!!!

Aloha and Mahalo always,

Jr Ortal

Doing the Unexpected

During my recovery, I learned that the blood thinner Lovenox was at the center of numerous malpractice suits. Lawyers were advertising for people with experiences like mine to contact them and bring lawsuits against hospitals and doctors. Even some of my visitors suggested that I sue the hospital.

So I decided to do the unexpected and give the hospital a $10,000 gift. The confused Major Giving Director at Virginia Mason came to my home to ask why I would do such a thing when everyone else was suing hospitals at the slightest opportunity.

I told him, "Because I want to." He was shocked.

Brenda later told me she thinks it was my way of saying, "I know there was a little mishap, but I forgive you. Just don't let it happen again!"

Time Out for a Celebration

Meanwhile, my aortic valve continued to close, taking the opening down another notch to only nine millimeters in diameter. Surgery had become more necessary than ever. I was finally stabilized enough to schedule open-heart surgery in the spring of 2015.

However, against doctors' orders, I postponed the procedure until after we celebrated the fiftieth anniversary of Papillon Helicopters, which would be held April 16, 2015, in Nevada.

It was an exciting, full-fledged, once-in-a-lifetime celebration, highlighted by most of my immediate family members flying in formation to the Papillon base in three beautiful helicopters.

Three of my five children were in attendance at the event: Lon and his leadership in the helicopter business, Kent and his entrepreneurial strength in the construction business, and Brenda with the leadership she had shown as my partner in building the Papillon Group.

One of the many brilliant decisions Brenda made was to bring in her son, Geoff Edlund, who grew up with a front row seat in the tour industry. He has the leadership skills to lead a Fortune 500 company, and at the celebration, he was named president of Papillon Grand Canyon Helicopters.

Brenda also brought in my grandson-in-law Jacob "Jake" Tomlin, who serves as president of Grand Canyon Scenic Airlines, another Halvorson company. When he joined us half a dozen years ago, he already had nearly 15 years of experience in professional aviation.

Going Under the Knife

After the celebration, and with the help of my friends at EvergreenGreen Health, we chose Seattle's Virginia Mason Hospital for my aortic valve surgery and scheduled it to take place on April 28, 2015. That hospital is a national leader in providing appropriate care, which means you get the tests and treatments you need and aren't put through the ones you don't need. Its heart specialists are recognized nationally in the treatment of heart failure and heart attacks, and their cardiac surgery outcomes are in the top 10 percent in the nation.

The night before my surgery, Randy and Rod let me know how much they loved me and would be praying for me. Words cannot describe the closeness that Barbara and I felt as we went to bed for much-needed rest before the crucible ahead of us.

Every member of my family was at Virginia Mason Hospital by 6:00 that early spring morning. I walked into the hospital on my own with no fear; just a determination to get the job done. After I was taken to a room and prepped for surgery, I asked my family to join me. We prayed, and as they started to roll me away, I called out to Brenda, "Don't forget to call Kash [the owner of a men's apparel shop in Scottsdale, Arizona] and order that shirt, just like mine, for Uncle Irv!" I learned later that everyone was dumbfounded I was thinking of something other than the surgery ahead. But I'm not the type to let much slow me down.

Friends showed up, and more family members came by. E-mails and phone calls kept arriving from people all over the world saying they were dropping everything to pray for me and mentioning how much they loved me and had been impacted by my life. Even business partners who weren't particularly religious sent some of the most beautiful messages.

When the anesthesiologist came out to give some explanations regarding the procedure that was expected to take from three to four hours, Brenda and Kent reminded him and the intake nurse of my helicopter crash and how they should expect some surprises when they opened me up.

After the operation began, the hospital kept everyone informed. They said I was responding well on the cardiopulmonary bypass pump. Brenda's Flagstaff physician friend, Dr. Carmen Alfonso, had flown up to be with us, and my grandson's father-in-law, Dr. Jeff Tomlin—anesthesiologist and Chief Medical Officer for EvergreenHealth—was also there. Both offered explanations regarding current procedures, as well as suggesting possible alternatives. Everyone was concerned I wouldn't pull through, and that even if I did, my mental capacities might never return to normal.

Surgery was expected to last from three to four hours. About an hour and a half after it was expected to be over, the assisting surgeon, thoracic and cardiac specialist Dr. Mark Hill, went to the waiting room to give an update. He said the procedure had gone well, and they had even gotten me breathing on my own. But then things went south. So much scar tissue remained from my helicopter accident that one of my lungs had separated. I was bleeding uncontrollably and had to be re-intubated. Two doctors had been working on me, along with many nurses, everyone taking turns to spell those who were tiring out.

Later, Brenda said, "Our hearts stopped, our tears began to flow, and we quickly called Randy and Rod to let them know what was going on. They came as fast as they could."

They told me later that they cried all the way to the hospital. When they arrived, Randy said, "I don't want my dad to die. I still need him." Rod kept talking about trusting God for a miracle.

Even the presidents of Virginia Mason and EvergreenHealth came by to visit my family, each asking if there was anything they could do.

Meanwhile, surgery stretched on. Bleeding continued to be so profuse, I remained in great danger. Barbara had held on for a long time, but finally she reached the end of her strength. It was agonizing for my family that nothing they tried to do would console her.

The medical team, in an attempt to stop the hemorrhaging, tried a new Israeli-developed technology designed to save victims of traumatic gunshot and shrapnel injuries. The bandage, made out of cellulose (plant cells), can absorb over 2,500 percent of its own weight. Once applied, it turns into a gel-like membrane, trapping platelets and coagulants so a biological clot can form. Because it breaks down naturally within the body, the bandage can be left in place.

Even in the face of this marvelous invention, my family wondered if my aortic-valve surgery could be completed.

When the retired anesthesiologist in our family group explained everything concisely, everyone returned to earnest prayer—including doctors and hospital administrators. After that incredible symphony of prayer, my family and friends were still concerned, but the burden had been lifted. They knew I was in God's hands.

New Complications

My gifted heart surgeon, Dr. Gautam R. Velamoor, was eventually able to complete the bypasses and replace the valve, but I wasn't out of the woods yet. My heart refused to restart, so they put in an aortic balloon. But that resulted in further complications, requiring more blood thinners and my being put back on the cardiopulmonary bypass pump.

I received countless frozen platelets to counteract the blood thinners and multiple blood transfusions to replace the blood I was losing. The outlook was grim for most of the day.

Around 8:30 that evening, Randy texted a friend. "Dad's surgery is still going on. They are having a hard time controlling the bleeding. Please pray."

The frantic thoughts and confusion continued. Finally, around 10:00 PM, I turned a corner. The surgeon declared, "This is a miracle!"

After more than 13 hours in surgery, Dr. Velamoor entered the waiting room to give his report. With a huge smile, he explained that mine had been one of his longest surgeries ever, but it ended up well, and everything looked good. I had been removed from the cardiopulmonary bypass pump, and after I spent time in recovery, my family could see me.

Gloom quickly turned into elation and shouts of gratitude. No one thought they'd be getting that kind of news.

"However," the doctor continued, "we decided to put him into an induced coma to help the healing process, so I suggest that you all go home and get some rest. He wouldn't be aware of your visit anyway."

After sighs of relief went around the room, a couple of people began applauding the doctor, and everyone lined up to give him a hug and tell him thank you.

As Brenda walked out the backdoor of the hospital, she saw a vehicle from the blood center. She told the driver she thought he'd probably been delivering blood to her father. The man confirmed her assumption and asked how I was doing. She said I had survived the surgery. It turned out the man had never before delivered so much blood for just one person. Thirty-nine pints was enough for four people!

Delirious Days

Hooked up to a ventilator, I was moved from the surgical recovery room to intensive care around 1:00 Wednesday morning and was kept in a propofol-induced coma for 10 days.

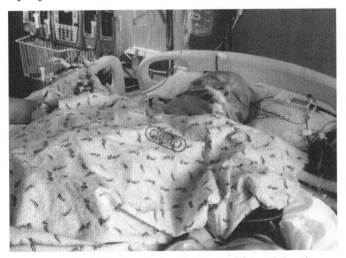

I'm told Barbara came to my hospital room every day. She would hold my hand, pray for me, and turn the television set to shows she thought I would like best. I slept on while the rest of the family made frequent visits, usu-

As my body lay motionless between life and death, I experienced vivid hallucinations.

ally daily. Brenda flew up from the Grand Canyon and for 47 days stayed by my side, using our house, and sometimes a hotel across the street from the hospital, as home base.

They tell me I woke up to some degree, but I was so groggy and disoriented, I still don't remember it well. Then, for many weeks I had difficulty moving the left side of my body. At one point, two occupational therapists tried using a hydraulic patient lift to get me out of bed. But the mechanism featured a vest fitted around my upper body and partly under my arms. Apparently, no one thought about the fact that I

278

was still healing from open-heart surgery. The pressure on my chest and ribs was so intense, I felt like I was being crushed.

Another thing I remember after I first woke up is Brenda stroking my head and telling me how strong I was. Even though it felt good, I couldn't figure out what she was talking about. Why would she be saying such things to me? My family's worries about my mental state increased.

Then the nurse gave them a brochure about delirium as a side effect of the drug propofol. They hadn't heard about this possibility as a result of induced comas and started questioning all the decisions that had been made in order to keep me alive. What if I never recovered from delirium? What kind of a life would I have?

Doctors would come in and ask me such questions as, "What's your name? Where are you? What city are you in? Where were you born?" Apparently, I always got my name right, but was all over the place with other answers—in more ways than one.

I consistently told them I was on a flying house that belonged to my brother Carl. It was very nice, had many rooms, and we flew all over Norway and the United States, including Montana, California, Minneapolis, Saint Paul, Salem, Seattle . . . all places from my past.

I'm told I described little hangars with small flying vehicles that we would use to go to stores to get me things, and Bill, a physician assistant, accompanied me on all the rides. This went on for weeks. When Barbara asked me where the flying vehicles landed, I said, "At the *airport*, of course!"

Dr. Velamoor was included in my hallucinations. I thought we were at a wonderful party, and we journeyed into my heart. I was in one half, and he was in the other.

When it was time for my shots, I was convinced the hospital was trying to kill me, so family members would have to help hold me down.

At night, I would phone family members and ask why they'd left me. I would order them to get in my car and come pick me up—*now!* "Just make a decision, and *do it!*" I'd say.

Due to the leak in my windpipe and the possibility of my choking to death, I was not allowed any solid foods, just liquids. Convinced that one nurse in particular was trying to starve me, I gave orders to my family: "Go to McDonalds and bring me a hamburger and milkshake!"

Later, Brenda said, "You don't understand how hard it is to not do what your father asks you to do when he's been so logical all his life."

My family feared I would never be normal again.

Then one day, Barbara, Brenda, and Mark were sitting in my hospital room when my head suddenly dropped. They thought I had died. Actually, I'd become hypoxic—deprived of adequate oxygen supply at the tissue level. They slapped me around while nurses rushed in with oxygen and returned me to consciousness. (Rumor has it that the night nurse wasn't making me use my CPAP machine.)

At midnight that night, the doctor on duty called Brenda, informing her they wanted to intubate me again to control my breathing. Brenda desperately wanted to talk to Dr. Velamoor first in case something else could be done, but the hospital was adamant.

Brenda then called her doctor friend in Flagstaff, and they discussed the risks. I'd been coughing up some pretty large clots of blood. Would a tube down my throat further damage my trachea, bronchus, and vocal cords? They also worried that the longer I was on a vent, the more difficult it might be to wean me off of it. But in the end they realized that due to my current situation, the benefits of intubation outweighed the risks, and they needed to give permission.

Brenda informed her brothers, and they rushed to my side, not knowing what to expect. Later, she admitted, "I felt like I was getting an ulcer!"

On the Road to Recovery

Then, to everyone's surprise, the tube was removed just two days later. I was breathing on my own and had finally reached the point where my stamina and that old Viking stubbornness began to kick in.

Physical and occupational therapists came in every day now, and I pushed myself in between sessions. When it came time to move me out of ICU, my children—all Type A personalities—were concerned that if I was moved just to another floor at the hospital, time would be wasting for my healing. They wanted me to be moved directly into EvergreenHealth's Acute Rehabilitation Unit.

Then we learned that before authorizing patients to enter acute rehab, Medicare requires those patients to be strong enough to do rehab exercises. The hospital, in good conscience, didn't believe I was at that point yet.

My family argued and argued about it. And then a good friend who works for an insurance company that specifically covers Medicare patients wrote the perfect letter for my doctor to sign. Brenda took it to the doctor to sign, and he did so in a kind and supportive manner, no questions asked.

To the surprise of two hospitals, Medicare approved the move, and I was launched into the next phase. This was the breakthrough we all needed. And EvergreenHealth was so impressed with the letter, they offered our friend a job!

While all this was going on, Lon talked with Pastor Tim about a meeting that had been called so key people from a few of my businesses could discuss how they were going to continue while I was recovering. Lon said, "I know I'm prejudiced, Pastor Tim, but I'm very proud of my big sister, Brenda. She walked in and took leadership in that meeting and quieted everyone's fears. She kicked butt in getting the companies going again. It was a God thing."

My road to recuperation was a long one. My cardiologist called me Lazarus because I had come back from the dead. Later, in physical therapy, my trainer kept comparing me to a football player because I took the recuperation process and daily workouts seriously. I did not want a miracle to be waiting on me.

As I grew stronger, I began to dream again. I talked with friends over the phone, including a lifelong friend who faced his own tragedy. After everything I had been through, my heart was especially tender toward him.

I started reading through financial reports and e-mails, held business meetings in my room, and called in different employees. Barbara, ever supportive of me, told the nurses, "This is the best thing in the world for him. He has to get on with living." It's a blessing to have a life-mate who understands me almost better than I understand myself sometimes.

After being in acute rehab for four weeks, I was finally released to go home. What a special—almost surreal—day it was for us all! I can hardly describe how excited I was to sleep in my own bed, sit in my own rocking chair, eat normal food, and eventually drive my own car.

Perhaps for the rest of my life I will be piecing together the miracle of my survival. I now have the sense of a new lease on life—and a new understanding of how much my family loves me and how much I love my family. I am indeed a blessed man.

This was our Christmas card photo in 1964.

EPILOGUE
REMEMBERING RODNEY JAY HALVORSON
JUNE 23, 1958 – JANUARY 21, 2017

In January 2016 I was still recuperating from my near-death experience during heart surgery when we received another heavy blow. Rod was diagnosed with liver cancer.

At first, doctors told us the malignancy was so slow growing, they figured he could live out the rest of his life expectancy. Instead, he turned out to have a fast-growing kind.

We fought it every way we could. Seeking help from Seattle's Cancer Care Alliance, Rod received treatment at EvergreenHealth's Halvorson Cancer Center in Kirkland, the Fred Hutchison Cancer Research Center in downtown Seattle, and embolization[18] at the University of Washington Medical Center.

However, nothing really helped, and Rod's oncologist appointments grew increasingly discouraging. Finally, we were gently informed it was time to prepare for his passing.

We had been through so many life-and-death challenges with Rod and Randy, it was hard to grasp that maybe Rod's time might truly be nearing the end. Each member of our family began to process this new reality. For Barbara and me, it was almost like reliving our time crying our hearts out at the Washington Park Arboretum upon the initial Duchenne muscular dystrophy diagnosis.

---

[18] The liver is unusual in that it has two blood supplies. Most normal liver cells are fed by branches of the portal vein, but cancer cells in the liver are usually fed by branches of the hepatic artery. Blocking the branch of the hepatic artery that feeds the tumor helps kill off cancer cells, but it leaves most of the healthy liver cells unharmed because they get their blood supply from the portal vein. During embolization, substances are injected—in Rod's case they were tiny plastic beads—in an attempt to block or at least reduce blood flow to the malignant cells.

Rod's condition deteriorated rapidly, and hospice was brought on board. Since Randy and Rod already had round-the-clock medical care, hospice provided emotional support, along with help in getting the proper palliative drugs.

On January 20, 2017, I needed to be in California to receive a Living Legends of Aviation Award, and Rod was doing well enough that all of us—including our caregivers—thought we had time to slip away for the ceremony. Brenda, Kent, and Lon, along with their spouses, joined us at the awards ceremony. Upon our hurried return the next day, the 21ˢᵗ, we realized that Rod had been hanging on until we got home.

We all spent the evening together with Rod. At bedtime, Kent and Lon and their wives returned to their homes, and Brenda, here from Nevada, went up to a guest bedroom. Pastor Tim White had come by, and he and I secluded ourselves in my study.

It was after 11:00 PM when we heard Rod's nighttime attendant let out a scream. We hustled over to the room just as Rod was taking his last breath. Brenda raced downstairs immediately, and Kent and Lon showed up a short time later. As soon as the caregivers who weren't already on duty were called with the news, most of them rushed over to join us as we each grieved in our own way. None of us expected Rod to leave us quite so soon.

We held the memorial service on Saturday, February 4, at Washington Cathedral's Randy & Rod Halvorson ReCreation Center in Redmond.

Even though we realize that each of us must die someday and that Rod was ready for his transition to heaven, losing him was still a huge shock to us. We are comforted in knowing he is in a much better place, free from all physical restrictions.

Now, without his twin brother for the first time in his life, Randy has held strong. All their lives, both men exhibited tender hearts toward people, always more concerned about others than they were about themselves. One thing for sure—the house is much quieter now. Those two enjoyed such camaraderie and engaged in such lively discussions with one another, they kept our joint jumpin'.

Over the years, Randy and Rod became physically the most handicapped any person could possibly be and still remain conscious. Along with his brother, Rod could barely express himself due to vocal limitations, and he continually lost muscle control until the only way he could drive his wheelchair and operate computers was to touch his tongue to special controls. The progressive disease took everything from them except their minds. Yet, in spite of having virtually no muscular function, these ambitious and inspirational men have demonstrated an incredible will, not only to survive, but also to be contributing members of society.

Our family would be quite different if they had not been part of it. They have given to us understanding, patience, creativity, and trust in God's faithfulness. Those lessons have brought us through many difficult times and have given us the strength to endure.

Even on his final day on earth, Rod demonstrated his sense of humor, combined with his love of sports. As Kent hovered near his bed, Rod said to him, "When you get to heaven—if you make it—I'm going to kick your butt in basketball!"

Now, there's an example, if there ever was one, of the Halvorson legacy of creating a detour to destiny!

What seemingly insurmountable obstacle do you face today? My hope is that you, too, will look for a way to reroute detours into paths that lead to your own success.

APPENDICES

✦ ✦ ✦ ✦ ✦

APPENDIX A: HOW HELICOPTERS FLY

A helicopter's main rotor consists of a number of blades. Each blade is an airfoil (a wing) and generates lift. The rotor is driven by a motor, usually a turbine engine. The pitch of the blades can be changed, either collectively or independently or with a combination of both. Changing the pitch collectively will cause an increase or decrease in lift, making the helicopter go up or down. When the pitch of the blades is controlled independently, it is done in such a way that the pitch depends upon the blade's instantaneous position. If the pitch is changed so that the blade towards the rear has increased pitch and the blade towards the front has decreased pitch, this will tilt the whole rotor forward. This will result in the lift producing a force both upward and forward. Obviously, by changing relative pitches around the rotor in this manner, it is possible to move forwards, backwards and sideways.

A tail rotor is used to counteract the tendency of the helicopter to rotate in the opposite direction to the main rotor. Changing the pitch of the tail rotor allows the helicopter to be turned left or right.

A helicopter's main rotor or rotor system is a type of fan that is used to generate both the aerodynamic lift force that supports the weight of the helicopter and the thrust that counteracts aerodynamic drag in forward flight. Each main rotor is mounted on a vertical mast over the top of the helicopter, as opposed to a helicopter tail rotor, which is connected through a combination of drive shaft(s) and gearboxes along the tail boom. A helicopter's rotor is generally made up of two or more rotor blades. The blade pitch is typically controlled by a swashplate connected to the helicopter flight controls.

APPENDIX B:
DEVELOPING WHISPER JET TECHNOLOGY

In designing Whisper Jet technology on the Sikorsky S-55, I installed a much more powerful engine, the Honeywell TPE331-10. Ralph Alex told me he always believed the aircraft should have five blades, but the engine available didn't have enough horsepower, so they designed the aircraft around three blades. Since the Honeywell engine I installed was a screamer, here's how I reduced its noise.

First, my team and I measured the wavelength of the sound's frequency. Then, knowing that high-frequency sound cannot bend around a corner, we constructed a honeycomb structure to precisely match the length of the measured sound, and we lined the existing intake plenum (the screaming side of the engine) with a thin layer of a substance called felt metal, which has miniscule holes that allow sound to pass into the honeycomb. On the exhaust, which emitted a lower frequency, we used a thicker blanket of felt metal lining. The result was that sound waves bounced back within the honeycomb structure and self-canceled.

Over the life of the project, I brought in several engineers. My co-designer and I also successfully insulated the turbine engine compartment, which ended the radiating noise caused by the turning turbine. With that done, we focused our attention on the rotor blades. In fact, earlier, we had increased the rotor blade capacity by 67 percent. This allowed us to develop two different speeds of rotor rotation—one for takeoff and maneuvering, and a second (and lower) speed for cruise in flight. This idea was a breakthrough for helicopters, again reducing noise in a major way.

It wasn't long before the National Aeronautics and Space Administration (NASA) agreed to take an entire day to thoroughly test our new type of silent helicopter, making dozens and dozens of runs. In the quiet configuration, they determined it was the quietest helicopter ever built. Yes! That made our helicopter the only one in the world with quiet technology. And that distinction prompted me to come up with a trademark name for our bird—the Whisper Jet.

APPENDIX C:
WITNESSING THE BIRTH OF A VILLAGE

The history of the town of Tusayan, Arizona—an enclave of private property at the southern boundary of Grand Canyon National Park—dates back almost to when the park itself was first established in 1919. And of course, the nearby Native American ruins the community is named for are much older still.

My association with the town started when I began the Grand Canyon pipeline job. I noticed that amenities in the area consisted of a gas station and a small coffee shop/bar next door. Then, Robert Thurston, who owned most of the private property in area, started to build a small motel across the street from the gas station. I recognized from the beginning that if the area were sufficiently developed, it would be strategic in supporting Grand Canyon tourism.

This private property was a stretch of frontage of approximately 2,000 feet or so along Highway 64—a road leading to Williams, where travelers could head east to Flagstaff. Convinced that this small island of nongovernment land would be an excellent location for tourist lodging, I purchased a portion of it from Bess Thurston, Robert's former wife.

The first thing I built was a 36-unit motel. A trailer parked next door housed the reservation desk. About 24 months later, I constructed a two-story building with 53 more units, and the following year, we added a very large lodge building that included two restaurants, gift shop, six-lane bowling alley, and banquet facilities.

Whenever additional property was available for purchase, I acquired it, too, finally ending up with a significant part of the frontage.

But two main challenges prevented the community from growing: (1) the area had no satisfactory water source, and (2) it had no sewer system.

So, when we constructed the lodge, Bob Thurston allowed us to build sewage lagoons at the western reach of his property. From the lagoons and the lodge, we constructed a 12-inch-diameter sewer line about 1,500 feet in length.

It was important to me that this piping be deep enough to ensure proper drainage over the entire Tusayan community. Therefore, envisioning substantial hotel development and other businesses in the future, we bit the bullet, and, at great personal expense, overconstructed it. I wanted to make sure the sewer line would be capable of handling whatever demands were made upon it.

Back then, all water had to be trucked in, driving the cost to about three cents per gallon. Toilets used about six gallons of water per flush in those days, meaning that every time the handle was pressed, it was as if 18 cents literally went down the toilet.

An even more important reason for finding an adequate water supply concerned fire protection. Several months after we completed the lodge building, the 53-unit wood-frame motel caught fire in the middle of the night and burned to the ground. With no water to fight the blaze, the airport crew used an air tanker to drop fire retardant. Unfortunately, it was too little, too late. The bodies of two people were found in the charred rubble. I was devastated.

The two-story motel unit in the background—to the right of the original lodge building—burned to the ground one night due to lack of water to fight the fire.

When we rebuilt the property, I made sure it was constructed mainly of concrete to significantly decrease the chances of a similar disaster ever happening again.

Due to the fact that our lodge building was really too big for the small number of units we had, I brought in John and Elizabeth Seibold as partners and added another two-story, 53-unit building, giving us a total of 142 motel units. That ramped up our critical need for fire protection and a better water supply. We then constructed a 570,000-gallon steel water-storage tank for our motel units, but it wasn't sufficient for the rest of the growing community.

The Grand Canyon Squire Inn today.

Previously, many wells had been test-drilled without success to depths of 300 to 400 feet, so the Seibolds and I decided to attempt a super-deep well in an effort to locate a source of potable water. At great expense, an oil-drilling rig was brought in and drilled 24 hours a day for a number of weeks. This was a half-million-dollar gamble. We had no idea if we'd find water, and if we did, we didn't know if it would contain arsenic, like some of the wells down the road were getting. We held our breath.

At about 3,200 feet, we hit water. We test-pumped the well, had the water checked for minerals and arsenic, and everything passed.

Caramba! We'd hit the motherlode of good drinking water! Since then, we've constructed another water storage facility—this one with a three-million-gallon capacity—enabling us to service other properties, substantially reducing what everyone had been paying for water. Our company, Tusayan Water Development Association, Inc., now services the entire Tusayan area.

The well-drilling success gave us courage to move forward with additional improvements, and other people developed properties as well.

We soon added another 100 rooms attached to the lodge building, and we recently completed 68 more rooms, bringing the total, at what is now the Grand Canyon Squire Inn, to 318 units. This Best Western Premier property has three onsite restaurants, banquet facilities, a gift shop, bowling center, indoor and outdoor swimming pools and hot tubs, a 24-

hour exercise area, a 24-hour business center, onsite laundry facilities, and complimentary parking for cars, trucks, and RVs. At the time of this writing, out of over 4,000 Best Western hotels and motels in the US, only about 25 have the Premier Property designation.

In addition to all this, we partnered in developing an IMAX theater and producing the most viewed IMAX film of all time—*Grand Canyon: The Hidden Secrets.*

We also developed a freestanding steakhouse—named the Big E Steakhouse & Saloon at my daughter's suggestion—serving from 500 to 800 guests per day during the tourist season. We just completed the Chicken Kitchen, a sit-down restaurant that I expect to be just as busy for much of the year. Of course, we have plans for continued development in the future.

Some call me the town's father, but I'm not comfortable with that title. Instead, I prefer to honor my business partners John and Elizabeth Seibold, along with pioneers who came before us, including:

- George Reed, who homesteaded the 160-acre tract of land in 1920 and turned it into a productive farm.
- Rudolph "Chick" Kirby, who opened a store and campground in the area in 1928.
- Buford Belgrade, who led the American Legion in buying George Reed's original home, along with two surrounding acres.
- R. P. "Bob" Thurston, a Williams businessman and rancher, who purchased the balance of the Reed property.

Of course, there are other visionaries too, including the citizens of Tusayan themselves. They pushed through a number of hurdles to incorporate as a town in 2010.

You've heard the saying, "It takes a village to raise a child." Well, I'm convinced it takes people of courage to raise a village. I feel honored to have been part of those who have helped Tusayan become the wonderful little town it is today.

APPENDIX D:
AWARDS PRESENTED TO ELLING HALVORSON

Awards in the Field of Education

- Outstanding Alumni, Hillcrest Lutheran Academy, Fergus Falls, MN

- Outstanding Young Men of America, "In recognition of his outstanding ability, accomplishments, and service to his community, country, and profession," 1965

- Distinguished Alumni Award, Waldorf College, Forest City, IA, "For unique accomplishments in general construction projects, influence in the Christian church and regard for family and friends," 1969

- Distinguished Alumni Citation for Achievement in Business, Willamette University, Salem, Oregon, 2003

- The honorary degree of Doctor of Laws, Waldorf College (now University), Forest City, Iowa, April 18, 1998

- Inaugural Trustee Emeritus, Lake Washington Institute of Technology, 2018

Awards in the Field of Construction

- "A Splinter from the Pavilion" citation, "Recognizing Special Service and Support to Christian Witness in Century 21 World's Fair," Elling Halvorson Construction

- American Public Works Association, Washington State Chapter, Contractor of the Year, 1979

- Washington Aggregates and Concrete Association, Special Honor Award for Excellence in the Use of Concrete, 1983

- Honorary membership, Seattle Chapter, Associated General Contractors of Washington, September 8, 1997

- Construction Hall of Fame Inductee, AGC (Associated General Contractors of America), May 2004

Awards in the Field of Aviation

- Lifetime member of the Arctic Circle Club, April 12, 1976

- Meritorious Service Award in recognition and appreciation of outstanding service to the civil helicopter community, Helicopter Association International, May 25, 1993
- Member for Life, Helicopter Association International, June 2001
- President's Citation for Outstanding Achievement and Safety Leadership, "For inspiring and developing an effective industry coalition dedicated to improving the safety of passengers of helicopter air tour operators in the United States," Flight Safety Foundation International, 54th annual International Air Safety Seminar, Athens, Greece, November 7, 2001
- Lawrence D. Bell Memorial Award for "Saluting Excellence in Management Leadership," Helicopter Association International, 2004; presented at HELI-EXPO awards ceremony, Anaheim, California, February 7, 2005
- Meritorious Achievement Award, Tour Operators Program of Safety, February 2005
- Meritorious Service Award, Helicopter Association International, February 26, 2006
- Vertical Flight Hall of Fame Award, 2014
- Seattle Museum of Flight's Pathfinder Award, 2015
- Vertical Flight Hall of Fame Award, Living Legends of Aviation, 12th Annual Awards, January 16, 2015
- 20-Year Service Award, Tour Operators Program of Safety (TOPS), 2016
- Kiddie Hawk Air Academy, Living Legends of Aviation, 14th Annual Awards, January 20, 2017
- Elected as Fellow of the Royal Aeronautical Society, March 15, 2017
- Service on many committees and boards within the Helicopter Association International (HAI), including serving as chair for the years 2000—2001 and 2002—2003

Awards in the Field of Philanthropy
- Pacific Lutheran University Q Club, founder and charter member, 1972; Fellow, 2006

- Waldorf Society Dean's Club, 1996
- Lenny Wilkins Foundation for continuous support of the Odessa Brown Children's Clinic, 2009
- MDA Night of Hope Award for Outstanding Support in the Fight Against Duchenne Muscular Dystrophy, 2012
- EvergreenHealth 2017 Community Service Award

The Living Legends of Aviation award—along with my fondness for loud tux jackets—was featured in the event's full-color program on January 20, 2017.

APPENDIX E:
THE PRINCIPLE OF COMPENSATION THROUGH CHARITABLE GIVING

HOW THE HALVORSONS ARE GIVING BACK TO THE COMMUNITY

- Founder of the Halvorson Charities Fund with multiple beneficiaries
- Luther Seminary in Minneapolis, Minnesota: The Halvorson Memorial Endowed Scholarship Fund for four financially deserving MDiv middlers or seniors in good academic standing preparing for parish ministry

- Scholarship endowment as charter members of the Waldorf Endowment Society of Waldorf Lutheran College (now University) in Forest City, Iowa

- Instigators of and contributors to the HLA Legacy Club of Hillcrest Lutheran Academy in Fergus Falls, Minnesota

- The Halvorson Scholarship Endowment for qualifying students of need applying to Hillcrest Lutheran Academy in Fergus Falls, Minnesota

- Lake Washington Technical College, Kirkland, WA: (1) member of the Board of Trustees for 12 years, helping the school gain accreditation and providing momentum to change its name to Lake Washington Institute of Technology; (2) providing a lead gift in 2018 allowing the establishment of a Bachelor of Science in Nursing degree as well as the Elling and Barbara Halvorson Endowed Scholarship for Outstanding Nursing Students

- Honorary chairs of the Lake Washington College Foundation's annual Pathways to Learning benefit breakfast fundraiser on October 18, 2010, that raised $5 million.

- Contributing members providing leadership gifts to the President's Circle of Augsburg College in Minneapolis, Minnesota; also served on the Board of Regents.

- Lead contributors to the Randy and Rod Halvorson ReCreation Center in Redmond, Washington.

- Lead contributors to the Elling and Barbara Halvorson Cancer Center at EvergreenHealth Hospital in Kirkland, Washington.

- Substantial annual contributors to Seattle's Union Gospel Mission that provides support services for homeless people.

About the Authors

Elling B. Halvorson

Not long after graduating from Oregon's Willamette University in 1955 with a degree in economics and engineering, Elling Halvorson founded a company that specialized in construction projects in difficult locations. That led to him building a freshwater pipeline from the North to the South Rim of the Grand Canyon in the early 1960s, using helicopters to lower supplies to the canyon floor. Realizing the bigger opportunity, he began selling canyon air tours in 1965. Today he's chairman of Papillon Airways Inc., the world's largest air-tour provider, and has built up more than a dozen other family-owned businesses.

Elling and his wife, Barbara, raised four sons and a daughter and have eight grandchildren and 16 great-grandchildren. The Halvorsons are also active philanthropists. Learn more at EllingBHalvorson.com.

Gerald D. Gawne

Gerry Gawne has spent his life writing, creating, and producing every form of media. He began his career at a radio station in British Columbia, Canada, and then moved to Seattle to manage KING Radio, where he introduced a rock-music format in the early 1970s. He became involved in city and state political campaigns and then went to work for an ad agency. Soon he branched off into his own advertising and production company with clients that included local and national corporations, numerous Hollywood celebrities, and Presidents Ronald Reagan and Gerald Ford.

When he began working for Elling Halvorson, he developed multimedia projects for a traveling museum exhibition and for Papillon flight centers. He cowrote the documentary, *Wings Over Grand Canyon*, and then started to put together Elling's memoir before retiring due to health reasons. Gerry lives in Seattle.

296

Diana Savage

Diana Savage has written or contributed to 13 books and has published more than 200 articles, short stories, and poems. She speaks at a variety of venues in the US and abroad and for three years directed the annual Northwest Christian Writers Renewal conference near Seattle.

As principal of Savage Creative Services, LLC, she provides professional writing, editing, and speaking services. She earned her BA degree from Northwest University and her master's from Bakke Graduate University. She has served on the board of directors of four nonprofits, as director of women's ministries at a large West Coast church, and as development officer for a social-service agency working with homeless families. Learn more at DianaSavage.com.

Made in the USA
San Bernardino, CA
29 December 2018